Intimacy and mobility in an era of hardening borders

Manchester University Press

RETHINKING BORDERS

SERIES EDITORS: SARAH GREEN AND HASTINGS DONNAN

Rethinking Borders focuses on what gives borders their qualities across time and space, as well as how such borders are experienced, built, managed, imagined and changed. This involves detailed and often richly ethnographic studies of all aspects of borders: finance and money, bureaucracy, trade, law, new technologies, materiality, infrastructure, gender and sexuality, even the philosophy of what counts as being 'borderly,' as well as the more familiar topics of migration, nationalism, politics, conflicts and security.

Previously published

Migrating borders and moving times: Temporality and the crossing of borders in Europe
Edited by Hastings Donnan, Madeleine Hurd and Carolin Leutloff-Grandits

The political materialities of borders: New theoretical directions
Edited by Olga Demetriou and Rozita Dimova

Border images, border narratives: The political aesthetics of boundaries and crossings
Edited by Johan Schimanski and Jopi Nyman

Intimacy and mobility in an era of hardening borders

Gender, reproduction, regulation

Edited by
Haldis Haukanes and Frances Pine

Manchester University Press

Published by Manchester University Press
Oxford Road, Manchester M13 9PL

www.manchesteruniversitypress.co.uk

British Library Cataloguing-in-Publication Data
A catalogue record for this book is available from the British Library

ISBN 978 1 5261 5021 9 hardback
ISBN 978 1 5261 7462 8 paperback

First published 2021
Paperback published 2023

Typeset
by New Best-set Typesetters Ltd

To our daughters, Ania and Johanna

Contents

List of contributors

Sílvia Bofill-Poch is an Associate Professor of Social Anthropology at the University of Barcelona. Her main research focus has been on political and legal anthropology, feminist anthropology, and the anthropology of care. She currently focuses on ageing and policy making, economies of care and transnational migrations, with particular attention to legal disputes, political claims, and social justice. She is the head of the Study Group on Reciprocity (GER) at the University of Barcelona, together with Susana Narotzky; and is also a founding member of the Research Group on Legal Anthropology. She serves as scientific coordinator of the project 'Popular notions of social justice in the face of the crisis and austerity policies'.

Elżbieta Czapka is an assistant professor at the Institute of Sociology at the University of Gdańsk. Her current research concerns dementia in families with a minority ethnic background; care regimes and migration; transnational care giving and health of new labour migrants. She is a member of the European Sociological Association, Nordic Dementia Network, European Network of Intercultural Elderly Care, and Nordic Migration Network.

Radka Dudova works as senior researcher at the Institute of Sociology of the Academy of Sciences of the Czech Republic. She is an expert in the area of analysis of public policies and institutions. Her research interests are policy-making and practices of childcare and elderly care, women's bodily citizenship, policy-making on abortion, and changes in the labour market. She has published articles in the journals *Politics and Gender*, *European Journal of Industrial Relations*, *Sociological Research Online*, and *International Journal of Ageing and Later Life*, among others, and she is the author of several books.

Petra Ezzeddine is a social anthropologist. She lectures at the Department of Anthropology and Gender Studies, Faculty of Humanities (Charles University in Prague). Her ethnographic research deals with gender aspects of migration, transnational forms of parenthood, the globalisation of care for children and the elderly, female migrant domestic workers, and gender and ageing in migration. She cooperates closely with several Czech and Slovak non-governmental and international organisations working with migrants and refugees.

Anette Fagertun has a PhD in Social Anthropology, and currently holds a position as an Associate Professor at the Centre for Care Research West, Western Norway University of Applied Sciences (HVL). Her research interests in Norway, Europe and Indonesia include labour, gender, social inequality, healthcare services and regimes, the welfare state, and the political, policy, and political discourse. She teaches social theory, methodology, and theory of science and currently manages a large RCN project (ISP) aimed at developing services research as a field.

Christiane Falge is Professor of Health and Diversity at the University of Applied Health Sciences Bochum. Her work and research focus on medical anthropology, transnational migration, and health and collaborative community research. She has conducted long-term ethnographic research among Sudanese refugees in Ethiopia and the US between 1997 and 2006 and on migration in Germany. In 2016, she founded the City Lab Bochum where students and academics together with community researchers engage in collaborative research, co-production of knowledge, and activism against social inequalities. Her monographs include *The Global Nuer. Transnational Life-Worlds, Religious Movements and War* (2015) and *Migrants and Health. Political and Institutional Responses to Cultural Diversity in Health Systems* (2013).

Olena Fedyuk obtained her PhD degree from the Department of Sociology and Social Anthropology at the Central European University, Budapest, on transnational moral economies and distant motherhood in cases of Ukrainian female labour migrants to Italy. Her most recent project, RightsLab, deals with transnational labour rights, and the overlap of gendered employment, labour, and care regimes. Since 2012, Olena has directed two documentary films; 'Road of a migrant' (2015) looks at the role of the church in migrants' lives and 'Olha's Italian Diary' (2018) speaks of the taboos in personal stories for solo female migrants.

Hana Hašková is a senior researcher at the Institute of Sociology, Czech Academy of Sciences. Her research and teaching focuses on changes in the life course, reproduction, and care. She studies changes to the labour market and intimate lives, and explores relations between policies, discourses, and practices of care. She has coordinated research teams within international projects on gendered citizenship and women's movements, and headed research projects on childbirth, childlessness, postponement of childbearing, and changes in the life course. She has published in various journals including, among others, *Social Policy and Administration*, the *European Journal of Industrial Relations*, *Sociological Research Online*, and the *Journal of International Women's Studies*.

Haldis Haukanes is a social anthropologist and Professor at the Department of Health Promotion and Development, University of Bergen, Norway. She has been doing research in the Czech Republic since the early 1990s, publishing widely on the postcommunist transformation processes in rural areas, on food, gender, and care, and on young people's imaginations of their future. Since 2007, she has also been involved in gender-related research in Sub-Saharan Africa, including projects on reproductive health, sexuality, and fertility control. Her edited volumes include include *Memory, Politics and Religion: The Past Meets the Present in Europe* (with Frances Pine and Deema Kaneff), *Parenting After the Century of the Child. Travelling Ideals, Institutional Negotiations and Individual Responses* (with Tatjaja Thelen), and *Recasting Pasts and Futures in Postsocialist Europe* (with Susanna Trnka).

Hana Havelková was a sociologist and co-founder of the Department of Gender Studies at the Faculty of Humanities of Charles University in Prague, where she taught feminist and sociological theories, empirical research on gender in the socialist era, and gender in politics. She was co-author and co-editor of the publications *Waste of Talents. Turning Private Struggles into a Public Issue* (European Commission 2004), *The Politics of Gender Culture under State Socialism* (Routledge 2014) and *Vyvlastněný hlas. Proměny genderové kultury české společnosti 1948–1989* (Sociologické nakladatelství 2015). Hana Havelková passed away in the autumn of 2020.

Lise Widding Isaksen is a Professor at the Department of Sociology at the University of Bergen, Norway. Her research interests are gender studies, care practices, globalisation, transnational families, migration, and welfare politics. She has written extensively on gender, power relations, transnational families, egalitarian transformations, and welfare regimes with special emphasis on comparative organisations of family patterns and gendered care practices. She is coordinator of the Research Network 33 'Women and Gender Studies' in the European Sociological Association and a member of the Nordic Migration Network. Her publications include 'Egalitarian Ideologies on the Move: Changing Care Practices and Gender Norms in Norway' (co-authored with Mariya Bikova) in the *Journal of European Social Policy* 2019, Vol. 29 (5):593–599.

Agnieszka Kościańska is an Associate Professor at the Department of Ethnology and Cultural Anthropology, University of Warsaw. She is the author and (co)editor of several volumes on gender and sexuality, including the monographs, *Gender, Pleasure, and Violence: The Construction of Expert Knowledge of Sexuality in Poland* (Indiana University Press 2021, Polish edition 2014) and *To See a Moose: The History of Polish Sex Education from the First Lesson to the Internet* (forthcoming with Berghahn Books, Polish edition 2017), and a special issue of *Sexualities*, 'The Science of Sex in a Space of Uncertainty' (2016, with Hadley Renkin)

Carolin Leutloff-Grandits is scientific coordinator and senior researcher at the Viadrina Center B/ORDERS IN MOTION of the European University of Viadrina in Frankfurt (Oder), where she is currently acting chair of social geography. A social anthropologist by training, she focuses in her research on the interrelations of migration, borders, and family relations and has done extensive fieldwork in Croatia, Kosovo, Austria, and Germany. Together with Hastings Donnan and Madeleine Hurd, she edited the book *Migrating Borders and Moving Times. Temporality and the Crossing of Borders in Europe* (Manchester University Press, 2017).

Izabella Main is an Associate Professor in the Department of Anthropology and Ethnology at Adam Mickiewicz University in Poznań, Poland and Deputy Director of the Center for Migration Studies. She received her PhD on politics, religious symbolism, and protest in socialist Poland, from the Central European University. Her research focuses on medical anthropology, migration, and urban studies in Poland. She recently led the project 'Mobile Lives, Immobile Realms? Female Mobility between Poland and Norway', founded by the National Science Centre. In 2019/2020, she received Fulbrigh Senior Award at Georgetown University, Washington D.C. to conduct research on the access to healthcare of recent European migrants in the USA.

Gabriela Nicolescu is a postdoctoral researcher at the University of Oxford. She is a visual anthropologist and curator with research interests in ageing and care, migration, museum anthropology, and exhibition making. She gained her PhD in Visual Anthropology at Goldsmiths, University of London, and then worked on several projects as a curator and postdoctoral researcher at Goldsmiths and University College Cork (Ireland). She has curated exhibitions in Austria, Hong Kong, Hungary, the Republic of Moldova, Romania, the United Kingdom, and the Philippines and published in several journals, including the *Journal of Design History*, the *Journal of Material Culture*, *World Art*, and *Anthropology and Aging*. For links to pre-peer reviewed versions of articles, exhibitions, and research, please visit gabrielanicolescu.com/gabriela.nicolescu@anthro.ox.ac.uk.

Frances Pine is Reader Emerita in Anthropology at Goldsmiths, University of London. She has done extensive long-term research in various regions of Poland, and has published widely on kinship and gender, political economy, inequality, landscape and memory, and migration. Her edited books include *Surviving Postsocialism* (with Sue Bridger), *Memory, Politics and Religion: The Past meets the Present in Europe* (with Deema Kaneff and Haldis Haukanes) and *Transnational Migration and Emerging Inequalities* (with Deema Kaneff).

Acknowledgements

The authors would like to thank the University of Bergen (Bergen University Funds and Department of Health Promotion and Development, Faculty of Psychology) for financial support for the workshop 'Rights, Reproduction and Care: Gender, intimacy and mobility in the context of hardening borders and new populist nationalisms', held in December 2017 at the University of Bergen. The workshop, which all but one of the contributors to the book attended, was the starting point for this volume. We would also like to thank the series editors of 'Rethinking Borders' – Hasting Donnan and Sarah Green – for their support throughout the process of realising this book project; Tom Dark, Lucy Burns, and Deborah Smith at Manchester University Press for their professional and friendly help in the process of developing and finalising the manuscript; and two anonymous reviewers for valuable comments on the book proposal and the first draft of the full manuscript. Finally, we would like to thank Chris Hann and the Max Planck Institute of Social Anthropology in Halle for providing space and resources for us to work on the introductory chapters of the book.

Introduction

Haldis Haukanes and Frances Pine

This is a book about gender and reproduction, about movement and migration, and about boundaries and borders. We look at boundaries in terms of both geo-political borders (lines across which people and things move that are regulated by states), and ideological or conceptual/classificatory borders (that are also often developed and imposed from above by the state, the church, kinship). Our contributors highlight and elaborate on the parallels between these two kinds of borders, and show how they overlap and mutually reinforce each other. Underpinning the range of case studies discussed by the contributors is an overall concern with regulation in terms of law, policy, and ideology.

The chapters focus on different aspects of reproduction in relation to the (gendered) body, the person or citizen, and ideologies and constructions of communities and/or the nation. We take reproduction to encompass the biological, the economic, the social, and the ideological. We argue that looking at borders and boundaries, both external geo-political ones and internal ideological or regulatory ones, allows us to unpick the processes of social reproduction and specifically the reproduction of structures both of inclusion, which identify and define those with entitlement, and of exclusion, which relegate particular categories of people to the margins. As Izabella Main states at the beginning of her Chapter 9 'the politics of reproduction is an example of the ways individual choices and local contexts are being shaped by state policy, power relations between states and individuals, and ideological control of people by institutions imposing regulations and laws' (Main, this volume). How specific politics of reproduction relate to individual choices, local contexts, power, and regulation lies at the heart of this book. These entanglements are continually manifested in places and spaces where borders and boundaries are articulated and come into play.

Writing specifically about borders and boundaries in relation to the governmentality of migration, Didier Fassin points to the ways in which external territorial borders and internal social categorisations are 'tightly related' in racialised and ethnicised ways (2011: 214). These internal categorisations and external territorial frontiers have traditionally been considered separately by social scientists, but recent works which aim to extend analyses and understandings of political classifications (as developed by Douglas (1966), Levi Strauss (1966), Durkheim and Mauss (1970)) and governmentality (by Foucault (1977)) have tried to bring together these 'tightly related' social phenomena, creating and reproducing processes of inclusion and exclusion, and structures of inequality. Bridget Anderson, for instance, has re-analysed the dyad of Us and Them in the context of migration, showing that the 'Us' category covers successful citizens, while the 'Them' encompasses both non-citizens (migrants, refugees, asylum seekers) and failed citizens (welfare recipients, 'scroungers'). These classifications create the basis for the processes of governmentality and regulation of persons and bodies and the reproduction of 'communities of value' (Anderson 2013; see also Morris 2018).

In this book we follow a similar trajectory, focusing not only on migration but also on gendered bodies, sexualities, and familial ideologies. We argue that in all of these areas, both external geo-political borders and internal conceptual and ideological boundaries become vehicles of reproduction for the nation and the state.

The chapters in the book reflect on the profound differences currently creating divisions both between European states (in and outside the European Union) and between citizens and residents within these. As conceptual and ideological frames, borders and boundaries delineate and define what is permitted and forbidden; regulate dominant, counter, and subversive discourses and practices; and monitor and police human bodies and how, when, and in what ways they are able to be mobile (Foucault 1977, Bourdieu 1990, Butler 1993, Fassin 2011). Mobility may take place on a physical landscape, and involve moving from place to place and crossing political borders, or it may refer to status and identity, moving from one class to another through education or training (see Bourdieu 1990, Willis 2000), through a change in gender or sexual identification (see Butler 1993), or through change in status due to economic loss or failure (see Newman 1999, Mollona 2009, Hann and Parry 2018). In many instances, such changes disrupt established patterns of reproduction.

Thus, what we are looking at in this particular historical moment is the simultaneous development of different kinds of borders and boundaries, which we could loosely categorise as geo-political and physical on the one hand, and politico-economic and ideological on the other. Both generate and facilitate particular patterns of exclusion and inclusion. Both also give rise to imaginings, hopes, and dreams (see, for example, Jansen and Löfving 2008, Hage 2009, Kaneff and Pine 2011, Pine 2014, Kleist and Jansen 2016). From the individual to the family, from the community to the nation, all the sites of or frames for personal and group identity are tangled up and implicated in a grand narrative of what constitutes a nation and what makes a good citizen. Each chapter in this book is concerned with one or more of these aspects of hierarchical distinctions and imaginations of the future.

Book sections

Part I Gendered life worlds: migrants' imaginaries and obligations in contested contexts of intimacy

In this section, we present ethnographic and phenomenological discussions of people's changing lives as they cross borders for work, as refugees, as caregivers or dependent kin, or for marriage. The chapters examine not only the gendered dimensions of geo-political borders, but also how, in new environments, people shift, transgress, and reshape moral boundaries of proper gender and kinship behaviour, and moral economies of intimacy and sexuality. Women who cross borders are often seen as a threat to proper gender and generational hierarchies at home, and are commonly represented as betraying the reproduction of the nation, as being promiscuous, and as failing in their maternal duties – as Fedyuk shows in her perceptive and nuanced account of Ukrainian caregivers in Italy (Chapter 2). In the destination countries, they may be seen as sexually predatory, as some Italians see the Romanian *badanti* described so vividly by Nicolescu (Chapter 5). Or migrant women may be viewed as a threat to liberal gender orders, wearing the headscarf, looking visibly 'different', and generally evoking stereotypes which make them 'matter out of place', as Leutloff-Grandits highlights in her moving accounts of Kosovan brides waiting to join their spouses in Austria and Germany (Chapter 3). There is a tension between visibility and invisibility here, however. For example, many migrant careworkers, like those Fedyuk and Nicolescu describe in their ethnographies from Italy, are rendered invisible in their places of work. They remain hidden from public view in private or domestic spaces, but perform intimate care that many believe should be given freely, as a duty of love or 'blood', by family. Marriage migrants, on the other hand, like the Kosovan women in Leutloff-Grandits' study, struggle to become visible, overcome ethnicised and gendered barriers hindering their mobilities, and realise the futures they have imagined. Questions of when and why these migrants choose to be seen or make themselves invisible, and when and why invisibility or visibility is imposed upon them, are threads running through these chapters, as are questions of gendered transnational obligations to provide resources to those back home in the form of care, money, or love. Ezzeddine and Havelková's comparative exploration of

Bosnian refugees and Ukrainian migrants living in the Czech Republic (Chapter 4) shows that the women, although migrating for very different reasons (the Bosnian war and the post-Soviet economic collapse) and at different historical periods, have been regulated similarly by Czech border regimes and by kinship and gender hierarchies both at home and abroad. Ezzeddine and Havelková demonstrate vividly the women's struggles to gain control over their own bodies and lives. Similar struggles are identified by both Fedyuk and Nicolescu, in their respective accounts of Ukrainian and Romanian *badanti* striving to embody new kinds of personhood and femininities, and to occupy their chosen spaces and be visible on their own terms.

Part II Gender, entitlement, and obligation: migrants interacting with the state and voluntary services

The chapters in this section look at situations where people cross borders into other geo-political states and have to navigate their way around unfamiliar social services. Each chapter addresses questions about rights, limitations on citizenship, claims on and different kinds of access to and use of public services in the state sector. While some of those who change country, or move between countries, cross borders voluntarily with the possibility of continued mobility, others – forced migrants and asylum seekers without papers or home to return to – have limited choice. In all cases, however, when people cross borders their circumstances in relation to the rights and obligations of citizenship inevitably change. People may claim rights and benefits from state or voluntary sector services, such as childcare, health, and housing, as Main (Chapter 9) and Isaksen and Czapka (Chapter 8), demonstrate in relation, respectively, to Polish women seeking reproductive assistance in Norway and Germany, and Poles and Italians organising childcare in Norway. These studies reveal how their participants decipher and navigate local health and systems and maneuver to open new spaces and possibilities in their lives. Other migrants may be ambivalent about accepting state interventions, or struggle to gain access to the right kind of services, as in the case of the Syrian refugees in Germany in Falge's poignant account (Chapter 6). Migrant careworkers like those in Spain whose dilemmas and struggles are evoked brilliantly by Bofill-Poch (Chapter 7) are both caretakers and caregivers, both recipients and providers of financial and other kinds of social aid. On moving to a new country, people may be unaware of their legal entitlements, and local institutional and bureaucratic procedures may stand in the way of, rather than facilitate, their access to such resources, as Falge illustrates with her Syrian research participants. In these situations, intermediaries often play a significant role in transferring information. In

Falge's case study, based on principles of action research, the researcher herself became an important mediator between her research participants and different state players. On the other hand, experiences of injustice may spur political mobilisation and unexpected collaborations, like the joint struggle for dignity between migrant and local careworkers and their elderly clients described by Bofill-Poch. Taken together, the chapters show vividly the range of relationships which come into play in negotiation of state services and resources, and in encounters over these with the state, voluntary sector, and intermediaries.

Part III Shifting gendered policies: reproduction and care in national and historical perspectives

In the final section of the book, our emphasis shifts from case studies and ethnographic accounts to more theoretical analyses of regulation, policy, and borders and boundaries. The authors all discuss policy formation at the level of the state, in contexts ranging from regulation of sexuality, through sex education, to regulation of careworkers in institutionalised care facilities. In different manners, these chapters interrogate the ways certain domains become politicised and disputed at different historical junctures while others are kept outside the political. They document the creation of borders and boundaries, delineating what is acceptable, expected, or desired, and what is transgressive. Kościańska (Chapter 12), writing about sex education in Poland, and Hašková and Dudová (Chapter 10), addressing reproductive policy in the Czech Republic, are explicitly concerned with the regulation of biological and social reproduction and the imposition of models of normative heterosexuality in relation to these. Kościańska demonstrates the active role of the state and church in hardening classificatory borders and policies around sexualities and reproduction, while Hašková and Dudová highlight the implications of particular policies and legislations in promoting heteronormative reproduction and simultaneously constraining the reproductive options of Rom and other ethnic minorities. Raising similar concerns to Falge's and Bofill-Poch's discussions of activism and collaboration in Section II, Fagertun (Chapter 11) examines the field of institutional care work in Norway as a contested site of gendered labour. She shows how the flexible and 'absorbent' character of the labour force in nursing homes is predicated on under-politicised, unequal access to permanent jobs, proper contracts, and employment rights for particular categories of workers – often migrants or women with little education. Taken together, the chapters highlight how political (including religious and gender) ideologies are formed by, and in turn form, state policy and in so doing regulate significant domains of social, cultural, and economic life.

References

Anderson, B. (2013) *Us and Them: The Dangerous Politics of Immigration Control.* Oxford: Oxford University Press.

Bourdieu, P. (1990) *Reproduction in Education, Society and Culture.* London: Sage.

Butler, J. (1993) *Bodies that Matter: On the Discursive Limits of 'Sex'.* Abingdon, Oxon: Routledge.

Douglas, M. (1966) *Purity and Danger: An Analysis of the Concepts of Pollution and Taboo.* New York: Routledge and Kegan Paul.

Durkheim, Emile and Mauss, Marcel (1970) *Primitive Classification.* London: Routledge.

Fassin, D. (2011) 'Policing Borders, Producing Boundaries. The Governmentality of Immigration in Dark Times', *Annual Review of Anthropology* 40: 213–226.

Foucault, M. (1977) *Discipline and Punish.* London: Knopf Doubleday.

Hage, G. (2009) *Waiting.* Melbourne: Melbourne University Press.

Hann, C. and J. Parry (2018, eds) *Industrial Labor on the Margins of Capitalism: Precarity, Class, and the Neoliberal Subject.* London: Routledge.

Levi-Strauss, Claude (1966) *The Savage Mind.* Chicago: University of Chicago Press.

Jansen, S. and S. Löfving (2008, eds) *Struggles for Home: Violence, Hope and the Movement of People.* London: Berghahn.

Kaneff, D. and F. Pine (2011, eds) *Global Connections and Emerging Inequalities in Europe: Perspectives on Poverty and Transnational Migration.* London: Anthem Press.

Kliest, N. and S. Jansen (2016) 'Hope over Time: Crisis, Immobility and Future-making', *History and Anthropology*, Special Issue 27 (4): 373–392.

Mollona, M. (2009) *Made in Sheffield: An Ethnography of Industrial Work and Politics.* London: Berghahn.

Morris, L. (2018) 'Reconfiguring Rights in Austerity Britain: Boundaries, Behaviours and Contestable Margins', *Journal of Social Policy* 48 (2): 271–291.

Newman, C.S. (1999) *Falling from Grace: Downward Mobility in the Age of Affluence.* Berkeley and Los Angeles: University of California Press.

Pine, F. (2014) 'Migration as Hope: Space, Time and Imagining the Future'. *Current Anthropology* 55, Supplement 9: 95–104.

Willis, Paul (2000) *The Ethnographic Imagination.* Cambridge: Polity Press.

1

Reconceptualising borders and boundaries: gender, movement, reproduction, regulation

Frances Pine and Haldis Haukanes

Introduction

Borders and boundaries, and bordering as a process, are at the centre of this chapter. Our primary focus is on Europe, but we recognise that it is imperative to locate Europe in relation to history and to the rest of the world, and to identify the shifts which have taken and take place over time both in the borders of Europe, and in borders within and between different European nation states. We show that borders, and processes of bordering, are never static; they represent very different experiences for different people, for different kinds of bodies, and at different times. As has been repeatedly witnessed over the past century, people who live within a nation's borders as recognised citizens can suddenly find that, overnight, they lose the rights or status of citizenship, the right to live where they have long been settled, and/or the possibility of mobility between different states. One has only to think of the situation of European Jews in the 1930s and 1940s, of the Windrush generation who arrived in the UK from the Caribbean between 1948 and 1970 (and then found in 2019 that they had no rights to remain), of current changes in UK migration policy after Brexit, or of former Soviet citizens who found that national borders became hard in ways that changed life worlds unexpectedly and sometimes irrevocably. Borders do not mean the same thing for all people, and neither do they mean the same thing for the same people at different points in their lives and in history.

As we turn our attention to the processes of bordering and boundary making which have been taking place over recent decades, it is helpful to consider what constitutes a moral community or a community of value (Anderson 2013), who is considered to belong, and who is excluded. As we show, these notions of morality or value rest on shifting sands; people who are included for long periods may become excluded, as different economies and political ideologies emerge (for instance, in many European countries following the acceleration of migration globally leading up to the 2015 refugee crisis). For some of the world's population, in and outside Europe, established safety nets, based on state benefits, healthcare and social services, and care and support from family, kin, and community, have been eroded; this erosion has serious consequences in terms of the possibilities for mobility and for a reasonable quality of life both for those who want to cross borders, and for those within states where polarisation between rich and poor, often perceived as deserving and undeserving, widens.

In recent years there has been a plethora of work on borders and boundaries (see, for instance, Butler 1993, Donnan and Wilson 1999, Lan 2003, Constable 2007, Fassin 2011, Follis 2012, De Genova 2013, 2017, Green 2013, Donnan, Hurd, and Leutloff-Grandits 2017). Broadly, it falls into several loose categories: conceptual and theoretical work; work on practices, regulations, and consequences of material borders and boundaries; work on borders and boundaries as systems of classification; and work on borders of bodies, sexualities, genders. While much of the material is very rich, there has been, with a few exceptions (see for instance, Fassin 2011, Green 2013, Morris 2018), little attempt to address the areas of intersection where the different meanings, understandings, and theoretical and analytical uses of the terms meet, overlap, or converge. Ethnography offers a powerful tool for untangling these points of intersection, and the shifting sands on which borders and boundaries are erected, enforced, and differentially experienced (see Khosravi 2010).

In this chapter, therefore, we want to focus on these areas of intersection. We first identify the broad areas which are relevant for our topics, and then offer a brief review of the work which has most influenced or challenged our thinking. We are not aiming to provide a complete or comprehensive overview of the literature on borders and boundaries, but to engage with that pertinent for the present volume and suggest how the different approaches can usefully be combined to widen our understanding of the complexities of bodies, borders, and regulation.

Migration is not a new phenomenon. Humans have always moved (see Castles and Miller 2009, Kaneff and Pine 2011). What is striking, however, about the current 'age of migration' (Faist 2000, Castles and Miller 2009) is its intensity, its ubiquitous nature, and the speed with which information about it and images of it appear throughout the world. This speed of communication and instant access to images and knowledge (of sorts) also takes place in the spread of political movements and ideologies, ideas about personhood and bodies, and understandings of sexualities and genders. As is the case with all kinds of social and political movements, whether of people or of ideas and classifications, these processes must be contextualised and historicised. We would argue that in the aftermath of the 2008 financial crisis in the West, and acceleration of war and violent conflict in the Middle East, we witnessed not only a full blown global refugee crisis but also – related to these phenomena – the rise of the new right and populist politics in much of Europe, and increasing attempts by some states to regulate both sexuality and reproduction. These processes are all in different ways implicated in the commodification of bodies and the financialisation of certain kinds of 'intimate' labour (i.e. childcare, elder care, sex work). This process of market expansion and commodification is intricately connected to the changing locations of production and the values attached to labour, the growth of global capital investment in privatised care institutions, movements of both labour force and commodities/products of labour, and global growth of precarious labour.

With these points in mind, we want to look back at the very busy twentieth century, and the events and movements which led to critical change in ideology, reproduction, and regulation. What becomes apparent when such a timeline of history is laid out is the frequency with which new ideas are introduced, resisted, and then incorporated, leading to changes in political regimes and social classifications. What at one period might look like a definitive move to the right may be superseded by a widespread embrace of leftist socialist ideas or feminist principles, which in turn may be eroded by a sweeping tide of neo-liberal individualism. Neither time nor history ever stands still; what is striking about the past two decades, though, is the speed and pace of change, and the resultant sense of anxiety and uncertainty that marks many people's daily existence.

Background

Critical moments, resulting in regulation and alteration of both geo-political and ideological/conceptual borders, recurred throughout the twentieth century. Between 1914 and 1918, the First World War laid the foundations for the realignment of European imperial powers, and the creation of some new (or newly merged) nations and the geographical redefinition of others in the Treaty of Versailles in 1919. Politically, the European world was split from the mid 1930s into countries aligned with the fascism of Italy and later Spain and Germany, those opposed to fascism and its spread, and those which remained neutral. From the time of the Spanish Civil War to the end of the Second Word War, allegiances were formed and broken, states were incorporated into the political realms of more powerful others, and all of Europe, as well as much of the rest of the world, existed in a state of uncertainty and rupture. In 1945, the Yalta Conference and the Potsdam

Treaty again re-drew the boundaries of Europe, and at the same time, resistance movements in Africa and Asia against colonial power grew. Between 1945, when the division of Europe between the Soviet and the Western Blocs was made, and 1961, when this division was materialised in militarised metal and bricks, the Iron Curtain dividing the socialist and capitalist worlds solidified. In 1989, the states of the Soviet Bloc one by one fell, and eventually, in 1991, the Soviet Union itself began to disintegrate.

All of these alignments and re-alignments were accompanied by movements of people, sometimes forced and sometimes chosen. Simultaneously, other people were trapped behind militarised borders, frozen, unable to move even when they wanted to. These regime and border changes all created extreme economic, political, and affective changes in people's daily lives and livelihoods. And they all generated new attempts by states to impose particular ideologies and to regulate people's bodies, families, reproduction, and ways of being in the world. This was by no means confined to European space and Europeans. In the same postwar period, movements of people, opening and hardening of borders, and various forms of regulation led to new arrangements of people and ideas throughout the world. In the early postwar years, refugees continued to try to return to their homes, or find new homes elsewhere. Migration from Africa and the Caribbean, particularly, was encouraged by the UK in order to fill the holes in the British labour forces resulting from war; similar movements took place between other waning or former colonial powers and their territories, as in France and North Africa. War, anti-colonial revolt, drastic economic changes often categorised as 'development', and environmental change all led to instability and famine in parts of Africa, Asia, and the Middle East. Huge movements of people within and between countries and continents marked, for instance, the aftermath of civil war and ethnic cleansing in Uganda, famine in Ethiopia, and war in Viet Nam, the Cuban Revolution, and the periods of violent unrest and oppression across Latin America, notably in Chile and Argentina. In many ways, events of the second half of the twentieth century laid the foundations for the challenges facing the economy worldwide and the crisis in the environment which were to mark the first two decades of the twenty-first century.

As geo-political border enforcements and hardenings were taking place, and as migration increasingly became people's reaction to crises such as war, famine, and environmental disaster, as well as to entrenched poverty, ideas and ideologies concerning personhood and citizenship, bodies and reproduction, sexuality and gender were also undergoing enormous change. In the early twentieth century, concepts of citizenship in many countries widened as women received the vote. In 1948, the Universal Declaration of Human Rights was adopted by the United Nations' General Assembly, and the concept of universal rights, regardless of nationality, colour, or creed gradually became accepted. By the 1960s, in the West, developments in birth control were accompanied by a 'sexual revolution'. The women's liberation and new feminist movements challenged conservative ideas about sex and gender difference, 'proper' sex roles, and social and legal institutions such as marriage. Homosexuality was decriminalised in many places, again challenging entrenched ideologies and ideas about sexuality, morality, and the person. In the USA, the civil rights movement took on racism and racial inequality, challenging received values and norms concerning inequality, exclusion, and difference. Abortion, albeit subject to some restrictions in most countries, was widely legalised in Europe and North America. Although after the invasions of Hungary in 1956 and Czechoslovakia in 1968 there was widespread disillusionment with the Soviet Union and 'actual existing socialism' among the left, and the Cold War intensified from the late 1950s onwards, there was also a revival of interest in socialist theory, in communism, and in political revolution, demonstrated vividly in American (and indeed worldwide) opposition to the war in Viet Nam. Through these social movements and others, many of the ways in which rights were understood and enforced or denied, bodies regulated, reproduction (biological and social) controlled, and citizenship constructed, both by state institutions and legal structure and by popular beliefs and understanding, underwent significant change. By the end of the twentieth century, the collapse of the Soviet Union had to all intents and purposes ended the Cold War, but new, powerful divisions were developing with the rise of religious fundamentalisms, the spread of right wing nationalism and increased xenophobia in many nation states, and a seemingly endless series of small wars and violent civil conflicts throughout the world. These had huge effects in terms of loss of life, rights, and livelihood, and the movements of people which culminated in the 2015 refugee crisis. As we write, we are seeing the political consequences of the anti-migrant sentiment which became visible throughout much of Europe in the second decade of the twenty-first century, and has resulted in the resurrection of hard, militarised borders in much of eastern central Europe, amid the growth of anti-EU discourse in particular member states, including pre- and post-referendum UK. And as the Covid-19 virus spreads globally, resulting in lockdown in many areas of the world, new kinds of regulations and restrictions are being applied at national borders, placing constraints on travel and mobility in an unprecedented way. Simultaneously, as hundreds of thousands of displaced people continue to live in impossibly crowded and unsanitary conditions in refugee camps, increasing numbers are attempting to cross the Mediterranean, or to make the journey from Calais to the English coast, in small, unsafe vessels. The virus, far from being indiscriminate as some have claimed, is exacerbating the precarious existence of many of the world's most excluded people, and further limiting their possibilities for mobility, safe travel, and the most rudimentary forms of social welfare.

Border regimes – hard, soft, and permeable

This ongoing global crisis in migration, fuelled by war, famine, poverty, climate change, and other forms of extreme and critical events – like the spread of Covid-19 – tends to be viewed in terms of citizenship, hard and porous borders, and militarisation of boundaries between nation states. The perceived violation of geo-political borders by migrants (asylum seekers, refugees, and others) often contrasts with the necessity for porous borders that allow carers and others such as factory, agricultural, and construction workers to bring their labour to the domestic market. Country of origin and citizenship define who has freedom to cross borders and divides people into those who can move as they chose and those who are considered unwelcome or illegal. For instance, the countries which are enclosed by the geo-political borders of Schengen and the European Union define their citizens as Europeans who have freedom to cross those borders (both internal and external). On the other hand, people from outside Schengen and EU regions experience the borders very differently, as hard borders, the crossing of which takes place only after complicated negotiations, or illegally.

The time dimension is crucial in understanding how borders are established, develop, and disappear. Although they often appear to be 'natural' lines, dividing land and transforming it into territory by following a mountain range or a river, geo-political borders – like socio-political classifications – are actually created at particular moments, and eliminated or erased at others. However, it is often a strange kind of erasure. The physical border between East and West Germany had been incredibly *present* and extremely threatening. When it first was dismantled, and the corridors of fallow land watched over by military observation towers which separated the East and the West became overgrown and then disappeared from sight, people marvelled that something that had loomed so large in their lives could just dissolve, so quickly (see, for example, Berdahl 1999). As time went on, however, it was clear that it did not entirely disappear. People remembered where it had been and, like a lost limb, it was often experienced as if it were still there. Thus, borders are ambiguous spaces, which shift from being hard to soft and back again, and can be seen both as 'layers of political history inscribed in space' and as 'emergent from practices, flows and processes' (Hurd et al. 2017: 3). The post-Soviet borderlands between Russia, Estonia, and Latvia are one case in point; while the borders were porous during the Soviet period, they became gradually harder with the EU accession of Latvia and Estonia in 2004 and finally the Schengen agreement in 2008. As Laura Assmuth demonstrates in her ethnography of the Seto people living on the Estonian–Russian border, daily border crossings for trade, family, or other purposes became increasingly difficult, dependent on formal documents and thus on personal status and wealth in this period. Nevertheless, residents of the area on both sides of the (relatively hard) border continue their borderland interactions and exchanges (Assmuth 2013). Similarly, the Polish–Ukrainian border markedly softened in the years between 1991 and 2004, and then progressively hardened after 2004, when after Poland's accession it became the eastern border of the EU (Follis 2012).

These are also borders which always have the potential to be leaky – not only at different historical periods – as in the Polish–Ukraine example above – but also in the same period, for different actors in different spaces. A border may be closed to most foreigners, but open to a few with certain skill sets, financial position, or social relations and connections, and may present certain opportunities for slippage – it may become more permeable in the night, or when the guards change, or when a bribe can be paid so someone looks away. Aimee Joyce describes the Polish–Belarus border as ostensibly a hard border; however, the border guards are the sons and grandsons and life-long neighbours of old women who are habitual smugglers of certain goods such as vodka and cigarettes. These women have their own special seats on the cross border train, in which they make secret compartments in the seats to hide their contraband, secure in the knowledge that their boys will not search for them. But Joyce discusses how other dangerous or violent smugglers, who are reputed to move more valuable goods, and guns or people, are feared and the guards are said to attempt to harden and close the border to them (Joyce 2015).

Borders are thus simultaneously hard militarised places, and porous grey spaces. They are also affective spaces, across and around which sociality and social relations are developed, and memories and emotions evoked (see, for instance, Reeves 2014). Sarah Green points to a useful distinction between borders as objects, and borders as process. 'Borders regarded as objects, whether symbolic or material, are imagined as having thing-like qualities and are most often understood as mental or physical barriers or bridges. The borders-as-process approach argues instead that borders are, in effect, a technique: bordering, or the process of classifying and ordering space and relations between here and elsewhere in the world' (Green 2013: 350).

Nicholas De Genova has written about the obscenity of border regimes (De Genova 2013; see also Fassin 2011, Anderssen 2014, Bigo, Carrera, and Guild 2016), and we have great sympathy with this perspective. However, it is also important to consider and to engage with stories of those who manage to cross borders and to begin new lives. It is essential to look at both constraints and survival strategies, at ways that individuals and families plan, negotiate, and embark on migration, and at the consequences mobility and migration may have for various other people. Migration involves not only the person who moves, either as voluntary migrant or as refugee or asylum seeker, but also those who stay behind but facilitate or benefit from the migrations of others (i.e. remittances). Further, a range of people in the receiving countries interact with migrants, employing them, working with them, offering services and collaborations to them, and/or regulating and disciplining them. As well as crossing legal, physical, and often highly militarised borders between nation states, people often find that they face new boundaries and classifications when they arrive, and that they are subject to legal, moral and ideological rules, regulations and expectations aimed at shaping their behaviour and their agency. In other words, the same kinds of contradiction and ambiguity which surround the ideology and practices of geo-political borders also apply to migrants' bodies, in their capacity as workers (welcome) and alien others (unwelcome). Writing about governmentality and immigration, Fassin argues that 'borders as external territorial frontiers and boundaries as internal social categorizations are tightly related in a process in which immigrants are racialized and ethnic minorities are reminded of their foreign origin' (2011: 114). And further: 'harsh policing is not incompatible with tolerance regarding illegality of migrant workers who contribute significantly to several economic sectors' (2011: 218; De Genova 2013, see also Anderssen 2014, Uhde and Ezzeddine 2019).

While we are strongly in agreement with Fassin about the links between territorial and classificatory borders, we want to take this discussion one step further, and to look comparatively at types of inequality, and processes of inclusion and exclusion, which take place not only in relation to 'outsiders' who cross national borders, but also to citizens within those borders. We take seriously Bridget Anderson's argument that migration itself is not the only issue: she points out that non-citizens (migrants) and failed citizens (unemployed, living on benefit, etc.) are in many ways viewed and judged similarly, and are subject to the same kinds of moralised and politicised exclusions (Anderson 2013; see also Morris 2018). Following Anderson, we suggest that in discussions of questions of mobility, our focus should be on exclusion, inclusion, and regulation of particular kinds of persons, including migrants but also extending to failed citizens – what Lydia Morris referred to years ago as 'Dangerous Classes' (1994). Morris was writing about UK state discourse, in which single mothers and other welfare recipients – 'scroungers' – were seen as consuming the welfare goods and capital of society, without earning or deserving them. She showed how the arguments of the 1980s and 1990s, first articulated in the Thatcher years, producing by the turn of the century a view of the deserving and undeserving poor reminiscent of the Victorian poor laws. This served not only to blame the poor for their poverty, but also to identify a particular category of person – notably young, black unmarried mothers – as a scourge on society and a leech on social resources. Morris' recent work on borders, migrants, refugees, and asylum seekers, and rights to or exclusion from state benefits and other aspects of citizenship, shows how the tactic of blaming the most vulnerable for the predicaments in which they find themselves has been exacerbated in the UK in recent years by repeated attempts to introduce policy and legislation to curtail access to welfare and benefit payments for those merited undeserving. Writing about the new Universal Credit recently introduced in the UK, which replaces previously separate payments for housing, child benefit, etc. with one lump sum, Morris states:

> this reform of the welfare system also featured in political rhetoric as both the reason and the means to control migration, with domestic welfare and migration presented as "two sides of the same coin", and subject to an attack on the "something for nothing culture" ... Welfare provision is particularly amenable to boundaries of inclusion and exclusion, engaging as it does questions of resource, desert[1] and belonging, and the design and delivery of the whole system increasingly rests upon techniques of conditionality and control that extend across the three fields of domestic welfare, migration, and asylum. It therefore invites an approach that examines such policies together by means of a unified frame of analysis. (2018: 271–272)

Very similar discourses are developing today in many other European countries, most strikingly in eastern central Europe, as well as in the USA, aimed at strengthening the division between acceptable and unacceptable citizens or residents, and between proper and transgressive practices. As Thelen and Alber point out, the language of kinship (descent, blood, genetic ties) and kinship practice (marriage, parenting, affiliation) are used as instruments of both inclusion and exclusion in terms of rights to or denial of citizenship, as well as of migration and border crossing (Thelen and Alber 2018: 15). We would argue that emphasis on kinship stresses likeness and classifies people as like 'us', while perceived absence of kinship classifies people as 'them' and hence other. It does not involve a major leap of the imagination to see the parallels between anti-migrant (xenophobic or racist) and anti-LGBTQI (heteronormative) politics. We return to these questions later in this chapter, and they come up in various ways in several of the others, most explicitly in those of Hašková and Dudová (Chapter 10), and of Kościańska (Chapter 12). Here, it is perhaps enough to point out that just as an anti-migrant politics supports hard geo-political borders and severe regulation of or brakes on mobility for certain categories of people from other countries on the basis of colour, religion, place of origin, or, indeed, sexuality, an anti-LGBTQI politics builds up classificatory boundaries between people within a country and discriminates against some on the basis of criteria of sex, sexual preference, and gender.

It is important to remember, however, that movements across borders, from one EU country to another or from outside the EU into an EU country, may also generate possibilities for new life options and identities for individuals, and new landscapes of hope or imaginations of positive futures (see Jackson 2013, Narotzky and Besnier 2014, Pine 2014, Leutloff-Grandits, Chapter 3, this volume). In terms of sex and gender politics, while the move to the right and the implementation of repressive laws regulating reproduction, sexuality, and gender in some countries are cause for deep concern, in many other places state policies have followed public demands for more flexible categories, for recognition of different kinds of (non-binary) bodies and embodied practices. Here, for instance, we can think of legislation permitting same-sex marriage, allowing self-ascription in gender classification, and more liberal laws concerning assisted reproduction technologies, early terminations of pregnancy, and so forth. In relation to care, policies in some countries have broadened state economic and practical participation in childcare, healthcare, care for the elderly, and general support for individuals and families. We are thus witnessing a moment of polarisation in Europe (and beyond) in which on the one hand progress towards inclusion and equality (gender, sexuality, reproduction, labour) is being made in terms of both policy and popular understandings and discourses, and on the other hand ideologies of exclusion, separation, and right-wing nationalism are effervescing, fuelled by strong populist movements and sentiments that are reinforced and legitimated by state policies of regulation. To quote Morris, referring specifically to the management of migration in the UK, 'Again, we see stratified rights deployed as a means of social control, a supporting rational citing behaviours and abuse, and shrinking boundaries of entitlement justified by "fairness"' to the taxpayer' (Morris 2018: 279).

Geographical mobility is by no means a given for much of the world's population. However, when it is considered a right – for instance in the case of legal, EU-regulated mobility within the Eurozone – it may imply life-changing possibilities in everyday life, such as access to care services unavailable in the home context or escape from a regime that is repressive in terms of sexual and reproductive rights and practices (see Main, Chapter 9, this volume).

Regimes of intimate care

Borders and boundaries are gendered and sexualised. In terms of both gender and sexuality, the border between the public and the domestic/

private domains is significant, especially in relation to regimes of care – both economic and ideological – within the family and outside it. Since Arendt and Habermas first discussed these issues, we have been aware that the private (domestic) and the public are overlapping, ambiguous, and often changing domains. The writings of feminist theorists in the 1970s and 1980s reconceptualised these domains in terms of gendered spaces and gendered inequalities, and of visible and invisible labour (Rosaldo 1974, Reiter 1975, Barrett 1980, Harris 1981, Barrett and Mackintosh 1982, Pateman 1988, Strathern 1988). A key concern for these early thinkers was to highlight the value of reproductive labour in the overall political economy, but they also sought to emphasise the relation between cultural constructions of gendered labour and sexuality and the reproduction of unequal sex-gender systems (Rubin 1975, Strathern 1988).

The context of these discussions of gendered labour and reproduction shifted noticeably in the late 1990s and early 2000s, as the related phenomena in Western Europe of increasing numbers of women in the labour force and increasing longevity more generally led to a crisis in care. Simply, the daughters and daughters-in-law who had previously provided altruistic care within the extended family were no longer available to look after the elderly and the ill, who in turn were living longer and needing increasing amounts of care.

Unsurprisingly, discussions of care work as labour have widened in the past three decades to adapt to changing labour and demographic patterns arising from phenomena such as those mentioned above. Increasingly, in practice, domestic labour and caring have been separated off from kinship and family labour and have been made more visible, and rapidly more commercialised/financialised, as they are performed by non-family members, who are often migrant women (and less often men), for pay. Feminist scholars theorising gender and labour have taken great interest in care work as paid/professionalised labour, discussing among other things the rationales evoked for paying for care, the relational qualities underpinning various forms of care work – from family based to institutional care (Wærness 1984/2000) – and the role of the state in organising welfare services to advance a gender equal society (Hernes 1985, Fraser 1994). Similarly, attention has been paid to class and other social inequalities present in the more 'grey' areas of care work, such as unregulated, privately arranged and financed home-based care (Daly and Lewis 2000, Lan 2003, Pratt 2009, Lutz and Palenda-Möllenbeck 2011).

Whether care work is performed by paid employees working inside the household, or by state or other public actors, is partly determined by the particular state's policies concerning provision of subsidised external care facilities – nurseries, day care, support facilities, and residential care homes for elderly etc. In the Scandinavian countries, such provision is largely considered part of the state's duty of care (Fagertun, Chapter 11, this volume, Widding Isaksen and Czapka, Chapter 8, this volume, Bundgaard and Fog Olwig 2018). In other countries like Italy and Spain, where care has been increasingly privatised in keeping with neo-liberal market principles, carers are as likely to be brought into the household as they are to provide outside (institutional) care (see Bofill-Poch, Chapter 7, Fedyuk, Chapter 2, Nicolescu Chapter 5, all in this volume). And it is important to note that these countries are also *providers* of carers for countries such as France, Germany, and the UK, as well as for the Scandinavian countries.

Care of children and care of the elderly are emotionally and ideologically charged areas. In many ways, these two generations, the very youngest and the very oldest, are cyphers for the core of social and biological reproduction – the culmination of the economic life and resources of a family (hence links between and conflicts over care and (threats to) inheritance), and the embodiment of the hope for what is to be built in the future (hence the anxiety about outsiders caring for – and forming – these as yet unformed beings). With the separation of care work from domestic labour, the most intimate acts of care and reproduction are moving out of the family and household, and often out of the national workforce. Some of the moral panic erupting in the face of increasing migration must be understood in terms of these categorical and highly affective shifts in the labour, financialisation, and value of intimate care. The disjuncture between practices of care – for pay – by outsiders and the growing capitalisation and commodification of care facilities and persistent ideologies of care – for love and duty – by kin and family, fuels the panic and generally complicates both the affective and the socio-political public understandings of care.

In relation to the role of the state and the family in provision of care, the significance of mobility and border crossings in the economy of care as it has flourished in the past two decades cannot be overestimated. The work of care is regulated by both the state and the families who employ carers, and ideologies of kinship, gender, sexuality, and nation/state meet and intersect at specific times and in particular spaces. One consequence of this is that the labour of care itself, and the persons and bodies of the careworkers, are often hidden from public view in the domestic or private domain. And because of the ambiguities surrounding their position, the critical part they play in the process of reproduction – of the person, the family, the community, and the nation – is often obscured. At other times transnational care work is highly visible and organised, as in cases of global nursing care chains, where transnational agencies play a key role along with 'sending' states, the latter being paramount in ensuring that 'local' nursing education systems are compatible with Western standards and thus that careworkers can be exported (Yeates 2012: 139). There is an inherent contradiction in transnational divisions of labour and affect – the global care chain (Pratt 2009, Hochschild 2013), where women (particularly) leave behind their most morally binding obligations, the care of their own children and elderly parents, in order to provide care for the children and elderly relatives of strangers in other countries. The emotional labour carried out by the women involves two very different efforts: one part is 'to address her relationships with those she cares for and who hire her, and another part addresses the wrenching ruptures with those she leaves behind' (Hochschild 2013: 128; see also Isaksen et al. 2008, Pratt 2009). In parallel, ambivalence arises from the emotional conflict which confronts employers who need to see the carers as 'family members' to justify or rationalise their intimate roles, but who also wish to maintain and regulate hierarchical relations with them.

Boundary work, a term developed in cultural sociology by scholars such as Nippert-Eng and Lamont (see Lan 2003, Barua 2018), has been taken up in domestic work research to identify precisely this regulation of relationships in the 'contact space' of the home (Lan 2003). Boundary work in this context focuses attention on the daily life strategies – the micro-politics (Lan 2003) – of creating and maintaining symbolic boundaries, physical and social, between the employer and the employee; for example, through the use of deferential language or hierarchical/exclusionist organisation of space and eating patterns (Lan 2003, Barua et al. 2016). As Lan demonstrates so well in her study of migrant domestic workers in Taiwan and their employers, boundaries can be created through contact just as well as through distance; she suggests that 'employers may develop an intimate relationship of maternal benevolence with domestic workers to affirm their own class and ethnic superiority' (Lan 2003: 532–533). Further, the maintenance of hierarchical boundaries is smoother when the domestic worker is a migrant as 'foreignness' seems to justify discriminatory treatment (Lan 2003: 532). This way of thinking goes hand in hand with exclusionist migration policies that deny migrant workers citizenship and permanent residence (Lan 2003: 532). Still, there is a constant need to work on the maintenance of boundaries in relations between domestic workers and their employers. Boundary work often involves ambivalence and fear of 'inappropriate' transgression; for example, in the form of sexual relations (Constable 2007; Fedyuk Chapter 2 this volume, Nicolescu, Chapter 5 this volume). Especially, sexualised or sexual relations between elderly men and younger women carers are commonly viewed as highly problematic and are often morally condemned (see Fedyuk, Chapter 2, this volume). These relations may be consensual, and entered into freely by the women (see Fedyuk, Chapter 2, this volume, Nicolescu, Chapter 5, this volume). However, female domestic workers, living in a strange land often with no support network of their own, and with few resources outside the employers' house and immediate circle, are often vulnerable to sexual advances, pressure, and not infrequently violence (Figuereiro et al. 2018). Again, the idiom 'like family' which surrounds much care work often masks a much darker reality of inequality, exploitation, and risk or danger.

Social reproduction, class and status, and capital – the place of moral economy

The growing commodification of types of care formerly[2] carried out by kin evokes ambivalence and hence ambiguity. Kinship and family relations are infused with expectations and evocations of emotional attachment, reciprocity, and (inter)dependence, all underpinned by a strong assumption of morality. And even the kind of exploitation, unequal power relations, and gendered or generational violence referred to in the section above tend to be justified by an ideology of proper kinship or family order. The concept of 'moral economy' can be helpful in unpacking some of the complexities implicit in the entanglements of kinship, state, and economy. Since it was first proposed by social historian E.P. Thompson (1971) as a more substantive alternative to or dimension of the formalist, rational economy, the term has been used widely, often rather loosely, and as a result has been sharply critiqued and criticised (not least by Thompson himself 1991; see also, Hann 2018). Palomera and Vetta (2016) argue for the retention of the concept, with an increased emphasis on social reproduction, class dimensions, and capitalist accumulation. In terms of discussions of borders, care, social reproduction, and regulation by state, church, and other institutions, moral economy can be used to look both at the entitlements (socio-economic and other) claimed by specific categories of people – in relation to the state, community, or family – and at the ideas and ideologies invoked to make particular demands or claims on the state, the border regimes, and providers and institutions of care. A moral economy can perhaps be viewed as the flip side of the political economy: two complementary and often overlapping domains rather than opposed regimes of morality and affect on the one hand and rationality on the other. Importantly in the context of this chapter, both political and moral economy imply hierarchical power relations, and shared understanding of entitlements arising from these, which are driven by particular conceptualisations of value and desert. In this section we consider these contexts of moral economy in turn.

The critical events of the last decade have brought into stark relief deeply rooted and felt differences – and indeed rifts – in society. These are increasingly evident at both a worldwide and a community/family level. Globally, the sharp contrast between quality of life, possibilities of life, affordances and options for mobility and survival between the North and the South, and the East and the West, are paralleled by contrasts and gaps within countries and regions, between political right and left, between the included and the excluded, between those who are fiercely regulated and those who are above regulation (see De Genova 2013, Jackson 2013, Bigo et al. 2016). In all of these different contexts, individuals, political parties, and state and religious institutions evoke principles of morality, and the kinds of implicit moral and social contract Thompson described in his seminal article, to make claims and to justify and promote their own positions. Thus, the rise of the populist New Right in the United States, in the United Kingdom, and in much of southern and eastern central Europe is linked to fears and uncertainties about entitlement – who is entitled to work, who is entitled to social benefit, who is entitled to health, education, and housing services? From the point of view of the political right, these are legal entitlements of citizenship which are linked to worth or value, and which should exclude non-citizens, undeserving citizens, and outsiders (back to Anderson and to Morris). What is important here is that these are claims made from a strongly moral perspective; the fear of encroachment and strain on resources from outside is an argument of limited good, which assumes that there is never enough to go around, and which comes from an experience or perception of being left out, left behind, and excluded 'in their own land' (Hochschild 2016; see also Pasierka 2017). In other words, the state and its agents are perceived at best as ineffectual and at worst as corrupt and self-interested; by opening borders, by supporting non-deserving insiders, and by failing to regulate the moral bankruptcy and avarice at the top of society as much as failed citizenship at the bottom, the state is seen as failing in its obligation to care for its own people. From the point of view of the political left, on the other hand, the legal and moral premises of universal rights, and of human rights, demand the opposite; here the obligation of the state is to provide for people who are vulnerable, who are at risk in their own countries, who are facing political or 'natural' crises which endanger life and livelihood. The emphasis is not on limited good, and hence restriction of access from the outside, but on obligation to share resources. The problem is that the two positions – and we are deliberately oversimplifying them here for the sake of argument – appear to be, and often are, experienced as unreconcilable, and hence possibilities of negotiation and reconciliation – of opening rather than closing and hardening borders and boundaries – are severely limited. We have only to think of the paralysis in dealing with Brexit in the United Kingdom, of the Wall wars around Trump's ambition to build a militarised, impenetrable wall all along the US–Mexican border, or of the Hungarian government's border closures and highly politicised distrust of 'others', refugees, Roma, or Jews like Soros, to see how these divisions are being played out. What is important to remember is that both sides, or the various sides, are claiming moral high ground, and are, in effect, invoking the notion of moral economy to support their claims (see Hann 2010, Pasierka 2017).

When we turn from the broad political picture to individual cases, we can see the same contradictions in play. Here we consider two areas where this is very clear: care, and sex/gender relations. Both of these areas are concerned with reproduction and are subject to particular types of regulation. Both entail reconsiderations of concepts such as value, entitlement, and desert. We look first at care.

Care in some ways lies at the centre of the morality of kinship; across cultures and historical periods, ideas about the proper care reciprocities among kin and families, and the delegation of obligations and responsibilities between family and state, are core to the understanding of personhood, relations of hierarchy and equality, and entitlements (see Thelen and Alber 2018). The implicit contradiction between the privatisation of intimate care and its provision by outsiders, and the ideology of altruistic care provided freely by kin and friends, stems from the position of carework as both *outside* a moral economy of kinship, or even anathema to it, and *at the heart of* a new financialised economy of care, in which outsiders are paid by the family or by the state to behave 'like family'. Hence, ambiguous relations and representations of care commonly involve leakage between categories. At stake here, at least in part, is on the one hand capital accumulation, which separates those who control capital and the labour of others – and those who sell their labour to others – in a hierarchical relation, and on the other the financialisation of freely given, unpaid family care. Both of these aspects of care have implications for 'traditional' moral economies of kinship, and suggest their replacement, at least in part, by a different kind of economic relation involving payment and inequality, but also evoking claims of morality and affect.

Similar issues are immediately apparent when we turn from kinship and care to sex and gender relations. As Foucault showed, these are embodied relations, morally as well as physically. Marriage, the family, and reproduction rest on core moral concepts about the nature of proper bodies and proper unions, and their purpose/s. For Marx, humans created their value through productive labour, and ability to control the products of labour (productive and reproductive) determined social and economic (class) position; for Foucault, church and state introduced and regulated a discipline of the human body which again reflects the value of productivity: non-(re)productive sex – heterosexual or same sex – was viewed as deviant and had to be disciplined (Foucault, 1984). Simultaneously, however, and increasingly in the past century or so, sex, reproduction, and fertility have become marketable commodities, with a price (see, for example, Schurr and Friedrich 2015). In a capitalist or neo-liberal market economy, then, the question is whether entitlements to various aspects of care are universal, or only accessible to those who can afford to pay for the services.

Reproduction of bodies and domains

Conceptual borders and boundaries emerge from processes of regulation (by state, religion, family) and result in policies or discourses which differentiate types of bodies and types of persons and dictate whether and when sexual and reproductive behaviours and practices, particularly in areas where they overlap with intimate care and paid work, are desirable or transgressive.

We argue that it is necessary to interrogate the relation between subjects that become politicised, and those that remain outside the imagination of the political. As Edholm, Harris, and Young (1978) pointed out more than 40 years ago, reproduction takes place on various levels: biological reproduction (the physical reproduction of living things – in the case of the present work, people); social reproduction (the reproduction of norms, roles, practices, and social structures and institutions – the transmission, from generation to generation, of the social); ideological reproduction (the transmission of a particular dominant narrative, in the context of this chapter of proper families, proper persons and bodies, and following from that, of the idealised nation). In terms of biological reproduction, one of the most obvious and pressing questions concerns who is encouraged and allowed to reproduce, and who is discouraged or prevented from reproducing (see Stanworth 1987, Edwards 2018). As Rayna Rapp argues in her account of stratified reproduction (Rapp 2011: 703), the question is 'why, how and with what consequences the reproductive aspirations, practices and outcomes of one group of people are valorised, while the parenthood of another is despised or unsupported'. The role of nationalist, religious, and state ideologies in shaping policy is critical here; people whose sexuality is viewed as transgressive or whose ethnicity is unwelcome may not be allowed access to reproductive assistance and technologies. Birth control and reproductive choices may be negatively regulated in the same contexts, defining a rigid profile of an ideal family. It is important to remember that these processes of regulation are historically specific and may be contested and change over time. Reproductive governance, a concept introduced by Lynn Morgan and Elizabeth Roberts (2012: 241) 'for tracing the shifting political rationalities directed towards reproduction' in a Latin American context, is useful here. The concept draws attention to the various mechanisms through which loose configurations of actors – the state, the church, non-governmental organisations, international policy actors – struggle to shape and regulate reproductive practices, often through a focus on rights. The 'rivalry of rights' (Morgan and Roberts 2012: 243) may concern parental rights, rights of the foetus, indigenous people's rights, and natural (divine) rights. Activists on opposite sides invoke 'duelling laws and international accords' (Morgan and Roberts 2012: 243) casting 'their opponents' position as immoral, frivolous, profane, undemocratic or seditious' (Morgan and Roberts 2012: 243). Recent debates and emergent regulations currently unfolding in particular national settings, such as the right to life movement in the USA and the anti-abortion movement in Poland, reveal the reach of transnational networks linking religious, political, and economic processes (see Mishtal 2015).

The global rise of a New Right demonstrates the close links between policies of migration and ideologies of reproduction; not only are right-wing populist movements anti-immigration and xenophobic, their rhetoric is also often strongly anti-feminist. As Graff and colleagues (2019) argue 'Gender conservatism … is what brings together right-wing activists from otherwise distant walks of life; believers and nonbelievers, nationalists and universalists, populists who demonize global capitalism and traditional Reagan/Thatcher style conservatives with a neocon love for the market' (Graff et al. 2019: 541). On the recent European political landscape, this opposition to 'gender ideology' has become a 'symbolic glue' for illiberal forces, increasing their strength against the backdrop of neo-liberal reforms and increasing inequalities (Grzebalska and Peto 2018: 165, Kościańska, Chapter 12, this volume). The anti-gender movement can be understood as a countermovement, which has emerged in 'direct response to feminist and queer attempts to insert new understandings of gender, sex and sexuality into international policy' (Corredor 2019: 619). The religious right have been very effective in spreading New Right and populist ideas in Europe (although not all of the latter movements are religious). For instance, a platform called Agenda Europe includes a plan to overturn existing laws related to sexuality (LGBTQI rights) and reproduction (contraception, abortion, all assisted reproductive technologies) among others (Graff, Kapur, and Walters 2019: 542–543). May Ann Case argues that the conceptual foundations shaping the Vatican's war against 'gender ideology' were 'fully developed already in the early 1980's' (Case 2019: 640), but also demonstrates how it later evolved in intense interaction with and opposition to feminist deconstruction of gender stereotypes and sex-gender binaries (see also Corredor 2019). Pope Benedict formulated his responses to 'gender theory' comparing 'natural' (i.e. hetero-sexual) male–female human beings to endangered species. Pope Francis has also 'propagated his opposition to Gender theory in apocalyptic terms, and has, moreover, used the language of ideological colonisation to critique those who spread ideas about reproductive rights' (Case 2019: 649, see also *The Economist* 6 February 2014). Polish Archbishop Marek Jędraszewski of Krakow compared 'genderism' to Stalinism and Fascism and was specific about what he saw as the importing of ideas against the Polish church and nation. And, according to *The Economist* (2014), 'a newly created parliamentary group called "Stop Gender Ideology" invited (Theology) Professor Oko to Parliament where he criticised the World Health Organisation for "teaching toddlers how to masturbate" and linked the "atheist" Jean-Paul Sartre and Simone de Beauvoir with the Cambodian genocide perpetrator Pol Pot' (see also Kościańska, Chapter 12, this volume). In the recent illiberal turn in Polish and Hungarian policies, gender activists and experts frequently have been presented as agents of a transnational lobby – penetrating (and implicitly violating) national borders with their ideas (see *The Economist* 6 February 2014). Again, this has gone hand in hand with a construction of the refugee crisis as a threat to national sovereignty, epitomising the dangers of a borderless society. A recent article in the *Irish Times* pointed out that in Poland 'five years after an anti-immigration campaign helped PiS (Prawo i Sprawodialwosc/Law and Justice, the right wing ruling party) secure an absolute majority, party leader Jaroslaw Kaczynski has described the LGBTI movement as a threat to Polish values, and the state itself' (Scally 2019).

Concluding remarks

In the current climate of political unease and unrest which has been enveloping much of the world over the past decade, it seems particularly important to interrogate and highlight the strong parallels, overlaps, and intersections between the political and economic functions of geo-political state and regional borders, and the ideological borders and systematic classifications which now increasingly regulate gender and reproduction, different kinds of people and bodies, values and practices attached to care. Particular types of persons/bodies, including sexualised and gendered bodies, reproductive bodies, 'welfare-dependent' bodies, unemployed bodies, and migrant, refugee, and asylum seeker bodies, have very different routes of access, if any at all, to state benefits and civil, civic, and human rights, from full citizens deemed deserving, entitled, and 'natural' (whether in terms of citizenship, sexuality, race, age, or some other factor).

Our aim in this chapter has been to focus on care, labour, and reclassifications of different kinds (i.e. affective, economic) of value. Here we want to reiterate our starting points in a slightly different formulation. We have tried to show that by looking at different strands of apparently distinct although related phenomena and areas (migration, care work, regulation of movement, regulation of reproduction, gender, and sexuality) together, we create a different kind of map. We see that the rules and regulations developed to delineate and enforce geo-political borders between nation states, as well as between regions within them, parallel regulations and policies within different states created to order and control the social and physical worlds of their citizens. Sexuality, gender, reproduction, labour, and value all combine as pieces in this complex map which identifies and seeks to perpetuate proper citizens meeting particular norms and expectations. These borders and boundaries may prove just as difficult as geo-political borders to challenge or to cross.

Many of the practices of inequality and processes of inclusion and exclusion which continue to shape and dominate the social and geo-political maps of Europe, both internally and in relation to the rest of the world, are linked to, or are a direct result of, border and boundary making. These processes and practices regularly have an impact on people's access to wellbeing and the possibility of a reasonable life – what Michael Jackson (2013) refers to as 'the wherewithal of life'. One of the strengths of anthropology and other social sciences with qualitative methods is their potential to historicise these processes and to reveal the forms that they take in people's lives and lived worlds (see Khosravi 2010, Willis 2000) in a rapidly changing and increasingly complex global political economy.

The authors in this volume address complex questions surrounding inequality and its making, classifications of entitlement and exclusion, and relationships between the state, the private and voluntary sectors, and the family. Some use ethnographic methods to record and document the experiences of migrants, and the stories that they, many of whom are carers, recount of their life worlds. Others look at relations between migrants and local activists, presenting ways that a truly public anthropology might be imagined and carried out. And finally, some analyse conceptual and theoretical questions arising from examination of these complex relationships between state, families, and households; between labour, commodification, and regulation; and between ideologies and practices of inclusion and exclusion. In sum, they comprise a rich and vivid archive of some of the processes and practices which are shaping the economy, rights, and citizenship locally and worldwide, and of ways that individuals experience and live through these.

Acknowledgements

We would like to thank both Victoria Goddard and our anonymous reviewer for their careful and critical reading of an earlier draft of this chapter and their clear and thoughtful suggestions which helped us to reformulate some sections and certain ideas. Any remaining shortcomings are of course our own.

Notes

1 In this chapter, we follow Morris in using 'desert' in the sense it is used in philosophy and political sociology, to mean deserving in a moral sense. It is thus to be distinguished from entitlement, which refers to rights in law.
2 This did (and does) of course relate to wealth and class. Historically, throughout Europe, upper classes and wealthy families employed domestic labour, paid for childcare and or residential education, and so forth.

References

Anderson, B. (2013) *Us and Them: The Dangerous Politics of Immigration Control.* Oxford: Oxford University Press.
Anderssen, R. (2014) *Illegality Inc: Clandestine Migration and the Business of Bordering Europe.* Los Angeles: University of California.
Assmuth, L. (2013) 'Asymmetries of Gender and Generation in a Post-Soviet Borderland'. In: J.L. Band and W. Kavanagh (eds) *Border Encounters: Asymmetry and Proximity at Europe's Frontiers.* New York: Berghan Books, pp. 139–164.
Barrett, M. (1980) *Women's Oppression Today: the Marxits/-Feminist Encounter.* London: Verso.
Barrett, M. and M. McIntosh (1982) *The Anti-Social Family.* London: Verso.
Barua, P. (2018) 'Unequal Interdependencies. Exploring Power and Agency in Domestic Work Relations in Contemporary India.' PhD Thesis, Bergen: University of Bergen, Norway.
Barua, P., H. Haukanes, and A. Waldrop (2016) 'Maid in India: Negotiating and Contesting the Boundaries of Domestic Work', *Forum for Development Studies* 43 (3): 415–436.
Berdahl, D. (1999) *Where the World Ended: Re-Unification and Identity in the German Borderland.* Berkeley: University of California Press.
Bigo, D., S. Carerra, and E. Guild (2016, eds) *Foreigners, Refugees or Minorities? Rethinking People in the Context of Border Controls and Visas.* Abingdon: Routledge.
Bundgaard, Halle and Karen Fogg Olwig (2018) 'Producing "Good" Families and Citizens in Danish Child Care Institutions'. In: T. Thelen and E. Alber (eds) *Reconnecting State and Kinship.* Philadelphia: University of Pennsylvania Press, pp. 200–219.
Butler, J. (1993) *Bodies that Matter: On the Discursive Limits of 'Sex'.* New York: Routledge.
Case, M.A. (2019) 'Trans Formations in the Vatican's War on "Gender Ideology"', *Signs: Journal of Women in Culture and Society* 44 (3): 639–664.
Castles, S. and M. Miller (2009) *The Age of Migration: International Population Movements in the Modern World.* Basingstoke: Palgrave Macmillan.

Constable, N. (2007) *Maid to Order in Hong Kong: Stories of Migrant Workers*. Ithaca: Cornell University Press.

Corredor, E.S. (2019) 'Unpacking "Gender Ideology" and the Global Right's Antigender Countermovement', *Signs: Journal of Women in Culture and Society* 44 (3): 613–638.

Daly, M. and J. Lewis (2000) 'The Concept of Social Care and the Analysis of Contemporary Welfare States', *The British Journal of Sociology* 51 (2): 281–298.

De Genova, N. (2013) 'Spectacles of Migrant "Illegality": The Scene of Exclusion, the Obscene of Inclusion', *Ethnic and Racial Studies* 36 (7): 1180–1198.

De Genova, N. (2017, ed.) *The Borders of 'Europe': Autonomy of Migration, Tactics of Bordering*. Durham, NC: Duke University Press.

Donnan, H. and T. Wilson (1999) *Borders: Frontiers of Identity, Nation and State*. Oxford: Berg Publishers.

Donnan, H., M. Hurd, and C. Leutloff-Grandits (2017, eds) *Migrating Borders and Moving Times: Temporality and the Crossing of Borders in Europe*. Rethinking Borders Series, Manchester: Manchester University Press.

Edholm, F., O. Harris, and K. Young (1978) 'Conceptualising Women', *Critique of Anthropology* 3 (9–10): 101–130.

Edwards, Jeanette (2018) 'The Politics of "See-Through" Kinship'. In: T. Thelen and E. Alber (eds) *Reconnecting State and Kinship*. Philadelphia: University of Pennsylvania Press, pp. 153–177.

Faist, T. (2000) 'Transnationalization in International Migration: Implications for the Study of Citizenship and Culture', *Ethnic and Racial Studies* 23 (2) 189–222.

Fassin, D. (2011) 'Policing Borders, Producing Boundaries. The Governmentality of Immigration in Dark Times', *Annual Review of Anthropology* 40: 213–226.

Figuereio, M., F. Suleman, and M. Botelho (2018) 'Workplace Abuse and Harassment: The Vulnerability of Informal and Migrant Domestic Workers in Portugal', *Social Policy and Society* 17 (1): 65–85.

Follis, K. (2012) *Building Fortress Europe: The Polish-Ukrainian Frontier*. Philadelphia: University of Pennsylvania Press.

Foucault, M. (1984) *The History of Sexuality 1: An Introduction*. Harmondsworth: Penguin.

Fraser, N. (1994) 'After the Family Wage. Gender Equity and the Welfare State', *Political Theory* 22 (4): 591–618.

Graff, A., R, Kapur, and S.D. Walters (2019) 'Introduction: Gender and the Rise of the Global Right', *Signs: Journal of Women in Culture and Society* 44 (3): 541–560.

Grzebalska, W. and A. Peto (2018) 'The Gendered Modus Operandi of the Illiberal Transformation in Hungary and Poland', *Women's Studies International Forum* 68: 164–172.

Green, Sarah (2013) 'Borders and the Relocation of Europe', *Annual Review of Anthropology* 42: 345–361.

Hann, C. (2010) 'Moral Economy'. In: K. Hart, J.L. Laville, and A.D. Cattani (eds) *The Human Economy. A Citizen's Guide*. Cambridge: Polity Press, pp. 187–198.

Hann, C. (2018) 'Moral(ity and) Economy: Work, Workfare, and Fairness in Provincial Hungary', *European Journal of Sociology* 59 (2): 225–254.

Harris, O. (1981) 'Households as Natural Units'. In: K. Young, C. Wolkowitz, and R. McCullagh (eds) *Of Marriage and the Market*. London: CSE Books.

Hernes, H.M. (1985) 'The Welfare State Citizenship of Scandinavian Women'. In: K. Jones and A. Jonasdottir (eds) *The Political Interests of Gender. Developing Theory and Research with a Feminist Face*. London: Sage, pp. 187–213.

Hochschild, A. (2016) *Strangers in their Own Land. Anger and Mourning on the American Right*. New York: The New Press.

Hochschild, A. (2013) *So How's the Family? and Other Essays*. Berkeley: University of California Press.

Hurd, M., D. Hastings, and C. Leutloff-Grandits (2017) 'Introduction: Crossing Borders, Changing Times'. In: H. Donnan, M. Hurd and C. Leutloff-Grandits (eds) *Migrating Borders and Moving Times. Temporality and the Crossing of Borders in Europe*. Manchester: Manchester University Press, pp. 1–24.

Isaksen, L.W., U. Devi, and A. Hochschild (2008) 'Global Care Crisis. A Problem of Capital, Care Chains, or Commons', *American Behavioural Scientist* 52 (3): 405–425.

Jackson, M. (2013) *The Wherewithal of Life: Ethics, Migration and the Question of Well-being*. Berkeley: University of California Press.

Joyce, A. (2015) 'Good Neighbours and Bad Fences: Everyday Polish Trading Activities on the EU Border with Belarus'. In: I.H. Knudsen and M.D. Frederiksen (eds) *Ethnographies of Grey Zones in Eastern Europe: Relations, Borders and Invisibilities*. London: Anthem Press.

Kaneff, D. and F. Pine (2011, eds) *Global Connections and Emerging Inequalities in Europe: Perspectives on Poverty and Transnational Migration*. London: Anthem Press.

Khosravi, S. (2010) *'Illegal' Traveller: An Auto-Ethnography of Borders*. London: Palgrave Macmillan.

Lan, P.C. (2003) 'Negotiating Social Boundaries and Private Zones: The Micropolitics of Employing Domestic Workers', *Social Problems* 50 (4): 525–549.

Lutz, H. and E. Palenga-Möllenbeck (2011) 'Care, Gender and Migration: Towards a Theory of Transnational Domestic Work Migration in Europe', *Journal of Contemporary European Studies* 19 (3): 349–364.

Mishtal, J. (2015) *The Politics of Morality: The Church, the State and Reproductive Rights in Postsocialist Poland*. Athens, GA: University of Ohio Press.

Morgan, L. and E. Roberts (2012) 'Reproductive Governance in Latin America', *Anthropology & Medicine* 19 (2): 241–254.

Morris, L. (1994) *Dangerous Classes: The Underclass and Social Citizenship*. London: Routledge.

Morris, L. (2018) 'Reconfiguring Rights in Austerity Britain: Boundaries, Behaviours and Contestable Margins', *Journal of Social Policy* 48 (2): 271–291.

Narotzsky, S. and N. Besnier (2014) 'Introduction', *Current Anthropology* 55, Supplement 9: 95–104.

Palomera, J. and T. Vetta (2016) 'Moral Economy, Rethinking a Radical Concept', *Anthropological Theory* 16 (4): 413–432.

Pasierka, A. (2017) 'Taking Far-Right Claims Seriously and Literally: Anthropology and the Study of Right-Wing Radicalism', *Slavic Review* 76: S19–S29.

Pateman, Carole (1988) *The Sexual Contract*. Cambridge: Polity Press.

Pine, F. (2014) 'Migration as Hope: Space, Time and Imagining the Future', *Current Anthropology* 55, Supplement 9: 95–104.

Pratt, G. (2009) 'Circulating Sadness: Witnessing Filipina Mothers' Stories of Family Separation' *Gender, Place & Culture* 16 (1): 3–22.

Rapp, R. (2011) 'Reproductive Entanglements: Body, State and Culture in the Dys/regulation of Child Bearing', *Social Research* 78 (3): 693–718.
Reiter, Raynor R. (1975, ed.) *Toward an Anthropology of Women.* New York: Monthly Review Press.
Reeves, M. (2014) *Border Work: Spatial Lives of the State in Rural Central Asia.* Ithaca: Cornell University Press.
Rosaldo, Michelle (1974) 'Woman, Culture, and Society: A Theoretical Overview'. In: M. Rosaldo and L. Lamphere (eds) *Woman, Culture and Society.* Stanford: Stanford University Press.
Rubin, G. (1975) 'The Traffic in Women. Notes on the Political Economy of Sex'. In: R. Reiter (ed.) *Toward an Anthropology of Women.* New York: Monthly Review Press, pp. 157–210.
Scally, D. (2019) 'Polish Archbishop Compares LGBGTI Community to "Red Plague"', *The Irish Times*, 2 August 2019.
Schurr, C. and B. Friedrich (2015) 'Serving the Transnational Surrogacy Market as a Development Strategy?' In: A. Coles, L. Gray, and J. Momsen (eds) *The Routledge Handbook of Gender and Development.* London: Routledge, pp. 236–243.
Stanworth, M. (1987) *Reproductive Technologies: Motherhood, Reproduction and Medicine.* Cambridge: Polity Press.
Strathern, Marilyn (1988) *The Gender of the Gift.* Berkeley: University of California Press.
The Economist (2014) 'Suffering or insufferable? Poland's Roman Catholic Church is in a pickle over Gender studies.' www.economist.com/eastern-approaches/2014/02/06/suffering-or-insufferable. 6 February (accessed 30 September 2020).
Thelen, T. and E. Alber (2018) 'Reconnecting State and Kinship: Temporalities, Scales, Classifications'. In: T. Thelen and E. Alber (eds) *Reconnecting State and Kinship*. Philadelphia: University of Pennsylvania Press, pp. 1–35.
Thompson E.P. (1971) 'The Moral Economy of the English Crowd in the Eighteenth Century', *Past & Present* 50: 76–136.
Thompson E.P. (1991) *Customs in Common: Studies in Traditional Popular Culture.* London: Penguin Books.
Uhde, S. and P. Ezzeddine (2019) 'Transnational Migration: Borders, Gendered Global Justice Challenges', *Gender a Výzkum/Gender and Research* 20 (1): 3–17.
Willis, Paul (2000) *The Ethnographic Imagination.* Malden: MA Polity Press.
Wærness, K. (1984/2000) *Hvem er hjemme? Essays om hverdagslivets sosiologi.* Bergen: Fagbokforlaget.
Yeates, N. (2012) 'Global Care Chains: a State-of-the-art Review and Future Directions in Care Transnationalization Research', *Global Networks* 12 (2): 135–154.

Part I

Gendered life worlds: migrants' imaginaries and obligations in contested contexts of intimacy

2

Moral economies of intimacy: narratives of Ukrainian solo female migrants in Italy

Olena Fedyuk

Sexuality and affection are commodities traded not only by sex workers and not only for money.

L.J. Keough (2016: 170)

Introduction

Two newspaper articles set the scene for this chapter: 'The Boom', published in April 2008 in *Corriere della Sera*[1] and 'Simply Maria', published in a Ukrainian online newspaper *UkrTime*[2] in November 2007. Both articles discuss weddings of older Italian men to their younger foreign *badanti.*[3]

The Boom. A wedding, that was supposed to happen in Bologna Town Hall, was blocked *in extremis* until the prosecutor, together with the police, could verify that the future wife, a 44-year-old Romanian *badante*, was not trying to take money from her long time employer, an 83-year-old man whom she now wanted to marry. The investigation was initiated by one of the man's grandsons, who was concerned about his inheritance. According to the family, the old man wanted to put the apartment where he lived up for sale; he also went to the bank to make withdrawals from his account, not only accompanied by his 'little wife' but also seemingly mentally confused. The article then proceeds to a larger concern that 'in the past 10 years there has been an increase of 30000 weddings between elderly man between 70 and 85 years old, single, widowers or divorced, with very young foreign women'. 'This boom of weddings between elders and foreign *badanti*', states the paper, is producing serious inconveniences with inheritances, as 'these elderly men are devaluing their properties and pensions, harming their own families, with the ambition of rekindling their youth'.

Simply Maria. Named after a Mexican TV soap opera that was very popular in Ukraine in the early 1990s, *Simplemente Maria* (1989), the article tells the story of a Ukrainian woman, whose life 'was a horrifying labyrinth' until making a 'dramatic turn: the migrant woman has celebrated her wedding'. In her mid-40s, Maria is divorced, the mother of one son, and also a grandmother. Utilising passionate language, the article proceeds to tell the story of a woman who, because of unemployment and a lack of opportunities in Ukraine, had to move to Italy, where after a prolonged period of unemployment, fear of deportation, poverty, and psychological pressure, she found a job with a 67-year-old Italian widower, Salvatore. Maria was afraid to work for a single man, but 'her first tears were caused not by the offense but by the humane kindness; when Salvatore placed his food on Maria's plate. The Italian felt sorry for the woman exhausted from labour; he didn't know how else he could express his support and gain the trust of this foreign woman.' The article goes on in detail, describing the development of their relationship – Salvatore's help in getting Maria overtime employment, his encouragement of Maria singing Ukrainian songs in his home. When after three years of work Maria announced that she was returning to Ukraine, Salvatore blocked the doorway with his body and exclaimed: 'I won't let you go! If you want to go back, I'll come with you. I've never met anyone like you, Maria. Without you, I won't live.' The same day, the Italian man asked the Ukrainian woman to be his wife.

The similarity of these two stories of relationship and (planned) marriage contrasts markedly with the differences in the way they are told and the interpretation of motivations, actions, and events. 'The Boom' discusses the case as a threat to the very institution of the Italian family; the migrant woman is portrayed as manipulating the old man on his path to economic ruin. In 'Simply Maria', although the age difference between the couple is also quite significant (around 25 years), Salvatore stands out as 'signor Salvatore' whose proposal of marriage is presented as an act of humanity, manly strength, and dignity. The latter article is also conveniently silent about the consequences of Salvatore's marriage for the inheritance of his children. Presented in an emotionally charged language, neither of the articles gives the reader sufficient information to form an opinion about the motivations of either the Italian men or their *badanti*. But both articles point to the existence of highly contested interpretations of the personal relationships between foreign caregivers and their employers in Italy. In fact, both articles introduce their stories at the point when they step out of the privacy of Italian homes and care work and enter a public domain of matrimony and inheritance. Would these two cases ever make it to the papers if not for the weddings? Would the Italian press ever be concerned about a 'little woman' from Romania who gives a 'spark of youth' to an 'old Italian' man without any attempt to marry him, or would that just classify as a good care work? And would a Ukrainian newspaper dare to write about Maria's Italian lover if he was not to become her husband?

Based on interviews and ethnographic research with Ukrainian female domestic workers in Italy, this chapter looks into an often taboo topic – intimate, romantic, and sexual relations formed in the course of migration by women migrating alone. These relations are often seen as a side product of 'proper care work' and an 'inappropriate transgression' (see Pine and Haukanes, Chapter 1, this volume). The chapter aims to maintain the complexity of such encounters by contextualising a wide range of intimate relationships as power relations of uncertain economic situations, dismantling the dichotomy of paid versus unpaid sexual relations and scrutinising the boundaries of care work. Drawing a complex picture of sexual, romantic, and intimate encounters between migrant women and local men with various motivations, degrees of exploitation, and rewards on both sides, I take a step away from the 'trauma of separation from family' perspective that often dominates the discussion of the experience of female migration and shift the gaze towards women's personal ambitions and desires in migration.

Understanding the migration project

When I first started my research, as a 27-year-old Ukrainian woman, I feared that my age and cultural taboos would prevent me from effectively inquiring into the issues related to the private lives of older migrant women. My original research in Ukraine in 2006 fully supported this reservation; all my interviews with the women (temporarily) returned from Italy endlessly rotated around the painful issues of estranged families, family separation, and motherly sacrifice. Not that it was not of paramount importance to the participants of my research, but it was just a part of the story. This I understood literally the moment I crossed the Ukranian–Italian border near Udine, in a minivan full of women returning to work in Italy. The women who had said the most heart-breaking goodbyes at home in Ukraine some 15 hours before, exclaimed '*Viva Italia*', changed their telephone SIM cards, and chatted in Italian making arrangements to be met at the minivan stop. Some were picked up by Italian men. The narratives I had heard in Ukraine were not insincere; the women just (sub)consciously ignored the other important element – their life in Italy – which I discovered while continuing research there. The discourse of the women interviewed in Italy shifted dramatically to rotate around the paramount importance of work experience, economy of survival on minimal income, and relationships formed in migration.

Migration from Ukraine to Italy started increasing in volume in the middle of the 1990s, right after the citizens of newly independent Ukraine gained a constitutional right of freedom to leave and return to Ukraine in 1994 (Malynovska 2006). Immense economic restructuring in the country, including the collapse of many state supported industries, resulted in massive lay-offs, and year-long delays in salary payments, which pushed many women to take responsibility for supporting their families in a new way – through various patterns of labour migration (Malynovska and Vollmer 2015, Solari 2018). Since 2003, the flow of Ukrainians to Italy has become numerically noticeable, growing and peaking particularly around the years of state amnesties for irregular migrants, thus indicating both a steady growth and a degree of irregularity in legal status among Ukrainians in Italy. From about 2009, Ukrainians joined the top 5 immigrant groups in Italy, with 226,060 Ukrainian holding Italian residence in 2015 (Vianello 2015). From the beginning, the flows came to be shaped by a particular employment sector need – that of domestic and care work – with 48.4% of Ukrainians being employed in this sector (Vianello 2015). This trend is reflected in the particular gender and age composition: 80% of Ukrainian migrants are women with a mean age of 42 years and as many as 15.25% of all Ukrainian migrants to Italy are in the age group 50 to 54 years old. The literature shows that Ukrainians remain in the low wage bracket: 'only 22% have a monthly income higher than €1000 (vs 45% for other non-EU European immigrants) and the majority of Ukrainians are in the €751–1000 income bracket' (Vianello 2015). And yet, the established patterns and networks of this migration, coupled with the low average salary in Ukraine (approx. €150 in 2016)[4] and lack of employment choices – particularly for women over 40 – makes migration to Italy an attractive option for Ukrainian women.

For an absolute majority of the women in my research, the initial plan for migration was to stay in Italy for a year and then return to Ukraine. However, they found that they could not leave Italy after one year; some had pressure to pay back migration generated debts (visa and travel expenses), for others, a lack of travel documents prompted them to stay and make the best they could in one place. Many women went through a similar hierarchical professional migrant trajectory, finding a job as a live-in domestic and carer, and as they gained more legal, social, and economic stability, moving on to hour-based work in cleaning and caring. Many women found themselves carrying a triple burden: earning money (often under conditions of severe physical and psychological stress), maintaining contact with the family, and taking care of the unity and psychological peace of family members back at home. For fear of being misunderstood, or unsettling their family, many women choose not to share any information with them about their lives in Italy, let alone their difficulties. Some of this unevenness in exchange can be attributed to the guilt that many women feel for leaving their parents, husbands, and children behind (see also Ezzeddine and Havelková, Chapter 4, this volume).

The material for this chapter came from my 2007–2008 doctoral research in Naples and Bologna with Ukrainian women, and from over 10 years of repeated visits and follow ups with several of the women in particular, within the context of making a documentary film around the issues discussed here. My methodology included participant observation, in-depth life-story interviews, observations, and discussions in places of work, rented homes, as well as public gathering places, such as parks, minivan parking lots, or churches.

Moral economies of transnational intimacies

While 'The Boom' article cited earlier warns Italian families against lurking East European women seeking to snatch Italian men, the position of Italian men in pursuing East European women requires some reflection. In the early 2000s in Naples, the route between Piazza Garibaldi and the Ukrainian minibus parking lot on Sunday mornings was full of Italian men cruising around in cars, offering a chat, a coffee, or simply €30 for '*fare amore*'[5] to Slavic women who crowded sections of Via Benedetto Brin around the time of the departure of the Ukrainian minivans. Many Italian men were bringing Ukrainian women and their heavy packages prepared for home straight to the minibus that would take the packages to the women's families in Ukraine. The nature of the arrangements between these Italian men and Ukrainian women was impossible to decipher without knowing each individual case. From my research I knew many migrant women who would get a ride to the minibus from their employers or acquaintances with whom I knew they had no romantic or intimate relations. What was obvious on Sunday mornings on Via Benedetto Brin was the abundance of Italian men and virtual absence of Italian women.

Many of my interviews pointed to a certain existence of a gendered geography of attractions which had its rules: Italian men were eager to meet Ukrainian women, while Italian women never dated Ukrainian men; Ukrainian men preferred to date Ukrainian women in migration, while Ukrainian women usually preferred Italians or other immigrants. Ukrainian women in my research suggested that it was the Italian men who were most eager to meet migrant women outside strictly work relationships. Thus, one of my interviewees, Marijka (46), commented:

> Who else would try to make friends with a Ukrainian migrant woman? An Italian woman is usually not interested in becoming friends with her cleaning lady; she can be nice, kind and understanding, but would rarely find time to drink a coffee with her *badante* and to talk about her life. Italian men, they are curious and interested because they are attracted. They find more time and make more effort to meet a woman informally, maybe just for coffee, or a romantic adventure.

Indeed, Italian men seemed more often to engage in informal, unstructured interactions with migrant woman, providing opportunities for leisure activities, if not a romantic fling. I argue that these encounters, after the stress and shock of arriving in a new country, hard work, and often irregular status (experienced at least for a while), became important steps towards integration in Italy and in some ways gave a sense of 'normality' of flow of life to many women in my research.

On yet another level, this gendered geography of attractions was very physical and spatial – the city of Naples, like other Italian cities, was marked with areas, like via Benedetto Brin, where such encounters could and would occur in public. The power dynamics within such spaces were tangible, if not fully readable; to fully understand the nature of connections in such spaces one would need to know each particular story. Leya Keough, when writing about encounters of Moldovan women migrating to Istanbul with local men, uses the concept of 'sexscapes' (Keough 2016: 170), to account for the power dynamics within such encounters and to avoid falling into oversimplified dichotomies of paid versus unpaid sexual relations. Using the original concept Denise Brennan (2004) developed for understanding the encounters of Dominican women with sex-tourists, Keough invites us to see the multiplicity of forms of exchange of sex and intimacy 'as strategies for many different women to survive in uncertain economic situations' which should 'help us recognize the fluidity expected in all women's labours' (Keough 2016: 170). Seeing the power geography of such sexscapes, and how Ukrainian women work hard to define the terms and conditions of their intimate relations in Italy, allows me to unfold the economy of power relations, inequalities, and reciprocity in encounters of migrant women with local men.

The moral economy of migration is another analytical framework that will guide my inquiry into the role emotions, economy, and power play in encounters of Ukrainian women with Italian men. It builds on elaborations of the original work of E.P. Thompson (1971) that explored moral norms as a form of binding, informal contract between highly unequal classes of peasants and land owners. 'Moral economy' in Thompson's work opened up for examination the link between economic situation and behaviour of the individuals, and their sense of obligation or justice, accounting thus for collective political decisions. Since Thompson's article, the concept has been reused in migration studies, in particular with regards to transnational migration. Thus, Cinzia Solari (2018) in her recent exploration of Ukrainian migration to Italy uses a moral economy framework to study social and monetary remittances from both ends of migration as well as the intersections between the two types of remittances. My application of 'moral economy' is, however, closer to that of Jorgen Carling (2008) who uses 'transnational moral economies' to denote a complex, hierarchal, uneven, and contested system of duties and obligations between those who embark on migration and those who stay behind.

Following Carling, in this chapter moral economies are used to capture the experience of migrating women at the intersection of local and 'brought from home' norms of class, gender, age, and ethnicity. These norms, I argue, are challenged, transformed, and reinvented through transnational migration (see also Wolbert 2001, Keough 2016). In other words, the moral economies emerging in migration reflect fluid and transforming ideas about gender, class, age, and ethnicity in the context of migration (see Pine and Haukanes, Chapter 1, this volume). For this chapter, the moral economy of migration provides an important grid of economic, socio-cultural, and historic conditions, which allows us to understand women's decisions and practices beyond economic motives alone. I am using this concept particularly to unpack some of the dichotomies that have come up already (e.g. selfless vs economic motivations for a relationship) and to see how the notions of gender roles and motherhood brought from home shape women's interactions with Italian men.

The focus on intimacy in the title emphasises my claim that, regardless of whether money or sex transaction is involved or not, encounters of Ukrainian migrant women and Italian men create a space for interaction invested with hidden or straightforward power struggles. At times these encounters results in a sense of closeness, social and emotional inclusion. At other times they produce exploitation, abuse, and injury. Very often, however, they have elements of both. The experience of such contested but intimate encounters presents a part of the untold story of women migrating alone; their narratives are often dominated by loss of intimacies with their families back at home, such as estrangement from a spouse or a child left in Ukraine. Consideration of intimacy as this multi-dimensional factor highlights the power struggles forming migrant women's transnational social fields that cross borders.

I organise the discussion of my ethnographic findings in three main themes: expectations, work, and emotions. These themes overlap and mutually constitute each other and yet, as I demonstrate, the women in their daily working and private lives make an effort to keep them apart.

Expectations

Valentina (47), who hosted me when I first arrived in Naples, has a friend Irina (50), who often stoppped by for a chat. Irina was to marry a 75-year-old Italian widower, Gianni, whom she met a few years after her arrival in Italy.

She would stay long evenings gossiping with Valentina about the intricacies and lapses of her relationship. Irina often would say that Gianni was like a child; he used to call her, and ask 'Do you love me? Do you think of me, my star?' and while Irina saw these affective manoeuvres as a sign of infantilism, Valentina often scolded her:

> You should be like that too … It doesn't cost you anything to call him 'love' or 'star' but it makes him happy and that's it. […] He tells Irina: 'I am such a man in your life … you've been married but I made a woman out of you again after all these years.' I mean! He thinks he was the only man in more than 10 years since Irina got a divorce?! He is such a child … but let him be!

At this point I ask Valentina: what if Irina does not love Gianni, or perhaps even finds him repulsive? Valentina, however, does not seem to understand my question:

> What do you mean 'repulsive'? I mean, listen, we are almost 50 … what are we doing here, in Italy? We work, but how much longer can we do it? With all this rushing, cleaning all day, hands bleeding from the detergents we use daily … Don't we deserve something better, something what we need [for ourselves]? Irina will get her papers, she'll get the support. Otherwise, should she just go home now after all these years in Italy and do what? Start all anew? She already cannot work as hard [as she used to]. She has had surgery … what kind of prince should she be waiting for? Who else would like to spend his life with her?

Irina's story seems to echo perfectly one of the most prominent stereotypes, described with such concern in *Corriere della Sera* 'The Boom': an East European migrant woman who is trying to marry a significantly older Italian man for the benefit of papers and money. The question that *Corriere della Sera* does not address is what will happen to the migrant women who age in such care and domestic arrangements but do not have secure residence permits? Will they have to leave Italy even if they have lived there for years and have little to go back to in Ukraine? Should they have the right to choose to stay and age in Italy?

I had become so used to Valentina and Irina's frequent rituals of getting together and discussing this relationship that I started to see no more plotting in it than in the gossip many women share about their relationships. What was clear to me was that Irina and Gianni did not start their relationship on the same footing: while Gianni could focus whole-heartedly on the emotional and sexual side of the relationship, Irina (who unlike Gianni did not have a pension in Italy) still had to work long hours as a cleaning lady and had to make sure that every year she had a full-time contract that would allow her to apply for another year of residency. Under such pressure, a free, 'no-strings-attached' relationship with Gianni was out of the question, as her failure to secure her status would make her very presence in Italy and closeness to Gianni impossible. And yet, while Irina's prime concern was indeed a residence permit, she also clearly cared about the daily routine of their relationship, and the sexual and emotional side of their engagement.

Valentina seemed to appeal to Irina's moral obligation to make a practical choice in this relationship; she felt that it was Irina's responsibility to take care of her own prospects, not to be a burden, and she saw her relationship with Gianni as beneficial on all levels. In her understanding of the moral economy of this relationship, Valentine saw marriage to Gianni as a solution to the inequality in her friend's relationship, an ultimate sign of respect. Irina, for her part, was bringing her youthfulness and her willingness to be loyal and loving to a man more than 20 years older.

The right to think pragmatically and economically about the relationship was for Valentina, in fact, a hard won benefit of migration. Valentina articulated this in another example, this time from her own experience. She once went on a date with a retired widower in his early 60s, Francesco. It turned out that some time ago Francesco dated a Ukrainian woman for three years. Valentina recalls that Francesco spoke rather bitterly about his previous relationship, suggesting that even though they had lived together for so long 'she only sold him her body, as a hooker'. He then said that it was he, Francesco, who was her *badante*, as the woman worked but she sent all her money home without contributing anything to the household while Francesco cooked and cleaned for her, and gave her rides everywhere. Valentina recalls how she felt appalled by Francesco's interpretation of his previous romance:

> … I asked him what exactly did he expect?! I told him: 'Didn't she come to Italy to work?!' And what did he mean that she sold her body as a hooker? Didn't she love him, give him her love and emotions while they were together? What does money have to do with any of it? If she didn't have him in her life, she would do the same, just work and send all money home, so why did he think she was plotting against him and benefiting from him?

Francesco and Valentina here clash over moral economies in an attempt to divide the 'sacred' – emotions, relationships, intimacy, from the 'profane' – money. Francesco questions his ex-partner's loyalty on the basis that she 'sent all her money home' and, in fact, used him, highlighting the division known in the literature on emotional labour as 'paid employee vs. unpaid relative' (e.g. Hochschild 2003). In Valentina's case, she defends the woman by trying to take money out of the equation and introducing more important frontiers. 'What does money have to do with any of it,' asks Valentina, and immediately moves into a more significant divide, i.e. Italy vs. home: 'If she didn't have him in her life, she would do the same, just work and send all money home.' In Valentina's reading of the moral economy of migration, Italy is not a space for familial engagements. She already has a home, in which her work and emotional input is unpaid and a part of her family responsibility. Italy, on the contrary, is a place of paid work, where the fact that the woman has a lover does not change her family obligations.

About a year after I finished my fieldwork, I made another trip to Naples where I met Valentina again. When I asked her how Irina's wedding with Gianni went, Valentina replied:

> Oh, but there was no wedding! One of Gianni's children prohibited it. They already had all the papers, everything, but he finally said that he 'cannot get married.' Probably his daughters didn't allow him to, because of the flat [i.e. the fear that Irina will inherit Gianni's flat]. And Irina, she is still with him, she's just got used to him … she is with him because at least he is paying for her flat, but if he stops, where will she take money from? And what will happen later, if her residence permit expires? Nobody knows …

In Irina's story, her justification acquires a simpler but deeper meaning in the light of her prospects in life; Irina has been in Italy for many years, she feels that she lost her connection with Ukraine and family, she feels too weak to work the demanding hours of cleaning and care work, and she seeks some stability and guarantees for her future in Italy. Meanwhile, Irina's very pragmatic objectives do not seem as unsavoury as those mentioned in the articles cited above. As she fails in her search for legal security, she does not leave Gianni but stays, attached by emotions or habit. However, with Gianni's retreat from his initial engagement, Irina's own prospects are uncertain; it is unclear whether she will have to leave Italy or become irregular again.

Work

Most of the women I interviewed were completely unfamiliar with paid care or domestic work before arriving in Italy. Many of those who started their professional lives before the collapse of the USSR in 1991 had occupied high positions in Ukraine: I have met the director of a music school, educators, IT professionals, engineers. Among those who were too young to have had a career before 1991, many had an excellent education but had rarely worked professionally in their own field. Most women admitted being tempted by the option of working as a domestic worker precisely because 'at home we do this job for free anyway'. However, many of my respondents admitted that they had to learn to differentiate between unpaid household work for their own families and care work performed in the privacy of the Italian homes for money, and to professionalise their relation to work. In fact, paid work became one of the main frameworks for understanding, justifying, and moralising the harshness (and even harassment) experienced in migration, and for imagination of the migration experience in general.

To illustrate this connection, I turn to the story of Sveta, who was 53 at the time I rented a bed (*posto letto*) in her flat, which she sublet, as a sort of hostel, to other migrants. She had a university degree and considerable work experience as a school psychologist in Ukraine. Sveta, herself a mother of two sons (28 and 25), was an energetic, sporty woman with short hair, who rented a flat in Bologna with her elder son. The fact that she had managed to rent a whole flat and bring her son to Bologna placed Sveta among the ranks of the emerging elites of Ukrainian migrants. Sveta told me her story while eating ice cream in the kitchen of her flat, to the audience of myself and her son, interspersing her story with many jokes and a lot of laughter.

She had been in Italy for some time when she paid €700 to secure a job (which paid 900 a month) from an acquaintance (Ljuda). However, she soon recognised that the job was a fraud; the elderly bed-ridden *signora* for whom she was to care was about to be moved to a care home, which meant that after paying €700, Sveta could only keep the job for a month or so. Additionally, the 70-year-old husband of the bed-ridden *signora* asked Ljuda to find him a *badante* who would 'take care of his wife during the day and sleep with him during the night'. When he told Sveta about this arrangement, she felt cheated by her acquaintance. She recalled that she ran into her room, locked the door, and cried. However, she soon recovered and decided that she would not waste her tears on her employer but would also never give in to his wishes. She instead started developing strategies that would allow her both to maintain her job and avoid the harassment:

> Within just a few days I realised that he was very stingy, and he started cutting on my food, or throwing food at me, wanting me to pick it up. He was going crazy, watching me walking around and not having access to me. And I was going crazy too; I lost so much money on this job, I was not going to lose my dignity on top of that. [...] He would start scandals at 2–3 am. He would pick up the phone and tell me that he would call the police if I would not sleep with him. I would push the phone closer to him and say 'go ahead, call! The worst thing that will happen to me is that I go home for free [deportation]. But you, you will have to pay the fees for hiring an undocumented!'

Yet another form of pressure, a little more subtle but no less stressful and destructive, was treating Sveta in public as his lover, making affectionate gestures or buying coffee for her in front of the neighbours. All these forms of coercion could easily have made a weaker woman give up or become totally overwhelmed. However, Sveta turned the situation into a personal challenge and discovered her own capacity to deal with it. After she had realised that her employer was hiding her phone and was de facto trying to keep her under house arrest, Sveta recalls that she simply snapped at him: 'You think that you bought me? No, it's me who bought you and your wife, from Ljuda, who worked here ... I paid for the job, she sold you and your wife to ME!' Sveta then changed her strategy radically afterwards, telling the man that if he wanted sex, he should pay her another €900 per month:

> 'I will sleep during the day and have sex with you at night, and you cook for and clean and wash your wife.' But then he started whining 'But then what will I be paying you for if you won't do anything?' So, since he was so greedy, I insisted that he should pay for sex but since he always refused I was safe. It's just that to live through his night attacks and whining was very exhausting.

The role of the paid care work becomes crucial in this situation. Sveta decides to position herself as a worker by setting a price on her sexual services – one more monthly salary on top of her payment. The Italian man tried to destroy this boundary by merging all her services into one, i.e. 'then what will I be paying you for?' but Sveta clearly demarcated every task as a job operation and set a separate price on each. Thus, Sveta commented on her perception of the issue: 'I have a principle: either I clean a man's house, or I fuck him ... but to do both for one salary – never!'

In a sense, Sveta tricks the logic of global capitalism that brought her to Italy in the first place through building a form of moral economy in migration; local men are privileged to enjoy sexual and intimate relations, while migrant women have to face many aspects of precarity, among others legal irregularity, earning unstable wages, and sending money home. The moral thing to do for Sveta in this case is to make Italian men pay, to somehow even out this inequality at least. While a more affluent Italian household bought her care services, she refuses to give anything away for free; she separates her care, sexual services, and emotions into distinct tasks, and sets a price for them, thus gaining control over both her reward and the very choice of whether or not to perform those tasks. She completely reverses power relations when she screams into her employer's face: 'You think that you bought me? No, it's me who bought you and your wife [...]!' Just as Sveta's care and emotions have been 'bought', so she herself instrumentalises her employers, turning them into a resource which can be bought and sold.

In their attempts to maintain control over their services, work, care, and their bodies and souls, many women in my research had to learn to set a price for something that prior to migration was seen as within the one monolithic idea of intimacy. By separating out these tasks and attaching a price to them, women are often seen (especially by Ukrainian men) as descending into cynicism, desecration of motherhood and the feminine, and, ultimately, sliding into prostitution. In my own research it becomes clear that negotiating payment for various intimate services, including sex, helps a woman not only to get paid for it, but first and foremost, makes it possible for her to choose whether she wants to provide the service in the first place, whether the payment and the service are comparable, and whether she can do one type of work without doing the other.

Building the boundaries was a crucial issue for most women in my research, who even spatially were often thrown together with their person in care; several women in my research shared the same room, one lived in a hallway of the family where she worked, another spoke of a job where she shared a bed with a person in care. Barely visible boundaries between the work and private life of the Ukrainian domestic and careworkers in Italy often lead to (unwillingly) established intimacies, creating circles of dependencies of migrants on the person in their care and vice versa. However messy and unclear these dependencies are, they often open up a space for more tangible negotiations of such intimacies.

Emotions

As I discussed earlier, public discourses in Ukraine and Italy apply vigorous surveillance to migrant women's behaviour, often generating strain in transnational families and casting suspicion and shame on both migrants and their families. According to Ukrainian public discourse, the very trope of motherhood, as a primary role and fulfilment for women, has been already undermined by the women's decision to migrate. However, in the case of Ukrainian migrant women, motherhood has also become a double-edged sword; on the one hand, migrant women are often seen as the transgressors of the ideal of motherhood, on the other, most migrant women defend their choices precisely by claiming that migration is their sacrifice to secure a better life for their children. In her work on Ukrainian female migration to the Veneto district, Vianello (2011) observes that 'motherhood characterizes many migrants' discourses, because it is one of the strongest justifications a woman can rise in order to defend her decision. The sacrifice rhetoric is an alibi that hides a process of emancipation developed during the migratory experience' (2011: 12).

It is not coincidental that many women in my research felt trapped by migration. As a popular Ukrainian migrant proverb says: 'In one year, there is nothing to go back with, and in two years, there is nowhere to go back to.' This feeling, though in part described as 'in-between' in migration literature, has a gloomier undertone. Not only do women realise that they cannot be 'at home' in either their country of origin or the country of migration, they also do not see how they could abandon their often exhausting lifestyle as a labour migrant. Two women in their early 50s whom I interviewed in Bologna recalled bitterly episodes from their years in Italy (5–7 years); a few times upon calling home, they would hear, instead of words of support from their husbands, shouted accusations of prostitution, swearing, and even threats. However, both women consider their marital relationships functional and do not think of their husbands as abusive. In fact, both of them vigorously abstained from any romantic engagements in Italy, considering such behaviour against their moral and religious ideals. I conclude from these cases that women are often left on their own with their decision to eschew romantic engagements, while public pressure and family distrust condemns them anyway.

Some women, however, felt that there was very little left for them personally beyond their maternal sacrifice. Valentina, introduced earlier in this chapter, identifies the feeling of solitude, magnified by the need to earn money and to defend herself in the eyes of others, even family members:

> When a woman arrives in Italy, she has one thing on her mind – her debts with growing interest in Ukraine. Next, she needs to buy a flat or pay for school for her children, because we are all here for that reason. They say she is 'going around' here, but tell me please, when do you have time to do that? When do you have time to even think about love, and even if you meet love, you have so many problems on your mind, you can't even realise it is there, or think about it. And then, maybe with time, you manage to solve those problems and you happen to meet a nice person, it doesn't mean you are 'going around'! Why can't we believe that this person can feel love? Otherwise, what has she seen back there in Ukraine, when her own husband has sent her abroad, 2000 km away, to earn money? So I am not surprised that women here build their own lives, try to love … because, what do they have to go back to indeed? Maybe to her life in ruins …

It becomes clear from my interviews that life in Italy could not replicate life in Ukraine; emotional life, trust, attachment, and romantic engagements were all revisited and re-invented within the moral economy of a solo migrating woman, living with the need to earn, fear of sliding into irregularity, and the scarcity of trustworthy networks of support. In this moral economy, the majority of my research participants (both men and women) reserved their strongest criticism for those Ukrainian women who engaged in relationships with Italian men without benefiting from these relationships materially in one way or another. Several times during my research I encountered stories of women who moved in with Italian men or even married them and afterwards could not work full hours, thus limiting their capacity to earn and remit money. These stories were always told with a sense of the danger facing a woman following personal interest and neglecting the needs of her children; but at the same time, such dependence on a man makes a woman vulnerable. Thus, the inability to remit, to invest financially at home, might have a devastating effect on a woman's reputation – even making her chances of returning to Ukraine very slim.

On several occasions I heard stories told about such relations judged as shameful, implying a woman had lost control of herself and neglected all her principles for the sake of personal pleasure. Thus, Sveta told me a story about a friend of hers, who lived with an Italian man who did not give her any money:

> He saves his entire pension and they live on her money. They go to restaurants, she pays, they go here or there – she pays ... What is this?! Love?! What kind of craziness has got into her?! To hell with such a man! I am so happy that God gives me wisdom not to let any such Italian idiot into my life! I live for my children, and our common problems and that's it ... I appreciate my freedom ...

In her judgement of the woman's actions, Sveta completely discredits the possibility of strong emotional feeling, in which economic benefit would be less important for a woman than being with a partner. She in fact describes it as madness, a mental disorder, in which the woman is not capable of controlling herself. Sveta then continues, setting the 'right' priorities:

> You know I could have tried to arrange my life differently. At my age and with my looks I could have worked less, maybe find a man who would support me so that I don't have to work so hard. But I won't do it, until my sons get married and thus settled [...] I am not sure that if I went to live with some Italian man he would allow me to help and support my children.

Sveta's judgement speaks to two important points. It is a justification both for gaining material benefits from Italian men and for the need to remain unattached. A woman can be seen as justified in engaging in such a relationship as it can provide more stability, reduce her expenses, and increase remittances providing additional benefits (e.g. travel money home, presents for her children). On the other hand, motherhood is a 'stop-factor' that does not allow Sveta just to seek romantic fulfilment; she has responsibilities towards her adult children and, thus, has to choose carefully so as not to restrict her ability to provide for them. I see here a discrepancy between the carefree image that Sveta tries to present, and her actual carefulness. This discrepancy is a hint that even if presented as relationships for pure economic benefit, these intimate engagements might not be so effortless and insignificant for migrant women. Concluding with this point, I refer again to Valentina:

> I would recommend everyone to have their pride ... If someone wants you, why not? But you need to clearly understand what is the nature of this desire, that is whether someone just wants to use you for one day, or to make you really special; to be loved [by you] and to give you a chance to love. [...] So I would advise everyone to listen to their heart ... but sometimes, you can get a better understanding not with your heart but with your reason. I think one needs to harmonise them, but if that doesn't work ... maybe still better to listen to your reason. Yes, I follow my reason rather than my heart, because I am afraid to get hurt.

Conclusions

Expectations, the role of care work, and proficiency in mastering one's emotions were the three topics that guided my inquiry into how Ukrainian women experience relations with Italian men in migration. In my research, a gendered geography of attractions seemed to prompt Ukrainian women to see Italian men as gatekeepers to Italy: for various types of relationships that Ukrainian women establish in Italy (romantic or not, involving sexual intimacy or not), it was Italian men (and significantly less so women) who could provide an important informal network of support. While Italian men might appear to 'hold the keys' for migrant women, the question remained: what was the kind of Italy to which these men could open the doors? As I discussed earlier, migrant women often have no chance of entering romantic or intimate relations as equals. Numerous limitations in terms of migrant status, lack of resources and earnings push women to limit their choices, and create cases of abuse and dependency. However, as I have shown, this does not mean that such relationships are only a matter of calculation or that migrant women have no choice but to play their part in the existing hierarchies. While understanding the hierarchies can reveal a great deal about the existing inequalities, the personal accounts and testimonies of my interviewees reveal a great deal of the 'unexpected' and the 'uncontrolled' in such encounters.

Becoming a migrant in Italy involved not only the construction of a new self, but also participation in a different moral economy. Migrant women were often able to delineate clearly the space of migration from the space of home when I interviewed them about the competing pulls of intimacies developed in Italy and those of marriage or motherhood still existing in Ukraine. These could coexist, but only because there was a clear separation between the space/time of migration and the space/time of home. This does not mean that the spaces of home and migration are not interconnected. The objectives of migration, and the judgements made at home about its success or failure, link the two spaces, making them mutually constitutive. Thus, the decision to enter into or stay outside intimate relationships in Italy is often taken after careful consideration of the potential benefits or threats that these relationships might carry for their family in Ukraine. The shifts between these various regimes allow women to increase their flexibility and maintain a level of emancipation through stepping out of family bonds and through their economic independence. 'What happens in Italy stays in Italy', runs a migrant proverb, as women are trying to work out their personal and familial interests across the borders.

Notes

1 'Boom.' *Corriere della Sera*. 26 April 2008.
2 'Просто Марія'['Simply Maria'] *UkrTime*. Листопад 2008р [November 2008].
3 *Badante* [Italian] means 'careworker'; also used as a blanket term for many forms of domestic and care work performed usually by immigrants.
4 https://index.minfin.com.ua/ua/labour/salary/average/2016 (accessed 25 September 2020).
5 Italian for 'make love'.

References

Brennan, D. (2004) *What's Love Got To Do With It?: Transnational Desires and Sex Tourism in the Dominican Republic*. Durham, NC: Duke University Press.
Carling, J. (2008) 'The Human Dynamics of Migrant Transnationalism', *Ethnic and Racial Studies* 31 (8): 1452–1477.
Hochschild A.R. (2003) *The Commercialization of Intimate Life: Notes from Home and Work*. Berkeley: University of California Press.
Keough L.J. (2016) *Worker-mothers on the Margins of Europe: Gender and Migration between Moldova and Istanbul*. Washington DC: Woodrow Wilson Center Press.
Malynovska, O. (2006) 'Caught Between East and West, Ukraine Struggles with Its Migration Policy'. *Migration Information Source*. www.migrationinformation.org/USFocus/display.cfm?ID=365 (accessed 25 September 2020).
Malynovska O. and B. Vollmer (2015) 'Ukrainian Migration Research Before and Since 1991.' In: O. Fedyuk and M. Kindler (eds) *Ukrainian Migration to the European Union: Lessons from Migration Studies*. Springer International Publishing AG.
Solari S.D. (2018) 'Transnational Moral Economies: The Value of Monetary and Social Remittances in Transnational Families', *Current Sociology* 67 (5): 760–777.
Thompson E.P. (1971) 'The Moral Economy of the English Crowd in the Eighteenth Century', *Past & Present* 50: 76–136.

Vianello F.A. (2011) 'Suspended Migrants. Return Migration to Ukraine'. In: M. Nowak and M. Nowosielski (eds) *(Post)trans-formational Migration*. Berlin: Peter Lang, pp. 251–274.

Vianello. F.A. (2015) 'Migration of Ukrainian Nationals to Italy: Women on the Move'. In: O. Fedyuk and M. Kindler (eds) *Ukrainian Migration to the European Union: Lessons from Migration Studies*. Springer International Publishing AG.

Wolbert B. (2001) 'The Visual Production of Locality: Turkish Family Pictures, Migration and the Creation of Virtual Neighborhood', *Visual Anthropology Review* 17 (1): 21–35.

3

Borders within intimate realms: looking at marriage migration regimes in Austria and Germany through the perspective of women from rural Kosovo

Carolin Leutloff-Grandits

Introduction

For most non-EU citizens, marriage migration establishes one of the few possibilities to move to countries within the European Union. Unlike other migration options, in which the citizenship of the migrant and/or the needs of the local labour market are taken as the main measurement for the right to enter the EU and to achieve residency rights within the destination country, the right to family migration is – among other things – bound to the individual membership of the sponsor in society – in legal as well as economic respects. In Germany and Austria, only citizen sponsors or those with residence permits are entitled to apply for family reunification as a basic right. However, especially since the new millennium, this right has been increasingly reduced within many EU countries, although the exact legal measures vary from country to country.[1] Generally, legal requirements for bringing over non-EU citizens into EU countries are increasingly restrictive in many EU countries (even for naturalised EU citizens and migrants with residence permits), and set new boundaries through which sponsoring spouses as well as prospective marriage migrants (and underaged children) are forced to fulfil certain criteria in order to be able to bring over a partner or move. The arguments contesting the right to marriage migration are manifold and build on culturalised discourses within Western Europe which regard marriage migration as emerging from patriarchal and backward partnership ideologies. In fact, it is suspected that marriage migration supports marriages which are not based on 'love' and 'free choice', the ideal model of Western marriages, but rather on arrangement and force. As such, they threaten not only individual rights and freedom, but also the freedom and solidarity of receiving societies. However, such legal measures also pose a challenge to marriage migration, and often lead to a considerable postponement of the migration, or even render it impossible.

In this chapter, I focus on the proliferation of borders that are established to control the movements of prospective marriage migrants who are perceived as 'cultural others' within EU countries. Based on several ethnographic fieldwork sequences in the rural region of southern Kosovo, which I conducted between 2011 and 2014, this chapter concentrates on young women from this region who are planning to move to Germany or Austria via marriage, and who either have already married or want to marry a partner living in Austria or Germany. As these partners or (one of) their parents mostly originate from the same region in Kosovo and are Muslims, such marriages are classified as 'co-ethnic', Muslim marriages. As such they fit in with the widespread notion in Austria and Germany that marriage migration is a phenomenon found mainly among certain ethnic groups of Muslim background.

This chapter is based on material that I collected during fieldwork in rural Kosovo, where I lived with a family in the region and conducted extended narrative interviews with local inhabitants and visiting migrants. I ask to what extent the policies concerning marriage migration and the attendant societal discourses and legal frames for marriage migration within Germany and Austria inform and affect the realities, experiences, and strategies of marriage and family migrants. In order to understand the outcome of measures to control marriage migration, I take a de-centred, processual perspective on cross-border marriages which emphasises the emic views of prospective marriage migrants, and also highlights the gendered and affective dimensions of the various layered boundaries these women meet. Proceeding from the strategies to find a partner across the border, to the 'waiting' period preceding family reunion, which includes preparations for the move, the chapter charts the migrants' efforts to meet the requirements set by the migration regimes and at the same time cultivate partnership relations before actual migration takes place. My main aim is to highlight the measures taken by the migration regimes of Western EU states to control marriage migration, which unfold as boundaries that are established outside the territory of prospective states. I then link these measures, and the boundaries they uphold, to the experiences and strategies of young women in rural Kosovo willing to migrate via marriage. I show, with reference to my ethnographic material, that the new measures to control marriage migration create gendered barriers. Instead of helping women to free themselves from patriarchal domination and develop agency, as has been the declared goal of such measures, they pose a special pressure on prospective female marriage migrants and their partnership relations. As such, the crossing of geo-political borders is limited by gendered boundaries set up by the migration regimes of Western states. These boundaries are already experienced in the country of origin before actual migration takes place.

In the following, I outline the externalisation and proliferation of borders by the marriage migration regimes of Western European states, and its legitimation by reference to culture and gender. In the next sections, I move on to discuss the experiences and viewpoints of prospective female marriage migrants in rural Kosovo who make sense of borders and who struggle with borders long before moving abroad. I will start with their motives to marry abroad and outline ways that the geo-political border establishes an incentive for cross-border marriages. I then move on to the different dimensions of borders which prospective marriage migrants meet before migration, and especially the dimension of temporality. Finally, I concentrate on the pre-entry language test, which became an important hurdle for migration, and its gendered nature.

The proliferation of borders within the Austrian and German marriage migration regime

State borders cannot just be understood as 'lines' on a map which spatially distinguish one nation state from another, but must be seen as political, legal, social, and economic demarcations (Mezzadra and Neilson 2013, Schiffauer et al. 2018). In many cases, a state border also marks a welfare and income gap – and this is surely the case between Kosovo and states of the EU. For many people from Kosovo, EU countries embody the desired emigration destination, not least for economic reasons. While in Kosovo the average net income per month was about €350 in 2015,[2] in Germany and Austria, the favourite emigration destinations of Kosovans, the average net income was about six times as much. Similar divergences can be highlighted for unemployment numbers and welfare: while in Kosovo, the unemployment rate stood at around 30% in 2017 and reached almost 53% among young people,[3] Austria and Germany had very low unemployment rates of 5.5 and 5.7%[4] respectively. In Kosovo, state welfare provision is minimal (Sauer 2002), while Germany and Austria are traditionally strong welfare states (Esping-Andersen 1990).

In relation to the territoriality of the state, state borders also delineate the legal entity of the state and define who is allowed to cross and who not. As such, borders are not just barriers or walls, but membranes which filter who can and cannot cross, and according to what kind of criteria. For migrants, borders proliferate, as there is not only the political-territorial line surrounding the state to be crossed, but many other boundaries to be dealt with (Balibar 2002, Mezzadra and Neilson 2013). For quite some time now, the borders of Western European states have been externalised. For prospective marriage migrants this means that they have to apply for visas within their country of origin before migration; and to be successful they have to meet a variety of criteria. We also notice the increasing establishment of legal and administrative boundaries that migrants encounter after crossing the geo-political line. These boundaries are often legitimised in terms of ethnicity, culture, and gender (Balibar 2002: 82, Cooper and Perkins 2012). As such, difficulties in border crossing also relate to the drawing of social and cultural boundaries, which may be experienced before or after migration. The spatial location of borders becomes diffuse, as they are not just on the geographical borders of the state, at checkpoints and embassies, but stretch to the everyday life and can be found outside as well as within the state (Balibar 2002, Rumford 2006, Walters 2006). In order to securitise the external borders of the EU, the EU agency Frontex operates in the Mediterranean and various countries on Northern Africa collaborate with the EU in order to scrutinise migrants according to criteria set by EU states. When migrants have passed the geo-political line of their destination countries within the EU, they are still subject to social and cultural boundary work, which build a basis for allocating residency and welfare rights (Newman 2006: 179; see also Pine and Haukanes, Chapter 1, this volume).

In the realm of marriage migration, the borders of many states within the European Union, including Germany and Austria, increasingly proliferate. These borders are not meant to stop marriage migration fully, but to control and reduce the immigration of those perceived as 'not wanted' and 'not fitting' persons. Despite unclear statistics about the ethnic background of those who apply for family reunion, cross-border marriages are seen as a migrant and largely female phenomenon based on so-called culturally different notions of marriage, which are viewed as a threat to the cultural homogeneity of the nation, as well as to the integration of migrants into society (see, for critical discussion, Block 2014: 5, Pellander 2015, Bonjour and Block 2016).

In fact, it is assumed in the West that there is a cultural gap between 'Western' and 'non-Western' (Eastern and Southern, and especially Muslim) marriages. While the former are supposed to be based on love and free will, following emancipated and 'modern' partnership models, the latter are seen as following patriarchal and 'backward' models where women in particular are seen as being victimised and forced into instrumental marriage arrangements. This notion of a gap legitimates the introduction of various measures which are meant to empower women in such cross-border marriages – but these measures easily establish new barriers which bear gendered implications. While in Western countries 'love' is supposed to be the measure of a 'genuine' marriage, in cross-border marriages sponsoring spouses and their partners need to meet far more formal requirements, e.g. reaching a certain income level, in order to qualify for union than when marrying within the country, disregarding the fact that this may push emotions into background, or even negatively affect the relationship (Schmidt 2011). In various EU countries, this applies not only to residents with a migration background, but also to full citizens, and as such diminishes the basic citizenship right to live with the spouse and underaged children. This again builds on the notion that citizenship might be obtained by naturalised migrants who are still perceived as 'cultural others', something which justifies the devaluation of their citizenship rights (Bonjour and Block 2016).

Marriage migrants are also regarded as placing a possible economic burden on the welfare state in the receiving society,[5] because they are largely seen as dependent spouses. In order to minimise the risk that the welfare state has to care for and finance them, most sponsoring spouses[6] are required to demonstrate 'adequate housing' and an income level that disqualifies them from claiming social benefits. It is, however, not acknowledged that these requirements pose a special barrier to female sponsoring spouses, as women in Austria and Germany, on average, earn about 20% less than men (Danaj 2016) and have more difficulties meeting the economic criteria to bring a spouse over. The legal requirements for marriage migration therefore have a gendered bias, which negatively affects prospective female sponsors.

Next, prospective marriage migrants have to meet various legal and administrative requirements in order to join their spouse in Austria and Germany, ranging from an age requirement to a pre-language entry test, which are meant to protect individuals from possible exploitation within marriage. In order to understand the effects of the legal and administrative measures on prospective marriage migrants, the next sections will outline the perspectives of the latter. They contextualise the measures of the marriage migration regime of Austria and Germany on the basis of the social lifeworld and the local conditions prospective marriage migrants meet in rural Kosovo, as well as the expectations and imaginations prospective female marriage migrants have about marriage and a life abroad.

Geo-political borders creating marriage incentives

In rural Kosovo, international migration to Western Europe is nothing new; it has influenced family life and communities since the late 1960s, when men left for labour migration to Western European states in order to send remittances, while their families – including wife and children – largely remained 'at home', in the households of the migrants' parents and brothers.

This contributed to the continuity of the patriarchal household and family arrangements (Reineck 1991, Aarburg and Gretler 2008). In the 1990s, ethnic conflict resulted in war, leading to the outmigration of complete families. While some returned a couple of years later, others remained abroad, but often maintained ties with their home region and relatives, visiting them for holidays and building houses there. After the war ended in 1999, legal options for migration ceased, and cross-border marriages between villagers and those who originated from the region but who had migrated years or even decades ago became an important migration pathway (Leutloff-Grandits 2017). In fact, in 2011, according to information I received from a local administrator, about half of the marriages in the region of Opoja in Kosovo's south were cross-border marriages. In addition to the wish to enter a happy married life and to raise a family, these cross-border marriages are based on manifold and diverse reasons, expectations, and imaginations, which reflect the different spatial and social positionings of the prospective partners on either side of the border and create what I call a 'border–marriage–migration nexus'.

Migrants from rural Kosovo living in Germany and Austria who decide on a partner from their birthplace in Kosovo often want their children socialised in the Albanian language and local traditions, to learn 'where they are from and where they belong'. Others mentioned that the Albanian language competence of their prospective spouse was important for interacting with family, especially their parents. Generally, these young migrants had positive experiences during their holiday visits to rural Kosovo, where their migrant status was in itself seen as valuable.

Migrants seeking a marriage partner 'back home' in rural Kosovo are often those without higher education, who migrated in their teens or as young adults and discontinued their education in order to start working early. Having been socialised in two or more social contexts simultaneously, their decision to marry a partner 'from home' is often a deliberate step and sometimes a way of rediscovering and re-evaluating their own 'roots' and family values. This may go together with feelings of not fully belonging to the receiving society and being stigmatised as a 'cultural other'. Being aware of the dominant Western notion that cross-border marriages resurrect 'patriarchal' gender relations and impede integration, some also want to dismantle this notion and commented when we talked that their own marriages were based on 'love' and in line with the 'modern' partnership ideas of the receiving country. Some stressed, for example, that they wanted their wife to take up employment after migration (Beck-Gernsheim 2006: 120–123, Schmidt 2011, Leutloff-Grandits 2014).

Young people in rural Kosovo, men and women alike, also opted for marriage migration because of the income and economic gap between

Kosovo and countries like Germany and Austria, which contributes to imaginations of a better life on the other side of the border (Leutloff-Grandits 2019). Young women inclined to marry someone abroad often linked this to their wish to escape poverty and to create material prosperity, comfort, and a better future for their own children, including the prospects of a good education and healthcare system and more generally state social security.

Many young women contrasted their hopes of a marriage abroad with restricted economic possibilities and the 'patriarchal' gender relations in their home region, despite the major changes that occurred after the war. From media reports or accounts of visiting migrants, they were aware that elsewhere it was possible for women to leave behind traditional roles and enjoy greater freedom. A case in point is Vlora, who at 18 had just finished secondary school and remained at home as her parents could not afford for her to go to university, but did not want her to work. Although she considered herself too young for marriage, she regarded marrying abroad as her best choice, as it would allow her to leave village life, which she felt had become a prison. Marriage to a young man from a neighbouring village was not an option for her, as this would mean moving to her husband's home and remaining in a large patrilocal household, bearing children and caring for them and her parents-in-law. She thus saw marrying abroad as the better solution. The hope of a 'brighter future' is a common motive for migration from a poorer country to a more prosperous one (Appadurai 1996, 2004, Constable 2005, Beck-Gernsheim 2006: 117, 2011: 62, Timmerman 2006). In Kosovo's rural south, young women also hoped to achieve more individual freedom, take up employment and thus contribute to the household income, or even pursue their education goals and qualify for a better job abroad (Leutloff-Grandits 2014).

Meeting borders of knowledge and borders of time

The geographical distance, the income gap, and the legal barriers to crossing the borders, which may make it difficult for citizens of Kosovo to visit Western European countries, often impede the possibility of getting to know prospective marriage partners, or the lifeworld to which they would like to migrate. In fact, opportunities to visit the destination country before marriage are very limited, as it is difficult to obtain a visa. Another barrier prospective marriage migrants face is the legal requirement that – at least in Austria and Germany – administrative marriage documents must be obtained outside the EU, to ensure that the migrant does not enter the EU on a visitor visa with the intention to marry and immigrate. This may inspire imaginations, but makes it difficult to secure accurate information about migration and the migration destination. It does not enable prospective marriage migrants to make a thoughtful decision, but creates borders of knowledge and a 'risk of wrong decisions'; as Straßburger and Aybek (2015: 91) found in the Turkish case, a risk which prospective marriage migrants try to minimise with their own strategies. In rural Kosovo, young women who want to marry a spouse from abroad fear that these men want to find a submissive wife, or, even worse, that parents want to find a wife for their son in order to discipline him (Neubauer and Dahinden 2012); thus, women regard family counselling as a way to take their future into their own hands and to build a secure marriage and family life that would best suit them. In order to get to know prospective spouses who they can trust, despite the distance, they welcome the advice of family members who have information on prospective candidates and their families as well as their marriage proposals, before proceeding further by, for instance, chatting with the chosen candidate via digital platforms. In fact, when migrants visit rural Kosovo, young people turn to relatives or friends for support in finding or contacting the right match, as the migrants' stay in the village is short and public interactions between unrelated and unmarried men and women are carefully observed and commented on, which puts pressure on both sides. In this situation, young people willing to marry prefer meeting potential candidates away from the gaze of the village, often in café bars in town – but arranged by and in the presence of family members.

The geographical distance and the obstacles to crossing political territorial borders also limit the agency of prospective marriage migrants in finding the right spouse. This leads to ambivalent processes of waiting for the right match – often for a long time – and rushing into a decision as soon as a suitable candidate is in sight. In fact, due to the limited length of visits, prospective partners have little time for face to face meetings or, sometimes, to think over the decision. Adelina, 30, is a case in point, although the time frame which passed before she met a suitable partner was longer than in other cases I came across. After eight years at school, she had remained at home waiting for marriage for fifteen years and was already considered old compared to other unmarried women in the region. Finally, she found the right match. She had wanted to marry someone abroad who was family-oriented, but not greatly under the influence of his parents, in order to be able to provide her own children with better possibilities in terms of basic education and professional qualifications. She also wanted the potential to develop herself, e.g. by taking up employment. After various proposals and years had passed, she finally received a proposal via relatives that met her expectations. It was a migrant in his late 30s, originating from the region but living in Germany, who owned his own firm, lived in a nuclear household, and earned well. When he was on a holiday in rural Kosovo, the families organised a few meetings so they could both check if they matched and could imagine a joint future. In her own descriptions, the decision to get engaged was taken rather quickly, as the time he could spend in Kosovo and the opportunities to meet were limited. On one of the last days of his holidays, he came to her family to ask for their consent to the marriage, upon which they celebrated the engagement. Soon after, he left again for Germany.

Such a hurried decision to marry is further complicated by the fact that the waiting time for a visa is often long. Those who desire to move abroad immediately after the wedding in rural Kosovo often conduct a civil marriage in the municipal administration at the time of the engagement to allow for the administrative procedures, as an official marriage certificate has to be presented along with the application for family reunion – all of which can take months or even longer. Ideally, the traditional wedding ceremony, which usually involves hundreds of guests, is only held after the visa has been obtained, so that the young couple can move abroad together after their wedding. However, it does not always work out this way, as various other requirements also have to be fulfilled, which often take much longer than initially expected. This adds to the sometimes months-long time frame of the administrative processing of the applications (see also Grote 2017: 29). In fact, in various cases I explored, neither the young people living abroad who wanted to marry a partner from rural Kosovo, nor those in rural Kosovo who were willing to move abroad via marriage, had in-depth knowledge about immigration regulations and all the requirements awaiting them, and only later learned about the procedures and the attendant difficulties. As Straßburger and Aybek (2015: 95) have elaborated on in the case of marriage migration from Turkey to Germany, the extent of knowledge and awareness of such regulations and procedures may be related to educational level and economic status as well as to the committed involvement of a solid network of acquaintances as the source of necessary information. Inadequate information about marriage requirements and procedures time and again led to the postponement of migration on the basis of marriage and had the effect of inculcating pessimism and negative attitudes about Western bureaucracy in the prospective migrants as well as their partners.

Various EU countries have introduced an age requirement for prospective marriage migrants and their partners in order to control marriage migration (Block and Bonjour 2013: 207). Based on the assumption that (mostly female) partners within cross-border marriages are forced into and/or victimised within such marriages, the minimum age of partners within cross-border marriages was raised to 18 in Germany in 2007 (whereas marriageable age in Germany is 16) (Grote 2017), to 21 in Austria and in the Netherlands (introduced in 2004) (Strasser and Tošić 2014: 143 for Austria; Bonjour and Block 2016: 790 for the Netherlands) and even 24 years in Denmark (Liversage and Rytter 2015: 132), as it was assumed that more mature migrants would have a greater say in the marriage decision. In the rural south of Kosovo, this meant that young people, who were still 'too young' for marriage migration when they entered an engagement, had to wait for years in order to meet the age requirement and to qualify for marriage migration. People who were opting for a cross-border marriage were thus forced to wait and to stay immobile until they crossed the age threshold, which often had negative effects on the partnership, as such a long distance relationship was not easy to sustain over a longer time-space.

More generally, the insecurity of waiting because certain visa requirements were not met (checking the partner within the migration country, missing language certificate) and the lack of knowledge about life after migration created undue psychological pressure and disturbed intimate relations. Partners eagerly awaited their marriage life with excitement and happiness. However, with the need to wait – sometimes even for years – to realise those marriage plans, romance was often put in the background, and the whole idea of entering a cross-border marriage was subject to reframing. Sometimes partners found themselves drowning in doubts and worries, or the interest of (one of) the partners waned, so that the bond was put to test even before the wedding ceremony, or before partners had started living together.

Adelina, for example, confessed that as much as she was happy and excited about her future abroad, since the day of her engagement she had also become increasingly nervous about the prospects of an unknown future, away from her family, in a foreign country with a strange language. Her fiancé had returned to Germany soon after their engagement, and her personal interactions with him in the interim period had been minimal. Enduring the year-long waiting period between her engagement and her wedding, before she was to finally move abroad, was emotionally challenging. As she put it: 'Before my engagement, I wanted to live abroad, but after the engagement I had a bad feeling.'

These insecurities and burdens also tended to have a gendered component. During my fieldwork, I met several young women who had moved to the household of their parents-in-law after marriage (this is of course limited to cases in which at least the mother-in-law is living in rural Kosovo), where they waited for their visa to join their husband abroad, often with no clear idea about when they would join their husband or where they would live. They probably would have preferred to wait in the household of their own parents, but this was contrary to the patrilocal tradition in rural Kosovo, where women move to their in-laws' home after marriage. I observed that women silently suffered and endured their 'fate', often for months or even years, sometimes with growing depression. While these women seemed rather powerless, I observed a case in which the parents-in-law tried to accelerate the possibilities of reunion of the young couple and even thought about undocumented migration for the son's wife, just to enable a reunion. What remained clear was the fact that the marriage migration regime established new borders. However, these borders were diffuse, as they entered everyday life and penetrated intimate realms, which had not just spatial but also temporal dimensions.

The pre-entry language test as a new boundary in intimate realms

Another threshold which filters the movement of prospective marriage migrants and postpones — and sometimes even stops – their migration is the obligation of the spouse to prove proficiency at beginners' level in the language of the receiving state before entering the country. Prospective migrants who fail to pass the language test do not qualify for marriage migration. This means that the 'plea of integration' has been shifted from the place of destination to the place of origin or departure. While Germany introduced the requirement to prove a basic language capacity for non-EU citizens who want to migrate on the basis of family reunification in 2007, in Austria this law has been valid only since 2011 (Block and Bonjour 2013: 207, Gutekunst 2016, Grote 2017: 27–28). Potential marriage migrants must gain a language certificate from accredited language institutes, such as the Goethe Institute in the case of Germany, and must present it at the respective consulate or the embassy within the sending country in order to apply for a visa.

In Austria and Germany, sponsoring spouses who belong to a privileged stratum of economically preferred migrants within the receiving country, i.e. more highly qualified migrants and workers with an expertise in demand, have an easier track to family reunion as their partners are exempt from the need to provide a pre-entry language certificate. This means that the integration is increasingly measured by capacity and performance within the labour market (Strasser and Tošić 2014: 131–133). The justification for a pre-language test is, however, also based on culturalised and gendered arguments. In fact, both conservative politicians in Western European countries and various feminists assume that 'the language requirement (...) prevents forced marriages of incoming spouses, thus has empowering and preventive potential', as only with language capacity may marriage migrants be able to develop agency (Straßburger and Aybek 2015: 84; see also Gutekunst 2016). The notion that especially women may be held captive within their marriage and may not be allowed or not able to attend language classes after joining their husband abroad is seen as a further argument for pre-entry language tests. Conservative voices even raised the argument that persons could just fail the test as a means to free themselves from an unwanted marriage, and thus regain freedom and agency with the help of the test.

However, critical border and migration scholars have already remarked that the obligatory pre-entry language test is far from being a measure of empowerment only (Gutekunst 2016, Jashari, Dahinden, and Moret 2019). As a considerable number of candidates involuntarily fail to pass the test, while others do not even get the chance to take it, it also poses a barrier to migration and to joining their marriage partner. When observed more closely, the language test seems to reproduce social boundaries as it excludes those who have no means to visit language courses offered by official partners of the embassies and which are thus designed to prepare pupils best for the test. Offered mainly in bigger cities, such courses are difficult to attend for a significant part of the population who do not live in urban centres (Straßburger and Aybek 2015: 84), as is the case for women from Kosovo's rural south. This again reproduces urban–rural divides.

In the rural south of Kosovo, the need to gain a language certificate in order to migrate also changed the habits of prospective marriage migrants, as they have to pass the language test before migration and thus have to start learning German before migrating. Luckily, in one of the more than 20 villages which form a municipality, a local teacher offers a course to prepare for the official German language examination at a Goethe Institute in Prishtina – and even uses the same teaching materials as the courses offered by the Institute. While prospective male as well as female marriage migrants visit the language course in order to learn German and to obtain a language certificate, and seem to meet the same conditions, a closer look shows that in rural Kosovo, this unequally burdens prospective female marriage migrants. As such, it reproduces gender boundaries, which shows that the border regimes of European states themselves are gendered. However, these border regimes do not necessarily work for the achievement of equal rights of women – as they tend to claim – as they may disadvantage women in their attempt to migrate on a family basis.

This is first of all based on the fact that the language class cannot be easily reached by public transport. In contrast to young men, most young women do not have a driving license, and women learners have to rely on their family members to drive them to their language classes and to the final examination administered by Goethe Institute in Prishtina. During my fieldwork, I also realised that several young women had difficulties in learning, as they had only the obligatory schooling where they had rarely learned a foreign language (besides some basic English). In addition, many were out of the habit of learning since they had left school years ago. Based on the fact that in this rural region of Kosovo a higher percentage of male than female pupils finished gymnasium and entered university, the challenge of 'relearning to learn', especially in a classroom environment, in order to gain 'eligibility' for this cross-border marriage fell thus more heavily on the shoulders of prospective female marriage migrants. This went together with a strong emotional pressure to learn and pass the test.

Thirty-year-old Adelina had, for example, started to prepare for her German qualifying language exam after her engagement to a migrant from her home region. She was generally positive about it, as she wanted to learn German in order to be more independent and to take up work once she was abroad. However, during the German language course she attended in a neighbouring village, she became discouraged as learning on the basis of books turned out to be difficult. When I met her, she had been engaged for a year and this was also the time frame she had tried to learn German within in order to pass the language test; she complained about the stress and anxiety, as learning German made her eyes and head hurt, and after developing a severe toothache, she could not think about learning any more. Like Adelina, other prospective marriage migrants developed stress-related symptoms of illness, depression, and pain while trying to meet the requirements for marriage migration.

The fees for the language course and examination added to the difficulties, as prospective marriage migrants often have to rely on family support. It was not usually the young woman's natal family who paid for their enrolment on the German language course, but the prospective husband and his family; from engagement onward her education was considered to be the responsibility of her affines. This also created financial dependency on the prospective spouse and could burden the relationship, especially when women failed the course and had to repeat classes and tests.

In rural Kosovo, however, the need to provide a language certificate also sparked rumours about the possibility of buying such certificates and bypassing the burdensome language course, thus pointing to the weak state of law in Kosovo and the ongoing corruption in this sector. For young women whose sponsoring spouses did not offer to buy their certificate, but instead paid for the course, this became much more than just a simple language test: it proved whether they were indeed marriageable and eligible for a cross-border marriage. Adelina, for example, said that her fiancé in Germany also supported or even welcomed the pre-entry language training, as he saw it as proof of her capacity to learn the language and integrate. Adelina's performance in the exam would not only determine her visa eligibility but also her partner's verdict about her suitability for the marriage alliance – and this testing continued long after the engagement and the administrative marriage were held. Failing the test was thus extremely shameful, as it not only destroyed the plan for an imagined better future abroad, but also left her damaged, as she was then assumed not able to learn. This Damocles sword hung over her and increased her fear and nervousness, so it was not surprising that she could hardly sleep and developed all kinds of somatic reactions. Seen from this perspective, the pre-language test established a boundary which was inscribed onto the bodies of prospective marriage migrants and negatively interfered in the relationships of cross-border couples, long before the geo-physical border had been crossed.

To advance an intersectional perspective[7] on gendered marriage migration regimes, it is helpful to consider that in rural Kosovo, not only young, but also middle aged and elderly women wanted to move under the regulations of family reunion to join their husbands abroad. In the rural south of Kosovo, these women had not been able to follow their husbands who had migrated abroad in the 1980s or 1990s because they had to obey the demands of their in-laws who wanted them to stay in the village household and care for them. Once women finally reached the point when they no longer had care obligations, they suddenly faced a pre-immigration language test as a condition for family reunification in Austria and Germany, which they had a scant chance of passing. Few of them had received more than eight years of schooling in the 1960–1970s and, after 20–30 years away from school, it was nearly impossible for them to learn from books and pass the test.

Sixty-year-old Ilire, whose husband Artan migrated to Germany in the 1970s and provided financial support, had stayed back in her parents-in-law's household to care for them and her five children, and had visited her husband only occasionally on a temporary visitor's visa. When in the mid-2000s her only son followed his father abroad, and a bit later all her four daughters had married, Ilire wanted to join her husband and son permanently. But Ilire had limited options to join her husband on the basis of family reunion, as she needed to first pass the German language test, which was a challenge, owing to her advanced age and limited schooling. As her husband had been abroad for over 40 years, it was clear to Ilire that he would not return for good and that, more likely, they would maintain a mobile lifestyle as long as they were able to. Ilire is not an exception; there are numerous wives in the rural south of Kosovo who have spent decades providing care within village households. When they were finally in a position to join their husbands, the legal barriers were too difficult to cross.

Prospective family migrants from other non-EU states share the same fate, as reported, for example, in a documentary about marriage migration in Turkey (Priessner 2016). After an illiterate woman from Turkey lodged a complaint about the need to provide a language certificate, the European Court decided in 2014 that such a demand was contrary to EU guidelines for family unification as well as to the association agreement with Turkey (Gutekunst 2016: 236). However, individuals who experience such barriers have problems claiming their rights, as the decision of the European court did not lead to the annulment of the demand at national levels, and the affected persons often have too little knowledge and power to make their case heard.

Conclusion

Marriage migrants cannot 'just' cross the political territorial border of the nation state. In fact, the 'border' marriage migrants have to cross is not easy to define, as it proliferates and appears to have manifold dimensions – not only spatial, but also temporal, social, and gendered (Hurd, Donnan, and Leutloff-Grandits 2017). In order to become eligible for marriage migration to Germany and Austria, prospective spouses have to pass a certain age threshold and a pre-entry test in the language of the destination country. While this border regime is officially put in place to avoid victimisation of – and empower – female marriage migrants, in rural Kosovo the reality is different, as it unequally burdens women and interferes with their marriage plans and partnership relations.

A common motive of many young people in the rural south of Kosovo in deciding to marry a migrant from their region was to seek a more gender-egalitarian partnership that would open up employment possibilities and thus create more equal power relations. The increasingly restrictive legal measures against such marriages made marriage migration considerably more difficult and slowed down the procedure, which again affected interactions between spatially separated couples, creating stress and unease in the process. The need for a language certificate especially sets a high barrier for prospective female marriage migrants and family migrants in rural Kosovo, who are mostly economically dependent, and particularly for those who have only basic education or who are elderly. With this, borders proliferate and are felt bodily, as they enter intimate realms. In fact, due to their complex and fragmented nature, various prospective marriage migrants subjectivise their failure to cross the border as they link their symptoms to their own lack of abilities, and less to the border regime as such.

For purposes of integration and participation, it is therefore worth asking if it might not be better to attend language courses within the country of migration (Straßburger and Aybek 2015: 84). Such courses are offered and are in part already obligatory for new immigrants as a condition for secure residency rights (BAMF 2017). However, instead of 'forcing' migrants to attend courses, it should be regarded as a priority for policy makers to make such language courses more accessible and practical for migrants within the receiving states. Here, an intersectional approach which takes care not only of gender, but also of educational background, family situation, and age, and which offers different courses according to the diverse profile of migrants, would be useful.

Another possibility to empower marriage migrants would be counselling services for marriage migration in Kosovo, promoted through Kosovo media, which could elucidate the possibilities and barriers marriage migrants face abroad and also link them to counselling offers in Germany and Austria. This would contribute to dismantling the barriers marriage migrants experience, instead of setting up new ones even before migration has commenced.

Notes

1 For more information see AGF – Arbeitsgemeinschaft der Deutschen Familienorganisationen e.V., 2012.
2 See https://riinvestinstitute.org/En/riinvest-story/226/personal-income-by-sector-in-kosovo-who-pays-and-how-much/ (accessed 11 February 2019).
3 http://ask.rks-gov.net/media/3989/labour-force-survey-2017.pdf (accessed 11 February 2019).
4 https://de.statista.com/statistik/daten/studie/17304/umfrage/arbeitslosenquote-in-oesterreich/ and https://de.statista.com/statistik/daten/studie/1224/umfrage/arbeitslosenquote-in-deutschland-seit-1995/ (accessed 30 September 2020).
5 For Germany, see Grote (2017: 26). In the Netherlands, sponsors of marriage migrants needed to earn 100% of the minimum wage before 2003, while in 2004, this was changed to 120% of minimum wage. In 2010, this was changed again to 100% of the minimum wage. In France, this was similar (Block and Bonjour 2013: 207).
6 However, Block (2014: 8) writes that 'citizen sponsors must fulfil fewer conditions regarding housing, employment, and income than foreign resident spouses'.
7 For an intersectional perspective on migration, see Bürkner (2012).

References

Aarburg, H.P. von, und S.B. Gretler (2008) *Kosova-Schweiz. Die albanische Arbeit- und Asylmigration zwischen Kosovo und der Schweiz (1984–2000)*. Münster: Lit Verlag.

AGF – Arbeitsgemeinschaft der deutschen Familienorganisationen e.V. (2012) *Das Recht auf Familienzusammenführung. Die europäische Richtlinie und nationale Umsetzungen in der aktuellen Diskussion. Ein Fachgespräch der AGF am 22. Juni 2012*, www.ag-familie.de/media/docs/agf_doku_reunification_2012.pdf (accessed 30 December 2013).

Appadurai, A. (1996) *Modernity at Large. Cultural Dimensions of Globalization*. London: University of Minnesota Press.

Appadurai, A. (2004) 'The Capacity to Aspire: Culture and the Terms of Recognition'. In: V. Rao and M. Walton (eds) *Culture and Public action: A Cross Disciplinary Dialog in Development Policy*. Stanford: Stanford University Press, pp. 59–84.

Balibar, E. (2002) *Politics and the Other Scene*. London: Verso.

BAMF (2017) Deutsch lernen. Integrationskurse. Teilnahme und Kosten. www.bamf.de/DE/Willkommen/DeutschLernen/Integrationskurse/TeilnahmeKosten/Aufenthaltstitel_nach/aufenthaltstitel_nach-node.html (accessed 10 July 2017).

Beck-Gernsheim, E. (2006) 'Transnationale Heiratsmuster und Transnationale Heiratsstrategien. Ein Erklärungsansatz zur Partnerwahl von Migranten', *Soziale Welt* 57: 111–119.

Beck-Gernsheim, E. (2011) 'The Marriage Route to Migration. Of Border Artistes, Transnational Matchmaking and Imported Spouses', *Nordic Journal of Migration Research* 1 (2): 60–68.

Block, L. (2014) 'Regulating Membership: Explaining Restriction and Stratification of Family Migration in Europe', *Journal of Family Issues* 36 (11): 1–20.

Block, L. and S. Bonjour (2013) 'Fortress Europe or Europe of Rights? The Europeanisation of Family Migration Policies in France, Germany and the Netherlands', *European Journal of Migration and Law* 15: 203–224.

Bonjour, S. and L. Block (2016) 'Ethnicizing Citizenship, Questioning Membership. Explaining the Decreasing Family Migration Rights of Citizens in Europe', *Citizenship Studies* 20 (6–7): 779–794.

Bürkner, H.J. (2012) 'Intersectionality: How Gender Studies Might Inspire the Analysis of Social Inequality among Migrants', *Population, Place and Space* 18 (2): 181–195.

Constable, N. (2005) 'Introduction: Cross-Border Marriages, Gendered Mobility, and Global Hypergamy'. In: N. Constable (ed.) *Cross Border Marriages. Gender and Mobility in Transnational Asia*. Philadelphia: University of Pennsylvania Press, pp. 1–16.

Cooper, A. and C. Perkins (2012) 'Borders and Status-functions: An Institutional Approach to the Study of Borders', *European Journal of Social Theory* 15 (1): 55–71.

Danaj, E. (2016) 'Gender Wage Gap.' In: C.L. Shehan (ed.) *The Wiley Blackwell Encyclopedia of Family Studies*. New York: John Wiley & Sons.

Esping-Andersen, G. (1990) *The Three Worlds of Welfare Capitalism*. Princeton: Princeton University Press.

Grote, J. (2017) Familiennachzug von Drittstaatsangehörigen nach Deutschland. Fokusstudie der deutschen nationalen Kontaktstelle für das Europäische Migrationsnetzwerk (EMN). *Working Paper 73*. Nürnberg: Bundesamt für Migration und Flüchtlinge.

Gutekunst, M. (2016) 'Doing Gender und das Regieren der Migration durch Heirat. Eine ethnographische Analyse der Wechselseitigen Konstitution von Geschlecht und Grenze', *Feministische Studien* 34 (2): 226–240.

Hurd, M., H. Donnan, and C. Leutloff-Grandits (2017) 'Introduction: Crossing Borders, Changing Times'. In: Hastings Donnan, Madeleine Hurd, and Carolin

Leutloff-Grandits (eds) *Migrating Borders and Moving Times. Temporality and the Crossing of Borders in Europe*. Manchester: Manchester University Press, pp. 1–24.

Jashari, S., J. Dahinden, and J. Moret (2019) 'Alternative Spatial Hierarchies: A Cross-border Spouse's Positioning Strategies in the Face of Germany's "Pre-integration" Language Test'. Special Issue: 'Contesting Categories: Cross-border Marriages from the Perspectives of the State, Spouses and Researchers', *Journal of Ethnic and Migration Studies* (online publication) DOI: 10.1080/1369183X.2019.1625136.

Leutloff-Grandits, C. (2014) 'Transnationale Ehen durch die Linse von Gender und Familie: Heiratsmigration aus Kosovos Süden in Länder der EU', *IMIS Heft* 47: 163–193.

Leutloff-Grandits, C. (2017) *Translocal Care across the Kosovo Borders: Reconstituting Kinship, Gender, and Generational Relations in the Context of Opoja Migrations*. Habilitationsschrift: Universität Wien.

Leutloff-Grandits, C. (2019) 'When Men Migrate for Marriage: How Kosovo-Albanian Couples Cope with Gender Stereotypes and Immigration Barriers in Germany and Austria', *Journal of Ethnic and Migration Studies* (online publication) DOI: 10.1080/1369183X.2019.1625136.

Liversage, A. and M. Rytter (2015) 'A Cousin Marriage Equals Forced Marriage. Transnational Marriages between Closely Related Spouses in Denmark'. In: A. Shaw and A. Raz (eds) *Cousin Marriages Between Tradition, Genetic Risk and Cultural Change*. Oxford: Berghahn, pp. 130–153.

Mezzadra, S. and B. Neilson (2013) *Border as Method, or, the Multiplication of Labor*. Durham, NC: Duke University Press.

Neubauer, A. and J. Dahinden (2012) *'Zwangsheiraten' in der Schweiz: Ursachen, Formen, Ausmass*. Bern: Bundesamt für Migration BFM.

Newman, D. (2006) 'Borders and Bordering: Towards an Interdisciplinary Dialogue', *European Journal of Social Theory* 9 (2): 171–186.

Pellander, S. (2015) 'Collective Threats and Individual Rights: Political Debates on Marriage Migration to Finland'. In: P. Kettunen, S. Michel, and K. Petersen (eds) *Race, Ethnicity and Welfare States. An American Dilemma? Globalization and Welfare Series*. Northampton: Elgar, pp. 107–127.

Priessner, M. (2016) *650 Wörter*. (Documentary) www.martinapriessner.de.

Reineck, J. (1991) 'The Past as Refuge. Gender, Migration, and Ideology among the Kosova Albanians.' University of California, Berkeley, PhD thesis.

Rumford, C. (2006) 'Theorizing Borders', *European Journal of Social Theory* 9 (2): 155–169.

Sauer, M. (2002) 'Sozialpolitik im Kosovo: Liberalisierung eines Politikfeldes?', *Südosteuropa Mitteilungen* 5/6: 44–61.

Schiffauer, W., J. Koch, A. Reckwitz, K. Schoor, and H. Krämer (2018) 'Borders in Motion: Durabilität, Permeabilität, Liminalität', Working Paper Series B/ORDERS IN MOTION Nr. 1. Frankfurt (Oder).

Schmidt, G. (2011) 'Law and Identity: Transnational Arranged Marriages and the Boundaries of Danishness'. In: K. Fog Olwig, B. Romme Larsen, and M. Rytter (eds) *Migration, Family and the Welfare State. Integrating Migrants and Refugees in Scandinavia*. London: Routledge.

Straßburger, G. and C.M. Aybek (2015) 'Marriage Migration from Turkey to Germany: How Underprivileged Couples Cope with Immigration Regulations or Not'. In: E. Heikkilä and D. Rauhut (eds) *Marriage Migration and Intercultural Relationships*. Institute for Migration, Migration Studies C25: Turku.

Strasser, S. und J. Tošić (2014) 'Egalität. Autonomie und Integration: Post-Multikulturalismus in Österreich'. In: B. Nieswand and H. Drotbohm (eds) *Kultur, Gesellschaft, Migration. Die reflexive Wende der Migrationsforschung*. Wiesbaden: Springer, pp. 123–151.
Timmerman, C. (2006) 'Gender Dynamics in the Context of Turkish Marriage Migration: the Case of Belgium', *Turkish Studies* 7 (1): 125–143.
Walters, W. (2006) 'Border/Control', *European Journal of Social Theory* 9 (2): 187–203.

4

The gender of guilt: diversity and ambivalence of transnational care trajectories within postsocialist migration experience

Petra Ezzeddine and Hana Havelková

Introduction

In this chapter, we will analyse how specific transnational care practices are reflected in the personal life trajectories of women with migration and refugee experience in a postsocialist context in the contemporary Czech Republic. Our aim is to investigate the influence of gendered norms and expectations on women's transnational care practices and their feelings of care obligation, and to explore specific coping strategies for dealing with practical and emotional challenges arising from contradictory expectations.

The chapter is based on our two different research projects with women with migration and refugee experience living in the Czech Republic. We are placing the data from these two research projects into conversation with each other while identifying three types of gender specific phenomena of transnational care. These are: a) guilt over 'leaving behind'; b) a strategy of temporariness; and c) struggles to achieve a work–care combination with broader family structures in the transnational environment. We point to both commonalities and differences, trying to demonstrate the variety of transnational practices, reflections connected to them, and the specific underlying socio-cultural context that in our opinion contributes to the commonalities.

The first research project was conducted with 15 Ukrainian transnational mothers, all of whom come from rural areas of western Ukraine and are employed as domestic workers (Ezzeddine 2012). The second research project was a study working with 37 ageing women with refugee experience (who are at the same time the transnational daughters of their elderly parents) from the former Yugoslavia, most of whom came in the 1990s from Bosnia and Herzegovina and who belong to different ethnic groups (Ezzeddine and Havelková 2016). It should be mentioned, though, that the starting points of the studies were different: in one we are dealing with labour migrants and in the other with war refugees. However, in both cases migration was forced by external circumstances. As Zuzana Uhde has argued in her critique of the concept of 'voluntary' labour migration, 'many perceive their migration choices to be inevitable, rather than preferable, enforced by external circumstances that they cannot control. In many cases, migrants have a critical intuition that such circumstances are not even under the control of their national governments' (Uhde 2019: 196).

There are socio-demographic differences between the two groups: the participants of the first research project reflect the situation of Ukrainian female migrants who 'left' their children, husbands, and other family members in the country of origin; while the second research covers lives of women who were forced to flee their home country in the 1990s with their children and husbands and who left their elderly parents at home. Those in the first group shuttle between two countries while their families remain back home in Ukraine, while those in the second were forced to live in a new country and to develop life strategies immediately for members of their own nuclear family in the Czech Republic.

In our chapter we are looking at three postsocialist countries: Bosnia Herzegovina, Ukraine, and the Czech Republic. It is important to emphasise that neither the socialist past nor the postsocialist development of the three countries has been the same. On the contrary: the differences were and are considerable and we try to avoid constructing a homogenous picture of 'women in and after socialism'. What is nevertheless possible to theorise as common characteristics are the similar gender politics of actually lived socialism in the states of the Soviet bloc. In the discussions between 'Western' and 'Eastern' feminists which took place after the fall of the iron curtain, women from the former socialist bloc showed remarkable unity in claiming a fundamental difference in gender patterns between East and West (see Funk and Mueller 1993, Gal and Kligman 2000).

So, how do we project this common understanding of the socialist legacy of gender patterns into our analysis? In other words, what is 'the' socialist context we underline in our text? The very basic and in a sense 'banal' image is that of the super-woman, connected to the double or triple burden to which these women were accustomed and ready and able to manage; in other words, full-time employment and at the same time almost exclusive responsibility for family and household. Given the decades (four in the Czech case) that this gendered imbalance lasted, we suggest that it has been transformed into a cultural norm which forms the specificity of gender in former socialist countries. Though 'banal' it is highly relevant as the framework of our research, since the starting point of the strategies of migrating women in both groups is the expectations women have of themselves, or in other words what they regard as their 'duties', aligned with their families' similar expectations of them. These expectations mean responsibility for both care and breadwinning.

The gender patterns that developed in Balkan and other post-Soviet environments (including the Czech Republic) in combination with socialist norms and consumerism continued to be important in the transforming societies. As in other socialist countries, Yugoslav women actively participated in economic and production activities, which was meant to ensure their economic independence and liberation, but in reality it meant the 'double shift' duties we mentioned above (Jones 1994). As Bonfiglioli argues, the result of socialist politics in the field of women's emancipation in former Yugoslavia was mixed, since women's work outside the home continued to be considered secondary to men's work (Bonfiglioli 2013: 6). The labour market was segregated by gender, and women were mainly employed as unskilled workers or in 'feminised', low-paid work, for instance in agriculture, education, social services, and the textile industry (Mežnarić 1985). Women's presence in executive positions was also limited and further differentiated according to ethnicity (Reeves 1990).

The feminisation of Ukrainian labour migration could also be explained in terms of the socialist Soviet experience, whereby women participated in the labour market to a considerable extent, taking responsibility for the family economy while also continuing to fulfil their care duties in the household (Verdery 1994, Kiblitskaya 2000). Soviet men thus lost some of their patriarchal functions and responsibilities, something that also makes itself felt in present-day Ukraine. Because Ukrainian women today are marginalised on the domestic labour market, and at the same time are expected to look after their families, an ideal solution seems to be labour migration connected with the sending home of remittances (Solari 2010, Tolstokorova 2010, Fedyuk Chapter 2, this volume). Here, then, we see again not only the gender segregation of the labour market, but also the absurdity of the gender pay gap when women are often the main breadwinners.

This pattern was also partly true for the former Czechoslovakia. As Havelková argues, the gender segregation of the labour market if anything deepened during the socialist era, when both horizontal and vertical segregation in a peculiar way obscured the discrimination against women (Havelková 1995).

Concepts and methods

Care (including transnational care) has to be understood both as a resource and as relational practice (Buch 2015). Hromadžić and Palmberger (2018: 5) argue that 'transnational and migratory settings do not necessarily diminish but rather transform caregiving relationships and practices within and outside family'. The nature of long-distance care relations in the case of transnational families is, moreover, procedurally specific and fluctuating, since they are based on the bonds of kinship which define them, and their persistence over time and distance (Baldassar 2007). Baldassar suggests the notion of 'economies of kinship' in transnational families, developed and shaped across changing state, community, and family migration histories, together constructing 'ideal' family relations and obligations (Baldassar 2007: 280). 'Ideal' families are thus a specific form of 'imagined families' – conceiving themselves and other members of the family in a transnational context (Bryceson and Vuorela 2003). Similarly, Brah speaks about the transformation of family formation in the diasporic space where contemporary forms of transnational identities are constituted (Brah 1998).

An interesting perspective on transnational families is offered by Constable (2018), who proposes a non-normative view of family relations in terms of breaking the stereotype of a need for all family members to live in one geographical location. Instead, she prefers to speak about global assemblages of families that are partly conditioned by migration technologies such as governance of citizenship, social welfare regimes, and competing systems of morality (Constable 2018).

In this chapter we look at transnational practices of care as narrative representations that are localised in the life experiences of individuals (female migrants) and their families. Vertovec (1999) makes a similar argument when he develops the concept of the multi-local life-world. This is based on the assumption that various identities provide individuals with an everyday sense of their own position in various aspects of belonging in the society. Our research with both the Ukrainian and the Bosnian women was based above all on episodic biographical narrations and repeated in-depth interviews. According to Lutz (1995: 314): 'Biographies provide a connection between the actors of migration and the structure of society.' Erel (2007: 4) argues in a similar vein: 'By narrating their stories, migrant women can participate in the building of (imaginary) communities.' We see biographies as a social construction that 'shapes social reality and the world of the subject of knowledge and experience, and is continually confirmed and transformed in a dialectical relationship between the knowledge that features in a life story and the experiences and models presented by society' (Fisher-Rosenthal and Rosenthal 1997: 10). The goal of the reconstruction of a biography is thus to analyse life stories in various contexts where the social and the personal are very closely connected.

The guilt of 'leaving behind'

In our studies we identified among both groups of participants feelings of guilt caused by the fact that the migrating women had left behind close family members (children, husbands, and parents), albeit for different reasons. This is especially interesting in situations where the migrating persons obtain 'licence to leave', which Baldassar characterises as support for the migration decision as an appropriate life-course for themselves and their families (Baldassar 2007: 280). Although most of our research participants from both research projects had obtained such a 'licence', feelings of guilt still occur in their biographies as an integral part of transnational care, closely connected with a specific investment of emotions in an effort to fulfil expected gender roles in constrained conditions.

The biographical stories of Ukrainian migrant woman revolve around the central argument of ensuring a better life for their children (see also Fedyuk, Chapter 2, this volume). To do this, they have undertaken the difficult step of going abroad for work. They have had to deal with the fact that they miss their children, and with feelings of loneliness in a large foreign city. The future they imagined for their children was connected to narratives of the achievement of permanent financial security, higher wages (than their mothers), high-quality education for their children, and the opportunity to work and live abroad. In the former-Yugoslav case, feelings of guilt often emerged directly from the beginning of biographical interviews, whereas in the Ukrainian case, they were attached to the prolonging of the period of separation from children and the verbalisation of the date they left Ukraine. Speaking about the length of their time in the Czech Republic was something that reminded them harshly of the period that they had spent without their children, a time which would never return. This motif appears even more strongly in the stories of mothers who left behind infants and toddlers, i.e. children aged between 6 months and 3 years, an age when there are social expectations of close physical contact between mother and child. The introduction of uncertainty into normatively expected gender identity displayed itself in the way mothers cast doubt on their own maternal competence and childcare practices. An example of this is the story of Oxana who went to the Czech Republic together with her husband when her daughter was about 6 months old. When we were in contact with Oxana, her daughter was already 8 years old. Oxana was pregnant again, and she and her husband had decided that she would return to her daughter in Ukraine, while he would continue working in the Czech Republic. The last interview we did with Oxana was not finished, due to the emotional tension. It was the day before her departure, and it was clear that Oxana had spent a lot of time thinking about her daughter and how to re-establish her maternal role: 'I don't know what it will be like. I don't know ... I don't know any more what it's like to be a mother. We lived alone here, we got used to it. I can't imagine what it will be like getting up with a child, and how I'll live in Ukraine. I got used to it here ... I don't know what it will be like ... (cries).'

The motif of guilt and ambivalence appeared above all in connection with the argument over the decision to leave one's children and migrate, specifically in the description of the complexity of so-called push factors that lead women to migrate. The stories contained detailed descriptions of the economic crisis in Ukraine, levels of corruption, and unemployment and alcoholism in their families. In their narratives this picture of the bad economic system took a contrasting function to their current situation – an economically-improved living standard. It had come to embody the legitimisation of the 'rightness' of their difficult choice to migrate without their families. 'It was terrible in Ukraine. Inflation came, people had no money. We had little children, we were living with our parents, and you find yourself thinking how are we going to live. You do it for your family. For a better future.' (Irina).

Only two transnational mothers were reunited with family members during our collaboration. According to the OPU (OPU, *Organizace pro pomoc uprchlíkům* 2016), migrants seeking family reunification in the Czech Republic face a barrier in the form not only of the demands made of the sponsor, but also the unreasonably long time it takes to deal with their applications. In the context of migration policy, the Czech system is characterised by an uncompromising approach to the observance of rules by migrants, and an absence of sanctions on its own institutions when they themselves fail to observe the rules. The bureaucracy makes reunification complicated not only with children but also with seniors (which is exactly the case of parents from Bosnia and Herzegovina), since Czech law does not feature the legal concept of 'vulnerable person'.

In the case of the women with refugee experience from former Yugoslavia, the topic of involuntary departure, or rather escape from war-stricken Yugoslavia, was certainly the most delicate part of the interview process, both for the women interviewed and for us as researchers. Even though the women left their homeland more than 20 years ago, it was not easy for them to speak about this period of their life. The conditions in their country of origin at the time of their departure were, without exaggeration, life-threatening. When the war in Bosnia started, Mirjana decided to stay behind to take care of her mother. In this particular case, her husband and her daughter left for Czechoslovakia and she was reunited with them a few months later: 'Yes, I decided to stay. My mum was the main reason. My husband's sister stayed too because of her parents. The two of us arranged for water and wood. For several months we had no water, no electricity, no telephone connection, so we had no idea what was happening in the flat next to ours, and a lot of bad things could have happened. Actually, a lot of bad things really happened.' In other cases, women left relatives at home whom they never saw again, and experienced severe emotional distress when relatives died and they could not attend the funeral and say their last goodbye to them. Branka says: 'It was difficult to cope with the fact that my parents were ill and I couldn't be with them. I could send them money, but I couldn't offer the care I should have offered them as a daughter during the first hard days. This is a burden that lies heavy on my heart. They both died and I wasn't around.'

In the stories analysed, women with refugee experience often reflected sensitively on their feelings of guilt connected with the fact that they were among the few 'chosen' who were allowed to leave the war-stricken country and thus could provide safe living conditions for their children in a new place. At the same time, the women spoke about their ambivalent feelings related to their gratitude that they were able to provide a safe environment for their children as an important part of their care obligations during the fragile time of their war-torn life. Dženana says:

> In the first few days I was really happy that we were here, because I could feel that we had regained what we once used to have: peace, a normal life, basic foodstuffs, hygiene, water, electricity and so on. Later I started to suffer from a guilty conscience, I felt guilty about saving myself. I didn't feel that much guilt with respect to my family, parents and husband … I was thinking about my friends and people I knew who also had young children and failed to leave Sarajevo. So, at first I felt temporary happiness and satisfaction that I had left the city and managed to save in particular the children, but then feelings of guilt appeared as many people stayed even though they were in a more difficult situation than my family was.

Biographical interviews revealed that it was women who maintained, at every cost, the illusion of 'normality' in their families and summoned all their mental strength to create the feeling of safety for their children during wartime. The desire for *normal life* is also the main narrative motive of all stories about involuntary departure connected with satisfying the basic life needs of their family members – access to water, sufficient food, electricity, gas, job opportunities, a safe journey to school. In the interviews, we identified a significant strategy of 'ensuring that children have what they need'; women were doing their best to ensure that their children did not view forced migration as yet another negative change in their lives after having experienced the hardships of war. They were trying hard to sustain the family so that the children were saved from material shortage. Women thus remembered very well and in detail the biographies of the things (Kopytoff 1986) they provided for their new households – how they got the particular thing, from whom, what they had to do to obtain it, how much time it took them to save money to buy the particular thing.

Temporariness as a gendered survival strategy in migration experience

The feeling of guilt could, however, change into a strong moral commitment which helped them succeed and 'withstand' the emotional, social, and economic inconveniences that they were to face in the subsequent years of their migration. Besides this strategy, the migrating women used other strategies to cope with these feelings, one of which is connected to the dimension of time.

Time, in the study of migration experience, shows itself to be an analytical category as significant as space or place, although it tends to be, with a few exceptions, still underestimated in research into the personal experience of migrants (Andersson 2014). In our process of analysis of biographical interviews, we were intrigued by women's reflections on their own 'emotional work' related to the temporary nature of migration, implying a certain promise that the time would soon come when they could return home to family members. This specific temporal configuration helped women with migration and refugee experience to survive the difficult period at the beginning of the migration, when they were getting used to the new migration situation or were coming to terms with their inability to fulfil their normatively expected gender roles.

Among the Ukrainian women, we observed specific temporal regularity in the description of the strategy of female labour migration. At the beginning of migration, the women chose a three-month stay in the Czech Republic. This was more of a pragmatic decision which above all allowed them to enter the territory of the Czech Republic legally on a tourist visa; secondly, these three months allowed the women at least to orient themselves in their new society. However, this period also had an emotional significance for them. It became a trial separation, a test of how (if at all) they would cope with a long period of separation from their children. The women perceived the physical separation from their children as a temporary state and dreamed that it would 'one day end'. The motif of 'temporariness' was present in all the biographies analysed. The belief that eventually they would be reunited helped the migrant women to bear the difficult conditions in migration and to overcome the bureaucratic barriers that prevented the official reunification of the family in the Czech Republic. The strategy of conceiving migration as temporary also showed itself in the lifestyle of the newly arriving transnational mothers in the Czech Republic. During this phase of migration, the transnational mothers tried to reduce their living costs (and thus to save up as much as possible for remittances). It was for this reason that, at the beginning of their migration, many of them lived in shared, multi-occupant forms of accommodation, such as cheap workers' dormitories. Another reason why many of them chose this temporary form of accommodation was that, above all in the initial phase of their migration, they returned home relatively often. This temporary home in the dormitories gave migrant women space to decide whether they would stay and work in the Czech Republic, or would return home to their families. In their biographical stories we were able to observe that the women reflected on this part of their migration as the most difficult bit. Their social situation when they left Ukraine had been difficult, and they perceived their migration as a step towards a new 'bright future'. They tried to minimise the time they spent in the dormitories and to move out as soon as possible into shared sublet accommodation. It is important to remember here that the creation of a home in its material form (such as furnishing a flat or house) can also be perceived as a symbolic act of transferring oneself into another social space or social relationship (Miller 2010). We suggest that, along with economic reasons, this is the main reason that Ukrainian transnational mothers delayed the furnishing of shared flats, even though some ended up living in this provisional arrangement for years.

Women with refugee experience from former Yugoslavia also believed their forced departure was only temporary and provisional: 'we thought that it was to be a kind of holiday and that we would return soon'. By no means did they expect that the war would take so long and that the following 20 years of their lives would be so closely connected with the Czech Republic. This can be shown by Sanja's story:

> The worst thing was that it was really fast, I had no documents or anything. The only thing I had were the kids' medical cards that were of no use here. Actually, we took nothing! Apart from the passport which we had to have … We all believed that we would be away for just a little while and then go back home. Nobody knew that we were leaving our home forever. That was the problem. We left our home tidy and ready for our return.

Women were permanently overwhelmed by worries about the relatives and friends they had left in their war-stricken home country. Jasmina says: 'The worst thing was that we didn't know what was going on there. We only had some information from television and newspapers. We used to run to the post office and phone home to find out whether they were all right. You can hardly imagine what it was like.' It is also important to realise that they had left almost all the personal property they had accumulated over the years in their country of origin and they had no idea in what condition they would find it (or if they would find it at all) on their return.

We can thus see that the 'strategy of temporariness' could not last forever, and, indeed, it became temporary as well. Yet this also means, as we tried to demonstrate, that the invisible trajectory from guilt to commitment remained inside the women as an unprocessed emotional burden, accompanying their lives for a very long time.

Struggles to achieve a work–care combination

In the following section, we would like to consider various gender-conditioned strategies for combining work and (the still expected) long-distance care during migration. The research among transnational mothers from Ukraine showed that migration did not necessarily mean the loss of work fulfilment. In their country of origin, most women had no employment, because of high unemployment in their home region and the fact that they had become mothers at a relatively early age (around 20). Migrating to the Czech Republic meant, for most of them, getting access to their first paid job and the ability to decide about their earnings (Ezzeddine 2012).

Their ability to work was totally dependent on the care which their parents provided on their behalf in their country of origin, since most women could not rely on their partner because the relationship was not functional (only two women in our research had migrated to the Czech Republic with their partner). Ensuring 'replacement' care played a critical role in their decision to migrate for work. The women explained that they were able to rely on their family networks because, as one said, 'my mother brought me up well, too' and they knew that the children 'would be all right with them'. For all our research participants, care was provided exclusively by the grandmothers of the children; in some cases two grandmothers took turns to care for the children, or elderly parents cared for the children of two of their daughters. In particular, women who come from the rural environment of western Ukraine, where family ties are still strong, were already used to receiving help from their parents, above all from their mothers. 'I don't know how the children grew up, they were little, I had help. My mother, my sister, we all lived in one house. I didn't even get up to look after my son in the night, my mother used to go and look after him. They helped us a lot, because at that time we were beginning to build this house' (Alina).

In return for the provision of substitute care, it was expected that the migrant women would regularly send part of their earnings from migration, which were used not only to benefit the children, but also to support the carers themselves, both grandmothers and grandfathers. It was a suitable economic solution both for the transnational mothers and for the broader family unit. Ukrainian women sent part of their earnings not only to their children but to those who looked after them. In migration they thus transformed their gender roles and became the breadwinners of their families.

In the case of transnational mothers, therefore, there is an actualisation of motherhood, although within a framework of commodification of relationships. Remittances legitimised and materialised the validity of the difficult decision to go abroad to work, compensated for the physical absence of the mothers, and symbolically reconstructed and maintained, at a distance, family relationships (Ezzeddine 2019, see also Feduyk, Chapter 2, this volume). At the same time, these remittances visibly emphasised the new productive role of the women as the primary breadwinners of their families. The material practices of transnational mothers may thus be a specific display of the economy of dignity (Pugh 2009).

The case of women with refugee experience shows a different form of transnational practices of care. Transnational care for seniors is a kind of moral commitment which needs to be fulfilled regardless of one's own geographical location (Hromadzić and Palmberger 2018).

The situation with care for the elderly in former Bosnia and Herzegovina – where most of our research participants come from – is complicated. According to Hromadzić, 'both state and family in postwar and postsocialist Bosnia-Herzegovina materialize as semi-absent: the state is bureaucratically and politically ubiquitous but biopolitically shrinking, and family is materially present but physically elsewhere, or physically present and materially incapable of providing care' (Hromadzić 2018: 157).

Although the majority of women from former Yugoslavia did not find themselves in a good financial situation upon their arrival in the Czech Republic, they tried to support their families who were suffering at home in war-torn Yugoslavia. As soon as possible, they started to send home non-perishable and canned food. When the war ended, they continued to provide support, mainly financial, not only to their parents but also to other relatives who had stayed at home during the war, since the economic situation in Bosnia above all was (and continues to be) very difficult. In interviews the women emphasised that they had gradually got used to being a long way away from their relatives, who still lived in their homeland, and that it had become 'quite natural'. On the other hand, they stressed that emotional bonds 'go beyond borders' and separation only concerned their everyday life. They also mentioned how sorry they were not to be with their parents, particularly at times when the parents badly needed their assistance. This reflects the normative pressure in their country of origin where it was expected that daughters would 'naturally' take care of their old and ill parents.

Some women with refugee experience from former Yugoslavia were at the time of the our research in a vulnerable position on the Czech labour market due to their more advanced age, and it was therefore not easy for them to organise their 'caring' visits to their parents (Ezzeddine and Havelková 2016). They found themselves under a double pressure: to keep their insecure jobs (and thus ensure a more financially secure retirement for the future) and to meet the normative obligations of transnational care for seniors. Women thus organised their trips to their country of origin according to their job situation and their opportunities regarding paid holidays. Milica reflects:

> I haven't had a holiday for years, since I plan my holidays according to my father's visits to hospital or my mother's check-ups at various hospitals in Zagreb. They are both ill, so all my free time and plans are subject to this fact. That means driving them to hospital, taking them to the doctor and driving them back home as there is no hospital in our town. Also they have to live on one income, my mother is disabled and my father is retired. And they struggle to make ends meet from one pension ... So when I go there, I visit all the graves and I also bring them supplies for the winter – salt, flour, oil, other things, potatoes ... so that they don't have to go out. Winters are sometimes tough, the roads are slippery and they wouldn't be able to go out. I don't want them to catch something or have an accident. Because if they're not OK, I'm not OK here either. I wouldn't know what to do. I have to go to work, I can't go on holiday when I decide to ... I have twenty-five days of holiday. So I have to split that into four parts and it's absolutely insufficient. Of course they miss me. They need everyday care, really. Dad needs help getting into the shower, so they would need someone who lives nearby. The care is absolutely insufficient.

Although some of the interviewed women had obtained Czech citizenship, they are not guaranteed full access to and participation in all public services (e.g. full right to entry into the pension scheme) and their rights and demands are often questioned (Ezzeddine and Havelková 2016). Similarly to retired women from the majority society, older women with a refugee experience (especially if they are widows or divorced) find themselves on the poverty line (Sokačová 2015). As a result, some of the women in our research, in this vulnerable social situation and at the same time continuing to bear responsibility for care, deal with their situation by taking on additional jobs even after retirement age. This helps them to increase the resources necessary for long-distance care (travel costs, paying for care during their absence etc.).

Given the (traditional and/or socialist) norm of mutual support within the broader family and between generations, we find it surprising that women with refugee experience from former Yugoslavia themselves completely reject the idea that they might be supported by their own children, and that they might accept such care in the future. This strict refusal of offered help may also be explained by the fact that in migration these women had to put aside their own career ambitions and that their job opportunities in the new environment were limited; a number of women were overqualified for roles such as domestic workers. Therefore, they focused their energy on their children and expected them to succeed outside the family environment: both daughters and sons. Any request that might entail their children deviating from their career (for example, a request to look after their parents) would mean that this model of care would lose its meaning and interfere with the women's personal gender identity and dignity (Ezzeddine and Havelková 2016).

Conclusion

Our research findings show how geographical borders shape the life trajectories of transnational mothers and daughters, enabling the women to live parallel lives in a transnational space, where they move back and forth between their reproductive and productive roles. The borders of nation states also, however, determine their legal status as 'third-country nationals' who (with the exception of Croatian women) have limited opportunities for family reunification with their children or parents. This means that they have to search for other ways and strategies in order to fulfil socially expected gender roles.

Concerning feelings of guilt, women with refugee experience from former Yugoslavia related this mainly to the parents and friends that they had 'left' behind during the acute situation of their forced migration when they tried to find a peaceful place for their children. In the case of Ukrainian women, the feeling of guilt was related to the children they 'left' behind at home with their own parents as a result of their labour migration. As for the strategy of temporariness, it had varying results: in the case of women from former Yugoslavia, it gradually disappeared as a result of the evolving socio-political situation, so to speak – the involuntary prolongation of their stay in the receiving country – and also as a result of better life and career prospects for their children in the Czech Republic. In the case of Ukrainian women who were transnational mothers, the temporariness faded away with the continuance of labour migration, and also with hopes of a better life for their children 'left' at home.

The biggest difference between the women from Ukraine and former Yugoslavia participating in our two studies can be found in relation to the third issue, i.e. their position vis-a-vis other members of their families in relation to the question of life–work balance. The crucial aspect of difference is the professional career of the women. Women with refugee experience from former Yugoslavia, who had often had a successful career before they were forced to flee, gave up their careers in the host country in the sense that they 'shifted' their ambitions to their children's success. Yet we discovered a rather surprising secondary effect of this strategy, namely a refusal to receive support from their grown-up children, who they did not want to hold back in their promising careers. In other words, women with refugee experience again choose to remain in 'second place' and keep working until they are exhausted. Yet alongside this somewhat paradoxical attitude (paradoxical in the sense that it does not correspond with their tradition), they continue to support their family members in the country of origin (here keeping the tradition) partly due to the expectations of the receiving country but also based on their own deep commitment to help those at home. In the case of Ukrainian transnational mothers, labour migration often means new opportunities to grow professionally (although they often start in precarious jobs like domestic work) and to find new self-confidence (both of which keep them in the receiving country), but this is only possible thanks to a vast amount of help from their parents at home who take over the care and upbringing of their children. Here the support is mutual: migrating women also support their parents (and children) financially, but not at the expense of their own personal development.

The title of our chapter emphasises the concept of guilt as gendered. As a matter of fact, the complex and complicated decisions women from our two research projects had and have to make almost every day in connection with two forms of support to their families, i.e. both care and breadwinning, were gendered; men were not forced, by social rules and expectations, to do the same. The socialist legacy forms a very integral and important part of these socio-cultural expectations, meaning that women got used to meeting the typical socialist pattern which – unlike the bourgeois pattern – included both the responsibility for care and for breadwinning at the same time.

Acknowledgements

This publication was supported by The Ministry of Education, Youth and Sports – Institutional Support for Long-term Development of Research

Organizations – Charles University, Faculty of Humanities (2019) and by the research programme Global Conflicts and Local Interactions of the Czech Academy of Sciences (Strategy AV21).

References

Andersson, R. (2014) 'Time and the Migrant Other: European Border Controls and the Temporal Economics of Illegality', *American Anthropologist* 116 (4): 795–809.

Baldassar, L. (2007) 'Transnational Families and Aged Care: The Mobility of Care and the Migrancy of Ageing', *Journal of Ethnic and Migration Studies* 33 (2): 275–297.

Bonfiglioli, Chiara (2013) 'Gendering Social Citizenship: Textile Workers in Post-Yugoslav States'. CITSEE Working Paper No. 2013/30: https://ssrn.com/abstract=2388858 or http://dx.doi.org/10.2139/ssrn.2388858.

Brah, A. (1998) *Cartographies of Diaspora: Contesting Identities*. London: Routledge.

Bryceson, D. and U. Vuorela (2003, eds) *The Transnational Family*. New York: Berg.

Buch, E. (2015) 'Anthropology of Care and Aging', *Annual Review of Anthropology* 44: 277–293.

Constable, N. (2018) 'Assemblages and Affect: Migrant Mothers and the Varieties of Absent Children', *Global Networks* 18 (1): 168–185.

Erel, U. (2007) 'Constructing Meaningful Lives: Biographical Methods in Research on Migrant Women', *Sociological Research Online* 12 (4): 1–14.

Ezzeddine, P. (2012) 'Mateřství na Dálku: Transnacionální Mateřství Ukrajinských Migrantek v České Republice', *Gender, rovné příležitosti, výzkum* 13 (1): 24–33.

Ezzeddine, P. (2019) 'Sentimentální peníze – Jaká je cena transancionálního mateřství?', *Gender a výzkum/Gender and Research* 20 (1): 68–90.

Ezzeddine, P. and H. Havelková (2016) 'Women in Between: Gender, Refugee Experience and Ageing', *Urban People* 8 (2): 179–201.

Fisher-Rosenthal, W. and G. Rosenthal (1997) ' Narrationsanalyse biographischer Selbstpräsentationen '. In: R. Hitzler and A. Honer (eds) *Sozialwissenschaftliche Hermeneutik*. Opladen: Leske & Budrich, pp. 133–146.

Funk, N. and M. Mueller (1993, eds) *Gender Politics and Post-Communism: Reflections from Eastern Europe and the Former Soviet Union*. London: Routledge.

Gal, S. and G. Kligman (2000, eds) *The Politics of Gender after Socialism*. Princeton: Princeton University Press.

Havelková, H. (1995) 'The Gender Dimension of the Relationship Between Private and Public', *Czech Sociological Review* 31: 25–38.

Hromadžić, A. (2018) 'Where Were They until Now?" Aging, Care, and Abandonment in a Bosnian Town'. In: A. Hromadžić and M. Palmberger (eds) *Care Across Distance*. New York: Berghahn Books, pp. 156–170.

Hromadžić, A. and Palmberger, M. (2018, eds) *Care Across Distance: Ethnographic Explorations of Aging and Migration*. New York: Berghahn Books.

Jones, A. (1994) 'Gender and Ethnic conflict in ex-Yugoslavia', *Ethnic and Racial Studies* 17 (1): 115–134.

Kiblitskaya, M. (2000) 'Russia's Female Breadwinners – The Changing Subjective Experience'. In: S. Ashwin (ed.) *Gender, State and Society in Soviet and Post-Soviet Russia*. New York: Routledge, pp. 50–70.

Kopytoff, I. (1986) 'The Cultural Biography of Things: Commoditization as Process'. In: A. Appadurai (ed.) *The Social Life of Things: Commodities in Cultural Perspective*. Cambridge: Cambridge University Press, pp. 64–92.

Lutz, H. (1995) 'The Legacy of Migration: Immigrant Mothers and Daughters and the Process of Intergenerational Transmission', *Commenius* 15 (3): 304–317.

Meznarić, S. (1985) 'Theory and Reality: The Status of Employed Women in Yugoslavia'. In: L.S. Wolchik and G.A. Meyer (eds) *Women, State and Party in Eastern Europe*. Durham, NC: Duke University Press, pp. 214–221.

Miller, D. (2010). *Stuff*. Oxford: Polity Press.

OPU (2016) *Analýza k Problematice Postavení Migrantek a Migrant v České Republice*. Praha: OPU.

Pugh, J.A. (2009) *Longing and Belonging: Parents, Children, and Consumer Culture*. Berkeley: University of California Press.

Reeves, J. (1990) 'Social Change in Yugoslavia and its Impact on Women', *International Journal of Sociology of the Family* 20 (2): 125–138.

Sokačová, L. (2015) 'Chudoba a prevence chudoby v genderové perspektivě.' In: I. Smetáčková (ed.) *Stínová zpráva o stavu genderové rovnosti v České republice v roce*. Praha: Česká ženská lobby, pp. 130–132.

Solari, C. (2010) 'Drain vs. Constitutive Circularity: Comparing the Gendered Effects of Post Soviet Migration Patterns in Ukraine', *Anthropology of East Europe Review* 28 (1): 215–238.

Tolstokorova, A. (2010) 'Where Have All The Mothers Gone? The Gendered Effect of Labour Migration and Transition of the Institution of Parenthood in Ukraine', *Journal of Eastern Anthropological Review* 28 (1): 184–214.

Uhde, Zuzana (2019) 'Claims for Global Justice: Migration as Lived Critique of Injustice'. In: J.C. Velasco and M.C. La Barbera (eds) *Challenging the Borders of Justice in the Age of Migrations*. New York: Springer, pp. 183–204.

Verdery, K. (1994) 'From Parent-State to Family Patriarchs: Gender and Nation in Contemporary Eastern Europe', *Eastern European Politics and Societies* 8 (2): 225–255.

Vertovec, S. (1999) 'Conceiving and Researching Transnationalism', *Ethnic and Racial Studies* 25 (1): 21–42.

5

Celebrating invisibility: live-in Romanian *badanti* caring for the elderly in southeast Italy

Gabriela Nicolescu

Preamble

Ana, a Romanian migrant live-in careworker taking care of Italian elderly in southeast Italy, would often describe her work conditions as 'house detention' because her care job allowed only two outings of a maximum duration of three hours a week. She would say, combining bitterness with laughter: '*Badanti*, what are we here? Slaves! But what can we do!?'

In Italian, *badare* means to take care constantly and watch over somebody, usually an older person. As a reaction to her lack of freedom, one day in the summer of 2014 I suggested to Ana that I could organise a local workshop or a conference as a space to raise issues related to infringements of labour regulations. Ana rejected my proposal. She said that instead of lamenting, we should organise a party.

The idea appealed to me. I started to lobby for the party and explore the possibilities. A small Italian cultural association agreed to host the party and also proposed a name: 'The Party of the Counter Hour'. The name was supposed to indicate that the hour of the party was really unusual by Italian standards: 4 to 6 pm on a hot July afternoon was far from ideal. The name was also supposed to signal that this was the only time when migrant careworkers living in the town were actually free.

This chapter addresses several issues. Firstly, I discuss the invisibility and the poor – and partly illegal – working conditions of migrant domestic careworkers in Italy. Secondly, I show attempts made by these careworkers to become visible, display a public image, and exercise power vis-a-vis their employers and their families back at home through connectedness, liberation, and curation of a joint performance. Finally, I explore the party as a device for analysis of the inevitable limitations of these attempts.

Exploring these issues in the chapter, I simultaneously reveal the lived worlds of one particular migrant woman in both public and intimate realms, her sociality, and her attempts to create a visible self in the town of Grano, Italy. Through phenomenological descriptions, the chapter emphasises how this woman lives in and 'curates' her body and practices, how she moves through and knows the world she is in, how she engages with the world she has left behind by using social media as a prolongation of her space and time of 'freedom'. This Italian 'life in the present' is contrasted to the long-term economic, financial, and moral ties implicit in being part of a particular household and extended kin group in Romania.

Methods

The protagonist of this story is Ana (a pseudonym), a Romanian domestic careworker, aged 45. Ana came to work in Italy in 2005 when she was 36 years old. She had no children of her own, but had a niece, whose university education she supported financially. When the niece finished university, and found employment, Ana would divide all the money that she gained every month (€600/month) in two. She would give half of the money to her partner to finish building their house in Romania, and she would keep half for her own expenses in Italy: clothes, food, tablets, monthly internet and telephone passes, cigarettes, and alcohol. In the 11 years she had worked in Italy, Ana also contributed to the renovation of her parents' house, in a village in eastern Romania.

The chapter describes in detail the party we organised in Grano in July 2014, at Ana's request. The material presented comes mainly from this event but is also based on my previous research, between July 2013 and August 2014, on migrant care work with the elderly in the region.[1] During this period I interviewed 34 migrant careworkers. The interviews were conducted in both Italian and Romanian, both languages in which I am fluent. Over the following years, up to the time of writing this chapter, I conducted follow up interviews on Facebook and over the phone.

Interviews before and following the party were conducted with Ana and with another 11 migrant careworkers who participated in the event. I also interviewed migrant careworkers who refused to come to the party for several reasons: because they feared that they would be seen to be chasing men or be considered 'loose' women in the community, or because they were not allowed free time during that day, or for some, because they had no work contracts and were afraid of being incriminated afterwards. Some of the tensions and clashes related to their participation or lack of participation in the party are explored in the last section of the chapter, where I discuss the party in detail.

Background

Italy's growing ageing population is mostly cared for by family and kin (Bettio, Simonazzi, and Villa 2006). The limited availability of institutional care in the Italian context (Hugman and Campling 1994, Degiuli 2010) was traditionally solved in families by Italian women who would perform the job of care for the elderly, along with other domestic duties (Degiuli 2010). Following the Second World War, domestic care for the elderly was completely transformed due to industrialisation and new employment opportunities for women (Crafts and Magnani 2011). Starting in the 1960s, when Italian women joined the paid workforce, the demand for migrant labour grew and migrant careworkers started to be employed in care jobs (Catanzaro and Colombo 2009). Official data show that in Italy, in 2013, over 800,000 elderly were cared for by migrant careworkers of whom the great majority were women (Pasquinelli and Rusmini 2013), but unofficial figures suggest that the numbers might be much higher.[2] Bettio, Simonazzi, and Villa (2006) affirm that even low-income families could afford to pay €600 a month to a migrant careworker, as the share of the family revenues coming from the pensions and state subsidies of elderly members could easily reach €900 a month.

Following Romania's accession to the European Union in 2007, Romanian citizens gained full access to the Italian labour market. In just a few years, Romanians came to dominate the field of migrant care in Italy (Ban 2012), and by the early 2000s, Romanians had become the largest community of immigrants in the country. This was related to the relatively close geographical proximity of Italy to Romania, the similarity of the Romanian and Italian languages, and the comparable patriarchal social organisation in the two countries.

Meanings of invisibility

This chapter builds on previous research on the invisibility of (mostly female) live-in migrant careworkers in different domestic contexts across the world. It examines not only the gendered dimensions of geo-political borders, but also how, in new environments, people shift, transgress, and reshape moral boundaries of proper gender and kinship behaviour, and moral economies of intimacy and sexuality. Live-in careworkers are very often the subjects of house work immobility or what some scholars have called 'the naturalization of the household' (Harris 1984), pointing to the fact that household labour was seen as naturally female, which meant it was not work – and not visible. 'Housewifisation' refers to the subordinate and unpaid nature of women's (care) work inside the house (Mies 1998 [1986] and Frazer 2016), and to the total atomisation, lack of freedom, and lack of organisation of these women (Mies 1998 [1986]: 110). In the context of migrant care work, as with the ethnographic material presented here, one could wonder if 'housewifisation' could be also used in the context of paid migrant labour. Even if payment occurs, the (lack of) legal status of employment in different contexts impacts massively on working conditions. In the following examples I show how the lack of freedom of movement for intimate care is encountered in both Asian and European contexts.

Nicole Constable (2007 [1997]) has written about the docility and obedience of Filipino domestic careworkers in relation to the rules and norms of Hong Kong employers and their households. In her book *Maid to Order in Hong Kong: Stories of Filipina Care Workers*, Constable also writes about new forms of activism. In the Hong Kong case, employment regulations accord one free day, at the end of the week, to live-in migrant domestic careworkers. During that day, careworkers, the majority of whom are women, meet in the city centre, and occupy corridors inside shopping malls, buildings, bridges, and crossroads. This form of massive visibility, even for a day, is a paradoxical form of freedom. Usually, migrant domestic careworkers in Hong Kong are bound to the household and work uninterruptedly for up to 18 hours a day (Constable 2007 [1997]). More broadly, their work is highly stigmatised, mostly because care work and domestic labour are associated with 'the presence of dirt, bodies and intimacy' (Borris 2010: 2).

In the southern European context, Victoria Chell-Robinson (2000) encounters other examples of migrant domestic careworkers' (in)visibility. She describes Italians' treatment of migrant live-in careworkers historically, as Italy switched in the 1970s from a country of out-migration, from which Italians would leave to seek employment elsewhere in Europe or in America, to a country of in-migration. This shift generated a moral panic in 'the disjuncture between practices of care, for pay, by outsiders, ... and persistent ideologies of care, for love and duty, by kin and family' (Pine and Haukanes Chapter 1: 18, this volume; see also Fedyuk Chapter 2, this volume). Chell-Robinson maintains: 'The underground economy in Italy is an important factor fostering migration – short term, flexible' (2000: 105). This allows for porous borders, comings and goings, but also for a lot of uncertainty around the specific types of employment, questions of legality, and common practices associated with these. Following Chell-Robinson's (2000) observations, I argue that the underground economy of care work, so pervasive in southeast Italy, imposes on migrant careworkers even more fear, more constraints, and specific forms of restriction of movement, therefore creating even more invisibility.

In the same southern Italian context, referring to live-in Ukrainian careworkers, Olena Fedyuk (2006) discusses the importance of invisibility for migrants who do not follow the legal procedures of employment, usually because they urgently need a rapid change of their economic situation, but stresses the importance of visibility for migrants who work legally. Fedyuk argues as follows: 'In their invisibility, labour migrants present a group that lives and functions in-between nation-states and citizenships. They are willing to abandon their citizenship rights for a while in order to improve their life conditions, which would otherwise be very difficult to change' (Fedyuk 2006: 5).

Fedyuk contends that these migrants' lives in between states and 'abandonment of citizenship' is paradoxical if one considers that domestic migrant careworkers contribute massively to making societies work. On the one hand, they contribute by taking care of the elderly, allowing younger Italian families to make use of the surplus value of their work. On the other hand, they contribute to the societies they left behind, by sending remittances. The multiple outcomes of their domestic work are also paralleled by the complex ways in which they communicate their work, values, and contributions to society in both the public and domestic spheres of life.

In the following sections of this chapter, we discover some of the worlds inhabited by Ana on- and offline, in Romania and Italy – almost simultaneously – as Ana spends approximatively five hours daily on the internet, on different social media platforms such as Facebook (Messenger), WhatsApp, and Skype. In migration, times, spaces, and languages of representation collide and merge, intersect and impact on each other, and shift boundaries and border regimes – physical and symbolic – at home and abroad.

Three hours outside the house

Before coming to Italy, Ana worked for the Romanian Post Office. At the height of the economic crisis in 2009, when the state company was restructured, Ana was made redundant. At the age of 36 she decided to go to Italy and work as a domestic careworker for the elderly. She felt that if she remained in Romania, she would have no option but to work as a waitress in a village bar. 'I did not want all the drunk men's hands to be on my butt' she commented in 2013. During the same period, she posted on her Facebook page a photograph from her first employment in Italy in 2009–2010 with the message 'old days'.

The image shows Ana sitting on a chair surrounded by four other people, all holding glasses of white wine in their hands. She is dressed in working clothes, black top and brown trousers; her hair is long and tied in a plait. Close to her, we find her elderly client sitting in a wheelchair. The two of them are surrounded by smiling relatives, a woman and a man, standing. With her shoulders down, humble and tired, Ana seems to be totally submerged in the domestic careworker's condition.

Four years later, in 2013, Ana moved to Grano and started to take care of a woman aged 93, Nona. She liked Nona and after two weeks Nona started to like her and to appreciate the way Ana talked to her, bathed her, laughed with her, cooked for her, and took her outside. But another reason why Ana liked this job with Nona was that Nona lived close to one of the two main squares of the city. Despite regulations prescribing free hours every day, and one free day at the end of the week (Zarattini and Pelusi 2007, FIDALDO 2013), in southeast Italy live-in migrant careworkers for the elderly rarely manage to get out of the house for more than four hours every week. During my research, 20 of the 34 migrant careworkers I interviewed were only allowed out of the house twice a week, for two to three hours each time (usually between 4 pm and 6 (or 7) pm).

Living in the city centre meant that Ana, together with Nona, could get out of the house more often and meet other migrant domestic careworkers of Romanian origin in the public square, whenever the weather was good enough for Nona's health. As I have explained elsewhere, migrant careworkers in Italy are very careful to keep the elderly in good health, in order to keep their employment secure (Nicolescu 2019). In summer evenings, with Nona in her wheelchair, Ana would join the other women and experience some time of freedom, feeling the breeze of the afternoon, talking to other women, giving and receiving advice, exchanging recipes, news, and laughing over obscene jokes. The bench attracted most of the Romanian women working in the region, but not all. Some resisted the desire to meet others and talk, and preferred to remain inside the house, outside migrant sociality. Some would use their limited free time to visit Italian friends or work for other Italian families for extra money.

Ana negotiated with Nona's relatives to receive six hours of free time per week, every week, rather than the usual four that is the unwritten custom in the region. Every Thursday and Saturday Ana could go to the city centre all by herself. On those days Ana would start the day by taking a shower and preparing the clothes she would put on. The blouse would be matched with the trousers, the boots or sandals with the jacket, and, last but not least, the lipstick and perfume would be arranged on the bed in preparation for the afternoon. That day she would not cook, so that her clothes would not smell of food. She would assist Nona in the bathroom, feed her, dress her in clean clothes, and help her into the wheelchair to wait for her son or daughter who took turns every couple of days to give Ana a little bit of free time. When one of the two arrived, Ana would be fully dressed and ready to go out in order to make the most of the three hours of free time that she had. The way she dressed attracted the attention of other people.

For some of her outings, Ana would want to see more than the city centre. She would convince one of her friends to drive her to a different city or village nearby, to visit another migrant careworker, or to see a tourist destination. That summer, Ana asked me if I would be willing to take her out to see the sea, 15 minutes driving distance from the centre of Grano. I agreed. We prepared in advance the swimming costumes, towels, cream, and sunglasses. To my surprise, Ana refused to be taken from home. Instead she suggested that I pick her up from the main square, from the bench where most Romanian careworkers would come. This point of collection ensured that other people knew of her outing.

At the beach, we arranged our towels close to the sea. Ana laid down for a few minutes only. Immediately after she asked me to take few pictures of her, then of us, and then insisted that we should leave. I tried to persuade her that we should stay a bit longer, that she should bathe in the sea, but she refused. She said that she wanted to buy something to eat for herself, say goodbye to the other Romanian *badante* on the bench in the main square, and then go home to Nona 5 minutes before 7 pm. I realised that for Ana the pictures of her and of us at the sea were more important than the sea itself. But also this experience made me feel with my own body that Ana's economy of free time was very different from mine. Resting was an activity that she was able to do frequently when Nona napped or slept at home. The three hours of freedom for Ana were hours of exploration and action outside the house, not of meditation or reverie.

If no friend offered themselves to take her outside the town, Ana would first go to the bench frequented by many Romanian women. At 4 pm not many would be there since most would be free from 5 pm till 7 pm on hot summer days. After that, she would enter a few shops, to look for new clothes and possibly buy some, and then go to a bar to eat a hamburger and drink a glass of alcohol. The eating and drinking would always be followed by pictures. She would ask other people at the bar to take her picture, or she would take a selfie. By the time she got back to the bench, she would be in a different mood: she would talk, laugh, and tease other less experienced domestic careworkers. On her return home, at 7 pm, she would take care of Nona and put her to bed. From 9–11 pm, Ana updated her Facebook account with pictures of herself going out, receiving comments and responding to these.

Facebook as public sociality and as freedom

During my research in 2013–2014 Ana looked fit and very trendy. The pictures that she posted on Facebook showed her with short hair dyed black, slim, with plenty of make-up, always dressed in fashionable glasses and clothing and almost always wearing red lipstick. She would upload pictures of herself inside the house before going out, but also pictures taken outside the house. The pictures taken before going out show an Ana who puts a lot of effort and enthusiasm into making herself look fashionable and modern, almost not assimilable to her domestic work position. The pictures taken outside the house make Ana look like a tourist in Grano, surrounded by trees in blossom, or by old buildings in the town or other tourist destinations nearby. On her outings, taking pictures of herself in the places she went to – a bar or a bench in the main square – would always be followed by postings on Facebook.

The limited hours spent outside the house are prolonged by Ana and others like her in many different ways. For Ana, Facebook represented an opportunity to create a larger space and time of encounter and visibility. Ana would normally go on Facebook at least twice a day – at lunch time and at night – for a total of approximatively four hours.

Images of her outings outside the town of Grano show what anthropologist Răzvan Nicolescu described as 'access to places that only better-off people can usually visit' (Nicolescu 2016: 166). Such postings show the use of social media in contexts of social inequality but also of lack of mobility among live-in migrant domestic careworkers in southeast Italy. After such postings, online friends would leave comments and discussions might continue for a day or more.

Through Facebook, Ana combines the sociality of the Italian south with networking among many Romanian careworkers – an interaction in which she is socially comfortable and which makes her feel that she is not alone. Once or twice a week Ana starts her day with a Facebook posting 'Buongiorno!' and 10 to 20 people, Romanian migrant careworkers or Italian friends, respond.

For Ana, access to the internet means access to a space and time of freedom. After a holiday, when she came back to Italy from Romania, she had no internet connection and she asked me to renew her contract. As it was Saturday, I was not able to renew it and this made Ana really anxious. She told me that without the internet she would die. Her domestic condition was bearable to her only because she could exchange experiences with others.

When she eventually got online again, she posted a few pictures from her stay in Romania. One was with her parents in a green garden in eastern

Romania. Another was of herself on a sofa in her own house in Romania. On top of her lies a big dog. The Facebook caption said: 'Nobody touches me!' This Facebook image and the caption are of specific relevance for an analysis of ideas of freedom and control manifested in live-in migrant careworkers' lives, both in their home countries and abroad. One would expect that, in migrant careworkers' home countries, the house would be a proper welcoming place and a space of freedom. Ana's post and her implicit position show that this is not always the case. Ana symbolically played with ideas of power and vulnerability, by showing to her Facebook friends that she has a dog that protects her. For the next summer holiday, she decided not to go to Romania, but to spend her two week holiday in Italy – I did not ask her where. As she told me, even if she cared about her house in Romania, she cared more about being independent and being able to do what she wanted in Italy – apart from some obvious constraints. Some family members wished Ana would come back more often. Ana did not wish to do so. Such tensions, existing in many families in Romania, add to the economic explanations of the massive migration of Romanian women in Italy. In this context, the Italian houses where live-in careworkers live might be understood as places of ambivalence. On the one hand they enclose the migrant careworkers; on the other, they offer them a chance of autonomy and hope for improvement. As Frances Pine mentions, 'migration (…) can be both a symbol and an enactment of hope and faith in the future and an act of or reaction to hopelessness, despair and acute loss in the present' (Pine 2014: S96).

The relationship migrant careworkers have with social media is also illuminating in terms of their relation with space and time. Unlike the working conditions of live-in migrant domestic careworkers in Hong Kong, where lack of space is dramatic (Constable 2007 [1997]), in southeast Italy, live-in careworkers have a certain degree of freedom if they live with the elderly alone, especially in cases where the elderly are immobile. After they finish their duties with the elderly, many *badanti* are able to use their free time as they wish (except going out). Some spend time on the phone, watching TV or on social media talking to their families left at home; others make friendships with Italian men and women that come to visit. This freedom gets interrupted when the relatives of the elderly come to visit, sometimes every day for 5–10 minutes. From the interviews I conducted for my research, 80% of the live-in careworkers live only with their clients. The remaining 20% live with their clients and their clients' kin. In these latter cases, the space of the house is felt less as a space of freedom.

I started this chapter with Ana's comment on the condition of live-in migrant careworkers in Italy: '*Badanti*, what are we here? Slaves! But what can we do!?' To further explore the duality of the *badanti* work, between freedom and constraint, in the following section of this chapter I describe the party that we organised following Ana's suggestion. This party demonstrates vividly women's struggles to transform themselves, to show control over their own bodies and lives, and to embody new kinds of personhood and femininity.

The Party of the Counter Hour

At 4:30 pm on a hot Saturday afternoon in July, six Romanian careworkers, all dressed in their best clothes and wearing makeup, lipstick, and perfume, entered the grounds of the Italian association where the party was being organised. Ana brought me a red rose, as a sign of appreciation for my efforts in making this party happen. In reality, she was the one who should have been entitled to receive such a gift. But, as I found out afterwards, the rose she offered functioned more as a pretext. Ana wanted to mark the importance of the evening and, dressed in her slinky black dress and black high heels, she started to stroll around in the city as if she was doing something important. As she explained to me later, very confident and laughing about her own adventure, she was proud that she had gone to the most expensive flower shop in the town, at 4 pm sharp. When the city was slowly returning to life, after the hot hours following lunch and the siesta, she bought that rose to the absolute amazement of the florist who had very rarely seen somebody at 4 pm dressed for an evening party. Ana was happy that she could hold an intelligent conversation with the florist, and that she could express herself in impeccable Italian. When she walked along the main road holding that flower, it was a performance in itself. In the small town of Grano where everybody knows everybody else, she wanted to confound and amaze everyone that she knew. She thought that her action would provoke the following question in everybody's minds: where could a *badante* go, dressed like that, at that hour of the afternoon?

But walking at 4 pm on the main boulevard of Grano in her black dress and high heels, while being intended as a powerful performance, also turned out to be an awkward situation. After the siesta hours, not many Italians were around to watch what Ana was doing. To compensate for this, several times during the party she went out of the association's premises to a shop located in the old square of the city – once to buy cigarettes, another time to buy alcohol, and another time to film the passers-by.

At 4.30 pm some more careworkers joined the party and helped with the last preparations: arranging the chairs to create some space for dancing, blowing up balloons, and starting to eat the food I had cooked the day before. After eating a bit and drinking a glass of sangria prepared by an

Italian friend, we started to dance. Traditional Romanian music started to fill the association's premises and the Italian square. More Italian friends joined us and stood perspiring in the middle of our circle.

Around 5 pm, Paolo, a successful local Italian entrepreneur who was also a writer and film-maker, arrived with Samir and Omi. Samir and Omi were the only two Indian careworkers in Grano (Samir was taking care of Paolo's father). The three men joined the party in an atmosphere of relaxation, master and servants together. Immediately after they arrived they began trying some of the food and drinks, and they joined in with the circle dances. With their arrival the party became 'international' and Italian and Romanian music started to mix with Indian popular hits interpreted by Bollywood stars.

A photograph taken at 6 pm shows 10 live-in careworkers present at the party, the hour when most of the Romanian women working as careworkers were expected to return to their employers' houses. Unlike the female careworkers in Grano, the two Indian men present at the party were allowed to stay out later in the evening.

Looking at the picture one cannot tell who are the careworkers, who are the activists, and who are the researchers. Nor is their ethnic background discernible. Dressed in some of our best clothes, 10 careworkers of both Indian and Romanian origin stood close to six Italian people and myself. Paolo and a Romanian careworker stayed close to one another, very happily. Trying to make the introductions, I found out that the two of them already knew each other, from a time when the Romanian woman took care of Paolo's father.

The atmosphere of conviviality and friendship speaks of a very special moment when the picture was taken. It involved the kind of 'immortalisation' of a special (and perishable) moment that Hans Belting (2004) describes, particularly because of its unusual and fragile nature. Many of us took pictures of this, such a rare encounter. But what resides beneath the facade of this moment and the image itself? Ervin Goffman's concept of *persona*, seen as the front stage of how an individual wants to be perceived in public, is useful here. Goffman (1990 [1956]) says that, once in public, individuals perform in order to project a desirable image of themselves. In the case of the party, the *badanti* exaggerated their public face, and dressed not for an evening out, but for a night party. Outside the party environment, when going out twice a week from 4–6 pm, some *badanti* behave as if they are free to do whatever they like, as a reaction to how their individuality is restricted inside the house. While in public, they seem to find their freedom and they show off their desire to be seen as not conforming to their employment status. In this respect, the private houses and the public square are two important places where power relations, care, and control are enacted in quite different ways. While inside the private houses, *badanti* tend to exercise their authority as a means of both easing their workload and increasing the efficiency of their work (for example, cooking Romanian meals rather than Italian ones, or walking the elderly in public spaces, represent occasions during which *badanti* appear to exercise a certain level of control). This control is publicly perceived when Italian people scrutinise their gestures, attitudes, and the external appearances of both *badanti* and the elderly the *badanti* work for. In this context, the 'Party of the Counter Hour', which took place in a very central public space, represented a particular extension of the care and control relations that were taking place inside Italian houses. The *badanti* became curators of an event where their presence, appearance, and tastes were publicly appreciated.

At the same time, *badanti* who live in the same house with Italian family members are very often under close supervision and they regard the public square as their only private space. The very fact that migrants' free time from 4–6 pm does not coincide with the free time of Italians means that some *badanti* feel and act as though nobody really cares what they do and how they do it; they feel that they live in totally separate worlds from those of their employers. But this also attracts criticisms from other *badanti* who want to be appreciated and respected by Italian families and who are critical of those *badanti* who are ready to enter relationships with Italian men. Some of these tensions became visible during the party. At 6.15 pm farewell kisses were exchanged and the Romanian female live-in careworkers left the party. The two Indian men remained for a bit longer, until 7.30, close to their usual time to return to their places of employment. Four Romanian women who were paid as careworkers while being in relationships with older Italian men, stayed a bit longer, up to 9.30 pm.[3]

The blurred boundary between domestic work and sex work is considered problematic by many *badanti* (see also Fedyuk, Chapter 2, this volume). This caused other live-in careworkers not to come to the party for fear they would be associated with Romanian *badanti* who were in relationships with Italian men. Others could not come because they were not free on that Saturday afternoon or because they lacked work contracts and felt that coming to a domestic careworkers' party would incriminate them. Others just felt that this specific type of exposure was something that they did not need. These many reasons for being absent or for showing how visibility complicates the *persona* (the public face of an individual, be that of a domestic labour migrant or not) emphasise the need for more elaboration around the concept of domestic work and around the notion of care. Careworkers negotiate between different worlds, times, spaces, and languages of representation. Their work can remain strictly professional, when they work in institutional care settings, or turn into a live-in profession, where the space of work is also the space of life, a way of finding oneself useful in other homes in other parts of the world; it can be a tool for finding oneself a better-off partner, or just a way of providing basic needs and education for children left at home.

Following the suggestion of the Italian Association who hosted the party, we continued the event until later into the evening and more Italians joined us. To mark the absence of the careworkers themselves – and inspired by Eugene Ionesco's (1951) absurdist tragic farce, 'The Chairs' – the organisers and I glued 14 pieces of white paper onto 14 chairs. Each paper bore the inscription 'motivated absence'. In this way we tried to mark the absence of the protagonists, who were both actors in and the audience of this event. It is unlikely that many people who joined the event read the inscriptions or understood our message.

As in other examples of activism dealing with migrant careworkers (Constable, 2007 [1997]), I attempted to bridge the gap between public and applied anthropology. This proved to be a new research strategy in line with the experimentation with new ethnographic forms working at the borders of ethnography, performance, and exhibition making in the wake of the 'Writing Culture' critique and associated debates (Marcus and Fisher 1986). It also proved to be what Lezaun, Marres, and Tironi call 'a gathering of strangers around a common object of interest (…) an experiment in participation' (Lezaun, Marres, and Tironi 2016: 9), which looks like a situationist encounter between different stakeholders. This encounter makes visible tensions, to build in knowledge among different publics, and to create long-term impact in both social and more technical fields of research. But this encounter could also be seen as an experiment in relational aesthetics, as defined by art theoretician Nicolas Bourriaud et al. (2002). Claire Bishop (2004) has criticised Bourriaud's idea of commonality and friendship in relational aesthetic practices for not engaging sufficiently with politics. According to Bishop (2004), relational art does not resolve the social inequalities and works with discrete events that are separated from the social texture.

Even so, events like the party I organised have an impact on both migrant domestic careworkers and the societies where they work. Olena Fedyuk argues that 'by bringing more visibility, agency, and security to labour migration' the face of labour migration will change, as well as people's occupations and lifestyles (Fedyuk 2006: 4). She continues: 'However, under the nation states system, rights seem to be too tightly attached to the category of citizenship and by abandoning their civic rights, labour migrants lose their basic human rights for safe labour, healthcare and freedom of movement' (Fedyuk 2006: 5). In this chapter, I discuss both the immediate impact and the importance of duration in judging the outcomes of such experiments in participation. All these ideas combined with my previous interests in making exhibitions as processes of capturing 'public(s)' and as tools of negotiation in situations of conflict (Nicolescu 2016), with new material data in the field of transnational care (Nicolescu 2019). This interest was taken further in an exploration of the tension between care and curation, as two fields of expertise deriving etymologically from a similar Latin root, but assigned to two distinct fields of visibility.

Marilyn Strathern (1995) suggests that knowledge production in anthropology benefits from 'shifting contexts', such as transfers between local and global, between small scale and large scale, or between the individual and groups. In this case, changing the field of interest from the house to a public venue of encounter, from care to curation, allowed a very powerful shifting of contexts. As Strathern affirms, 'epistemology is not merely about the context, but also about understanding the shifting of the context, the possibility to navigate between separate orders of knowledge such as "level", "context", "structure" and "event"' (Strathern 1995: 11). Based on Strathern's arguments, I see the curation of this event as an ideal space and time where dislocation and relocation of both people and horizons of expectations occur.

Finally, I think it is useful for the framing of the chapter to mention the concept of 'house societies' (Levi-Strauss 1983, Carsten and Hugh-Jones 1995, Goddard 2000). Live-in Romanian careworkers in southeast Italy come from two very poor regions of Romania, from the deep south or the far east, close to the border with Moldova and Ukraine. Their home setting is similar to Frances Pine's (1996, 1999) description of the house society in mountain villages in the 1980s and 1990s in Poland, and the role of migration there. Much of the money migrant domestic careworkers earn funds the needs of extended families comprising several generations. With their live-in care work in Italy, these Romanian women on the one hand attempt to continue the tradition from home, and to care for the elderly as if they were their own kin, dedicating enormous time and energy to making sure that the Italian elderly live so that their employment remains secure for longer periods (Nicolescu 2019). Inside the Italian elderly's homes they reconstitute fragments of time and the personal space of freedom. On the other hand, these *badanti* women show the Italian community that they can dress in fashionable clothes and look modern and successful. In this way they seem to contradict their rather patriarchal home culture. But this is more like a transitory action, while their permanent destiny seems to be still rooted in the home context that they have left. Similar performative actions, and liberations, are very often encountered in situations of mobility, when home norms and regulations are transgressed. The party made visible how careworkers negotiate between different worlds, times, spaces, and languages of representation to bring into being worlds they imagine for themselves, or to separate themselves from those with which they do not want to be associated.

Conclusions

This chapter showed how anthropological knowledge is informed by shifting the contexts in which people we research normally live and work. 'The Party of the Counter Hour' made visible the temporal and spatial complexities of domestic work. It also showed the invisibility and the poor – and partly illegal – working conditions of migrant domestic careworkers in Italy in relation to the attempts made by these careworkers to become visible, display a public image, and exercise power vis-a-vis their employers and their families at home. Finally, the party as a display of all the above and as a key device of analysis showed that the act of participation was a collaborative task to which the domestic careworkers contributed to different degrees, reflecting their personal freedoms and motivations. Not many careworkers could remain after 6.30 pm. The time constrictions also reflected their specific types of employments. Some were tied to strict schedules. Others, notably those who were in romantic relationships with Italians, were allowed to stay a bit longer. Italian employers had no restrictions whatsoever, and mainly because of this, the party continued up to 9.30 pm in the absence of the caregivers themselves.

After the party, Ana became Facebook friends with the organisers at the association where the event took place. When Ana moved to work in another town in the north of Italy, their interaction over the years became restricted to liking each other's posts. The association intended to organise similar events to which to invite other careworkers, but according to Ana, this was not accomplished in the end.

The work we did together could be described, using the words of Geraldine Pratt, as a 'productively compromised collaboration' that 'tried to create a process of knowledge creation that answers to different communities of interest operating within varying protocols of accountability' (Pratt 2012: xxxii). I suggest that the 'party' managed to reach such a compromise and display it publicly in a self-reflecting way. The party not only made visible the distinct temporal and spatial relations that migrant careworkers and their employers have, but also that public spaces are not really 'public' outside temporal frames. But as Ana remarked, despite these differences and inequalities, she still enjoyed listening to different kinds of music, eating different kinds of food, feeling that her work is transferrable no matter the cultural and gendered boundaries between Romanian, Italian, and Indian contexts. There was a common humanity that she recognised.

Notes

1 All names of places and people are pseudonyms unless otherwise stated. To conduct this research, I received formal consent from all the migrant careworkers, and all Italian employers who participated.
2 The total number of migrant careworkers could be significantly higher, mostly because of informal employment. During my research, only 30% of the care work performed by migrant careworkers was backed up by a contract.
3 Four women came accompanied by Italian men. In the cases of two of them, where the relationship between the live-in migrant careworker and the family member is not recognised, the women are still paid. In the other two cases, they are not.

References

Ban, C. (2012) 'Economic Transnationalism and its Ambiguities: The Case of Romanian Migration to Italy', *International Migration* 50 (6): 129–149.

Belting, H. (2004) 'Towards an Anthropology of Image'. In: M. Westerman (ed.) *Anthropologies of Art*. London: Yale University Press, pp. 41–59.

Bettio, F., A. Simonazzi, and P. Villa (2006) 'Change in Care Regimes and Female Migration: the "Care Drain" in the Mediterranean', *Journal of European Social Policy* 16 (3): 271–285.

Bishop, C. (2004) 'Antagonism and relational aesthetics', *October*: 51–79.

Borris, E. (2010) *Intimate Labors: Cultures, Technologies, and the Politics of Care*. Stanford: Stanford University Press.

Bourriaud, N., S. Pleasance, F. Woods, and M. Copeland (2002) *Relational Aesthetics*. Dijon: Les presses du réel.

Carsten, J. and S. Hugh-Jones (1995, eds) *About the House: Lévi-Strauss and Beyond*. Cambridge: Cambridge University Press.

Catanzaro, R. and A. Colombo (2009, eds) *Badanti & Co. Il Lavoro Domestico Straniero in Italia*. Bologna: Il Mulino.

Chell-Robinson, V. (2000) 'Female Migrants in Italy: Coping in a Country of New Immigration'. In: F. Anthias. and G. Lazaridis (eds) *Gender and Migration in Southern Europe*. Oxford: Berg, pp. 103–123.

Constable, N. (2007 [1997]) *Maid to Order in Hong Kong: Stories of Filipina Care Workers*. Ithaca: Cornell University Press.

Crafts, N. and M. Magnani (2011) *The Golden Age and the Second Globalization in Italy*. https://core.ac.uk/download/pdf/6335033.pdf (accessed 12 July 2018).

Degiuli, F. (2010) 'The Burden of Long-term Care: How Italian Family Care-Givers Become Employers', *Aging and Society* 30 (5): 755–777.

FIDALDO (2013) *Contratto Collettivo Nazionale di Lavoro sulla Disciplina del Rapporto di Lavoro Domestico*. Roma: Tipolitografia CSR.

Fedyuk, O. (2006) 'Ukrainian Labour Migrants: Visibility through Stereotypes', *Migration Online*. https://aa.ecn.cz/img_upload/3bfc4ddc48d13ae0415c78ceae108bf5/OFeduyk_Ukrainian_Labour_Migrants_1.pdf (accessed 6 December 2017).

Frazer, N. (2016) 'Contradictions of Capital and Care', *New Left Review* 100 (July–August) 2016. https://newleftreview.org/issues/II100/articles/nancy-fraser-contradictions-of-capital-and-care (accessed 6 December 2017).

Goddard, V. (2000, ed) *Gender, Agency and Change*. London: Routledge.

Goffman, E. (1990 [1956]) *The Presentation of Self in Everyday Life*. London: Penguin.

Harris, O. (1984) 'Households as Natural Units'. In: K. Young, C. Wolkowitz, and R. McCullagh (eds) *Of Marriage and the Market: Women's Subordination Internationally and its Lessons*. London: Routledge, pp. 136–155.

Hugman, R. and J. Campling (1994) *Ageing and the Care of Older People in Europe*. Hampshire: Macmillan Press LTD.

Levi-Strauss, C. (1983) *The Way of the Masks*. London: Jonathan Cape.

Lazaun, J., N. Marres, and M. Tironi (2016) 'Experiments in Participation'. In: F. Ulrike, R. Fouché, C-A. Miller, and L. Smith-Doerr (eds) *The Handbook of Science and Technology Studies*. Cambridge, MA: Cambridge MIT Press (4): 1–59.

Marcus, G. and M.J. Fischer (1986) *Anthropology as Cultural Critique: An Experimental Moment in the Human Sciences*. Chicago: University of Chicago Press.

Mies, M. (1998 [1986]) *Patriarchy and Accumulation on a World Scale. Women in the International Division of Labour*. London: Zed Books Ltd.

Nicolescu, G. (2016) 'The Museum's Lexis: Driving Objects into Ideas', *Journal of Material Culture* 21 (4): 465–489.

Nicolescu, G. (2019) 'Keeping the Elderly Alive: Global Entanglements and Embodied Practices in Long-Term Care in Southeast Italy', *Anthropology & Aging* 40 (1): 72–88.

Nicolescu, R. (2016) *Social Media in Southeast Italy: Crafting Ideals*. London: UCL Press.

Pasquinelli, S. and G. Rusmini (2013, eds) *Badare non Basta. Il lavoro di Cura: Attori, Progetti e Politiche*. Rome: Ediesse.

Pine, F. (1996) 'Naming the House and Naming the Land: Kinship and Social Groups in Highland Poland,' *Journal of the Royal Anthropological Institute* (1996): 443–459.

Pine, F. (1999) 'Incorporation and Exclusion in the Podhale'. In: E. Papataxiarchis, S.M. Stewart and S. Day (eds) *Lilies of the Field: Marginal People who Live for the Moment*. Boulder: Westview Press, pp. 45–60.

Pine, F. (2014) 'Migration as Hope: Space, Time and Imagining the Future', *Current Anthropology* 55 (S9): S95–S104.

Pratt, G. (2012) *Families Apart. Migrating Mothers and the Conflicts of Labor and Love*. Minneapolis: University of Minnesota Press.

Strathern, M. (1995, ed.) *Shifting Contexts. Transformations in Anthropological Knowledge*. London: Routledge.

Zarattini, P. and R. Pelusi (2007) *Il Contratto di Lavoro: I Lavoratori Domestici*. Milano: Edizioni Fag.

Part II

Gender, entitlement, and obligation: migrants interacting with the state and voluntary services

6

Migrating bodies in the context of health and racialisation in Germany

Christiane Falge

Introduction

Across the globe we are observing an increasing number of apparently impenetrable and incomprehensible borders, both geo-political state borders and institutional, cultural, and gender borders which regulate and order social life. As people flee their homelands for reasons such as war, climate change, or discrimination, they face tremendous difficulties, embodied in pain and even death, in their attempts to cross policed and militarised borders, mounted by Western states against the global South and East. Similarities and differences emerge between borders drawn across contested territories, as in the US/Mexican case, or in a maritime divide based upon a long colonial and precolonial history, as we observe with the emerging Euro-African border. What these borders share politically are the illegal industries that accompany them, and the negative effects these generate on the health and life of bodies of migrants. In contrast to these insurmountable boundary regimes with their deadly consequences for bodies, we have borders that can be crossed by some people or by body parts and other commodities with relative or complete ease, moving from less wealthy 'donors' to more wealthy recipients. Global economies intertwined with and paved by colonial and postcolonial processes are central to these unequal, often contradictory and racialised dynamics, facilitating and accelerating the movement of some and decelerating or blocking that of others. In the case of Europe, racialised and apparently insurmountable boundaries even cut across the continent itself. De Genova (2016: 91) reminds us of the irony in the fact that heirs of the colonial subjects who built Europe's wealth are actually excluded by racialised borders erected between them and white, well-off Europeans. On the other side of these borders, migrants, irrespective of their actual identities, are imagined as non-white, usually Muslim, poor (De Genova 2016: 81).

Building on these perspectives on borders and bodies, this chapter presents findings from a collaborative project and is one of advocacy. Conducted in the Hustadt community in the city of Bochum, it gives an ethnographic account of a locality overwhelmingly occupied by people who have crossed borders from the global South and who in Germany face new boundaries with regard to their access to health and wellbeing. This chapter links with Fassin's (2011) writing about governmentality and immigration as presented in Chapter 1 (Pine and Haukanes, Chapter 1, this volume). In Hustadt, people experience the effects of a process in which the tight relation of borders as external territorial frontiers and boundaries as internal social categorisations affect them in the form of racialised, exclusionary discourses directed against them by members of the receiving society. Furthermore, this chapter refers to the gendered boundaries and borders between the public and private domain as experienced by women in the context of care. New migrants of all categories find themselves spatially disconnected from their formerly extended social network in the homeland and re-situated, in the arrival country, in a rather narrow bounded network which confines some of them to spending long hours in the private sphere at home.

By applying a collaborative ethnographic approach to the Hustadt community and its access to health, this chapter aims to grasp the critical vantage point of that community. This inside perspective constitutes an attempt to contribute to the critique of racialised, hardening boundaries and processes of exclusion that occur in the context of obligations and entitlements to health and wellbeing in Europe.

The research for this article was conducted by members of the City Lab Bochum (see below) and the results emerged from three years of intermittent ethnographic research the author conducted in this location between 2015 and 2019.

Introduction to the Hustadt community

Bochum, which is located in North Rhine Westphalia in Germany, is affected by a restructuring process that followed the collapse of the mining industry in the 1970s. In the early twenty-first century, major industrial enterprises were closed down, such as Opel in 2008 and Nokia in 2014. It is a city with a 9% unemployment rate (Stadt Bochum 2018b) and was ranked 27th out of 30 German cities in terms of level of unemployment (Nitt-Drießelmann, Wedemeier, and Schüßler 2015). Bochum has undergone different phases of receiving migrants and is today characterised by a highly diverse urban population. Among the first significant groups of migrants were Poles, who came in the late nineteenth century as labour migrants. Further migrants from Southern Europe followed (1960–1970s), whereas in the 1990s, the migrant population predominantly consisted of refugees and asylum seekers. In 2015, the migrant rate reached 19%; the number of refugees received rose to 4,962 but decreased again to 2,588 in 2018 (Stadt Bochum 2018a).

Bochum Hustadt, where the City Lab is based, is a socio-economically marginalised part of the city. Official statistical data for Hustadt are not available but exist for Querenburg, the wider administrative district. Today, Hustadt is inhabited by around 4,000 people, of whom approximately 90% are migrants of dominantly Kurdish origin,[1] and according to the research group's estimate it has an unemployment rate of approximately 50%.[2] Many people in Hustadt either depend on welfare or hold two jobs, working up to 18 hours a day in low-skill labour sectors facing physically challenging working conditions (see also Figgen, Evers, and Van Loocke-Scholz 2012). Some have also established small businesses as mechanics, kiosk-holders, or supermarket owners.

In the city's public discourse, the Hustadt community is labelled 'a community of poor Muslims' who basically don't 'integrate' within the so-called 'dominant culture'. This is manifested in media representations about Hustadt as a problem area with high levels of criminality, vandalism, and unemployment. As I regularly accompanied seven-year-old Lana to her local primary school, I often had the chance to talk to the parents who accompanied their children. Once I chatted with a couple who had recently migrated to Hustadt from the US – a German university employee and his American wife, both white. They expressed to me their worries in relation to their child's wellbeing in the new school: 'It was a tough decision for us to send our daughter to this school. Look around! [pointing to the other parents]. The European culture, our values are dying!' When I expressed my discomfort with this statement, the man continued: 'In Germany one cannot say anything any longer without being called a Nazi. But people here are not integrating!' I asked what he meant by the term, upon which his wife responded: 'Don't you see? [pointing to the head-scarfed mothers standing around us]. Why do they all have six children while we have only two? Besides, they are not learning our language!'

What exactly was the problem? The term 'integration', as applied by this white middle-class couple to the Hustadt community, emerges from a polarised perception about the community. This perspective reduces migrants to what is also termed as *Integrationsverweigerer* (integration objecters) in the conservative public German discourse. In summary, the term refers to a perceived 'refusal' to learn German, to 'assimilate' what are imagined as certain 'European' values, and to give up their 'un-European' reproductive pattern. When I visited Lana's classroom for the first time, I commented on the high density of migrant children in class. Looking worried, the teacher responded with a deep sigh: 'Yes, we have only two Christians here.' Though the Hustadt community is heterogeneous in terms of people's religious identities (e.g. Shiites, Sunnites, Alevites, Yasidis, Catholics, and Protestants) and countries of origin (including Kurds from Lebanon, Syria, Turkey, and Iraq and people from other countries), outsiders often draw a racialised line between a 'non-white Muslim Other' and a 'white Christian Europe'. From the outsiders' perception, a Muslim, poor and non-white 'they' as represented by the Hustadt community is opposed to a Christian, white 'we' represented by the dominant culture. This resonates with Czollek's (2018) argument about the German integration discourse as a basically negative narrative. Czollek interprets the integration discourse as a theatre in which Germans play the main character and the complementary 'they' is represented by two supporting roles. On the one side are the 'good/well integrated' migrants and on the other side the 'bad/gang raping, non-integrating' ones (see also Anderson 2013). The German's self-image feeds itself through their distance from the 'bad' migrants while the 'good' ones demonstrate German openness to the world. From the vantage point of the migrants living in Hustadt, what they share is, among other things, the loss of their country and a feeling of not being welcome in German society. The majority of people living in the Hustadt community have crossed borders, often fleeing from situations of severe danger and risking their lives. Hence, as a result of war and displacement, many people share the experience of trauma prior to migration. They also share the experience of racialisation in the arrival context which often leads to a second, even deeper trauma. However, a large proportion of the Hustadt community is affected by low incomes or welfare dependence, whether they or their family members themselves have actually crossed borders to reach Germany, were born in Germany, or have lived there for several generations. Hustadt is also characterised by a high level of hospitality, good cooks, and a very intense sharing of public social spaces. This is enacted in friendly, welcoming faces, laughter, solidarity, and vital conviviality, which shows itself most of all in the many children who revive the heart of Hustadt – the Brunnenplatz – the public square around which high-rise buildings are clustered.

The City Lab Bochum

The City Lab Bochum is a long-term collaborative health promotion project that was established in Hustadt in 2015 and is to last for 12 years. Methodologically, it is meant to provide a space where universities and urban people can meet face to face in order to grasp the complexity of actual people's lives (see also Niewöhner 2014). This health-related research location aims for structural transformations in low-income areas by creating favourable conditions for people to be healthy. It consists of medical anthropologists, migration researchers, and members of the Hustadt community. Part of the City Lab's aim is also to create new relationships between the university and the city. This endeavour was put into action by relocating university seminars to the site, which sensitises students to their future work with local communities. Teaching occurs in a room[3] rented by the university in the neighbourhood. On the basis of the theoretical framework established through coursework, students conduct applied ethnographic fieldwork and develop health projects with residents onsite. Collaboration in the City Lab specifically refers to designing questionnaires and discussing research results together with community researchers and jointly working to improve health conditions in Hustadt. This takes the form of a project organised by students and university staff together with people from the neighbourhood. So far, the interventions have included information and counselling services for specific target groups regarding prevention and health promotion in the areas of cancer, nutrition, long-term care insurance, media consumption, and exercise. The students set up or extend access to facilities for families with members in need of healthcare and provide sport or exercise options onsite.

Since 2016, three research projects have been conducted in the City Lab: (1) a pilot Vulnerability Assessment for Refugees and Migrants (RM-VA); (2) an ethnographic case study of a recently migrated Syrian family; and (3) student-led projects. All studies were designed to identify barriers that would restrict participants' access to healthcare, to foster health and wellbeing, and to identify the significance of the community in this context. This chapter presents only the family ethnography in detail, although at times it briefly refers to results from the other two projects.

To emphasise the methodological approach with the resultant deep immersion in the field, passages referring to the ethnographic study are written from the first-hand perspective. The family ethnography was mandated by the family, hoping for advocacy to improve their disabled son's condition. Field access developed during encounters with a woman in the Hustadt childrens' playground. A mother actively approached me to introduce me to her son. She pointed to the gastric tube that protruded from his belly and continued non-verbally by pointing to her son's teeth. They were decayed and black and, as she symbolised with her hands, a result of medication. Another woman translated her words for me; the boy was sick and although four years old, spent most of his time at home, for lack of a kindergarden place. A few weeks later, when the woman invited me to her house, I explained about the City Lab and my interest in collaborative research and its aim to improve people's health. I offered to include their family in my collaborative project by focusing on their son's health. The family agreed and a few weeks later I moved into their house. The resultant ethnography was based on weekly, three-day[4] field research visits to the family in Hustadt in the period between October 2016 and July 2018. Thematically it sketched out our joint attempt to gain better access to healthcare for the disabled boy and foster his health and wellbeing. The field was not limited to the family boundaries but extended to its wider social network, the Hustadt neighbourhood as a whole. Methodically, the collaborative ethnography included participation in the everyday private and public life of the family, such as in parental talks in the kindergarten and visits to the doctor, to the authorities, and to healthcare institutions. Immersing myself in the transnational social field of the family, I took part in WhatsApp video chats with relatives in Syria, Holland, and Wuppertal, spent time with the mother and other mothers watching their children in the playground, and accompanied the daughter to the elementary school in the district, where I met other mothers. At the end of the day, I wrote fieldnotes, which I analysed reflexively (Breidenstein et al. 2013).

Following the project's ethical guidelines, the family was kept informed at all stages of fieldwork about the progress of the research project. The study results were discussed with the parents and partly with the children. Any public presentation or publication was checked jointly and, if agreed upon by them, published in anonymised form.

Health and migration in the context of racialisation

Racialisation in the context of migration has entered health discourses as the current rise of nationalism and right-populist movements increasingly affects non-white peoples' health. Several studies report the negative effects of migration policies and hardening borders on migrants' health worldwide. Recent studies allude to the effects of a 'Trump Anxiety Disorder' (Lee 2017, Panning 2017) on the daily lives, wellbeing, and health of immigrant families in the US, including children, with short- and long-term negative effects of toxic stress[5] on their physical, mental, and behavioural health (Artiga and Ubri 2017). Further, racialised migration policies have been shown to create severe depression and suicidal syndromes among refugee children detained on the Pacific islands by the Australian government (Deutschlandfunk 2018, Deutschlandfunknova 2019) and it can be assumed that this is a more widespread phenomenon. Simultaneously, a racialised epidemic of police violence to non-white nationals in the United States that also affects migrants has been highlighted in recent public health discourse (Cooper and Fullilove 2016: 51) and again, there is no reason to believe that this is confined to the USA. As various studies show, migrants are often more vulnerable than non-migrants in terms of their economic status (Knipper and Bilgin 2009, Razum and Saß 2015: 513) which in combination with discrimination affects their health and wellbeing (Krieger et al. 2011). We also came across this in Hustadt as people reported discrimination at school, where children receive little support from their teachers while their parents' support is limited due to language barriers. Whereas our interviewees clearly identified with Hustadt as their home and felt a sense of belonging to the community, our data also indicate that people share a perception of non-belonging to large parts of the German society beyond the Hustadt boundaries. Lahing, the father of the family I conducted my ethnographic research with, argues that, ideally, Germans and migrants need to approach each other by taking a step towards one another. This, however, has not been his experience: 'If you head one step towards a German he goes two steps backward [laughter].'

When asked about her experiences of discrimination, Hatice, an elderly female informant from the Pilot Vulnerability Assessment, responded: 'Yes, of course. Especially as a Turk they don't accept us.'

With an estimated unemployment rate of 50%, people face economic hardship in Hustadt and, as the results from the VA-RM showed, financial pressure constitutes a barrier to healthcare for all respondents. A cancer patient, for example, argued that he could not afford certain treatments that he was obliged to fund.

Several people who live in Hustadt today grew up with their families under difficult conditions in nearby asylum seekers' homes before they entered the area. Nima, a young man whose family of five spent seven years in an asylum seekers' home sharing two rooms, before they were given a flat in Hustadt, remembered this as follows: 'The conditions in the asylum seekers' home were like in jail. Collective toilets, collective showers, bunk beds. All who were in that home turned criminals. Yes, they bred them [the criminals] there' (Nima, 27 years, male).[6]

Here, young asylum seekers are confronted with racialised boundaries at a very early stage in their life due to the exclusionary practices of their long-term confinements to asylum homes. This practice substantially affects migrants' life chances as well as ideas and ideologies concerning their personhood and citizenship in Germany. Studies show that employees of migrant background work in atypical, dangerous employments (Füsers et al. 2018) and that they frequently suffer from medical conditions resulting from their conditions of work (Oldenburg et al. 2010). Work-related health problems were also reported by people I interviewed during my ethnographic research, with disc prolapse being the most common. Many, mainly male, residents also report a high level of physical and mental exhaustion, as Ayse explained to us: 'My husband leaves at 8.00 and comes home at 9.00 pm. Sometimes he falls straight asleep. Though he is still young, he already is worn out (in German *kaputt*), suffering from backpain' (Ayse, 35 years).

Confronted with a healthcare system that does not sufficiently accomodate cultural diversity (Falge and Zimmermann 2014) or that excludes people with few financial resources, informal help and support from the community serve as a major facilitator to healthcare (Falge and Dilger 2019). For example, the community would provide translation services during health consultations and in other institutions. As explained by Can: 'There are people here who help each other mutually. I always help by translating, if they have problems with their children at school, if they need to fill in something somewhere, if a conversation needs to be held somewhere with a doctor' (Can, male, 50 years).

Hence, people in Hustadt practise what has been defined by Samerski and others as healthcare bricolage; that is, the ways in which residents of neighbourhoods with multi-diverse populations and sometimes difficult or restricted access to statutory health services piece or cobble together their healthcare, combining self-treatment, help from relatives or friends, and information from the internet (Samerski 2019). These results show that some barriers to healthcare are migrant-specific, such as the absence of professional translation services, the unfamiliarity with the healthcare system, and certain informal dynamics of exclusion (see also Falge 2018, 2019). However, it should be noted that there are barriers that might equally apply to non-migrants, such as the lack of information about healthcare benefits and financial pressure. A migrant-specific experience with healthcare will now be presented through an ethnography-based account of the family mentioned earlier, starting from the initial contact and following the research through to the results of the study.

The family ethnography

The entering of specific social spaces always generates certain reactions. It mobilises feelings, negotiates identities and creates relationships of power (Tornaghi 2010: 38). Carrying out fieldwork in Hustadt made me aware of and eager to confront relationships of power between individual actors, the family, and state institutions, associated with different levels of agency. The relationship between me as a German with professional standing and status, and various state institutions, was characterised by my relatively high level of agency. In contrast, the less powerful family of asylum seekers with low economic, political, legal, and social status was characterised by a low level of agency. My role with regard to the family became that of a mediator between them and powerful state institutions. As a collaborative researcher, I strove to meet with the family on an equal footing, an undertaking that was obstructed by the power imbalances that existed between us. Reflecting on these power hierarchies, my aim in terms of collaboration was to produce non-hierarchical relationships between us. However, I realised that a complete balance of power hierarchies was illusive. Instead, I tried to create non-hierarchical communicative situations to make my field participants feel that they were being heard and taken seriously and so that the power constellations became more balanced and our relationship more intimate. As a result, my status changed from that of a stranger to a family member; eventually I was being called 'sister' by the family father and 'aunt' by the children. When my husband came to visit with my children, he was addressed as 'uncle'. Over time, our encounters steadily increased the family's agency, mainly because of their increasing confidence and knowledge about how to gain access to resources from state institutions, as I will demonstrate in the following ethnographic account.

The Mohammad family's story

The Mohammad family[7] fled to Germany from Syria in 2015. The parents, Lahing and Leyla (both 35), have three children: Burhan (12), Hevidar (7), and Bilind (4). In 2011, their daughter Hamrin died from chronic renal insufficiency at the age of 8. Bilind was also born with chronic renal insufficiency in Syria. Lahing travelled first and left Syria alone in June 2015. He travelled the Balkan route, partly by public transport and partly on foot, and crossed various national borders from Syria to Turkey, Bulgaria, Serbia, Hungary, Austria before finally crossing into Germany. Once he arrived in Austria, he took a taxi to the German border and from there continued by bus to Hamburg where he was granted asylum. Thereafter he applied for family reunification and a few months later his wife and children followed by plane with relative ease. Once they arrived in Germany they had to deal with many bureaucratic and institutional barriers. During the first year they stayed in a refugee reception centre which they liked a lot as they experienced the extraordinary German 'Welcome Culture' of the year 2015.

The Mohammads' recognition and entitlement to asylum included entitlement to the same healthcare coverage as people who receive benefit from the statutory health insurance agency.[8] Hence, shortly after his arrival in Germany, their son Bilind had an operation at a hospital in Hamburg. A gastric tube (percutaneous endoscopic gastronomy [PEG]) was inserted and, since then, his medication and food have been administered via the PEG. He now has a chance to survive much longer, although at some point he might need a kidney transplant. The Mohammads would have loved to stay in Hamburg, but due to lack of affordable housing they moved to Bochum in February 2016. Lahing's sister found them an apartment in Hustadt where she herself lived and where she had recently found a flat in a nearby neighbourhood for their brother, who had arrived from Syria with his family. Eight months later I moved into their house to start my research. During the first weeks, I slept in the daughter's bed, who then moved to her parents' room until space was created for me in Bilind's unused room; he also slept with his parents. At the beginning of my research, Bilind did not have a place in kindergarten and spent eight hours every day with his smartphone or tablet or in front of the television. His motor, social, and linguistic development was slightly delayed, his attention span was low, and he seemed to alternate between hyperactivity and lethargy. He often slept early in the day and was awake through the afternoon until after midnight. Due to the time-consuming care regime, Leyla had built few social relationships outside the family and did not like being in public spaces. She seemed insecure when she was outside the apartment and suffered a small breakdown after a joint visit to the language café, where she became aware of her poor language skills compared to other refugees.

The family usually gathers in the apartment late in the afternoon. When I got there in the evening, the father Lahing was often asleep on the sofa. Neither the television nor the children playing around him seemed to disturb his deep sleep. At first, I attributed these phases to 'depression', possibly a consequences of post-traumatic stress disorder. Only later was I able to establish a connection between a combination of factors, one of which was the care for the son. This among other things entailed seven PEG dispensations daily every five hours, three of them during the night, and an injection shortly before going to bed. Bilind receives the nightly PEG dispensations via a drip, and an alarm goes off if the tube kinks, which happens several times every hour. He has to be diapered three times at night because of the liquid he receives, which means that the parents' sleeping phases are two to three hours and interrupted by the drip alarms, diaper changes, and Bilind's calls for drinks of water. Both parents directed a tremendous amount of care to Bilind, who received a high level of attention and hardly any prohibitions: he could take as much food as he wanted, and the best pieces, though he never ate them; he could turn the dining room lights on and off while people were eating or throw water on the floor as a sign of anger or possibly to get more attention.

For the father, Lahing, this care system paired with a constant worry for his son was added on top of his daily routine, such as his German class, household duties, school and kindergarten issues, and most of all the humiliating and time-consuming interactions with the Job Centre and the

Foreigners' Authority. As these institutions are not accessible by phone, Lahing had to go in person for any minor issue during the first 24 months of his stay in Germany, sometimes on a daily basis, which often involved long waiting hours in overcrowded, ill-equipped rooms (see also Weissköppel 2015).[9] He often received what was, in his opinion, contradictory information from apparently badly trained, overworked clerks whom he perceived as unfriendly and who seemed unfamiliar with current refugee law and migrants' legal entitlements. This combination led to chronic demoralisation and exhaustion and various aspects of this post-migration situation was inscribed on his body by weight increment.

Similarly, Leyla, who still mourned and frequently talked about her deceased daughter Hamrin, embodied the family's situation and life in Germany with weight gain. She confined herself to the house and barely showed interest in the outside world. Instead she spent time on housework, childcare, and video calls with her relatives at home. She felt comfortable in her transnational space, in the virtual presence of her relatives back home who 'accompanied' her while cooking, cleaning, drinking coffee, or smoking.

As a large portion of the parents' time and energy was taken up with Bilind's care, little time was left for the other siblings, and the apparently endless love and care Bilind received contrasted with that provided for the others. I often observed Hevidar's claims for physical and emotional attention, which she expressed by attempts to embrace or otherwise physically approach her mother. Burhan, the eldest child, claimed attention in slightly different ways. Due to the war-related school closure back home, his Syrian school career was abruptly terminated at grade two and, when he rejoined school four years later in Germany, the system categorised him in grade four. Aged 11, unable to speak German, and lacking two years of schooling, he had a hard time catching up. Despite his parents' objections he was moved up to secondary school, and the gap between him and the other students widened. Unlike in the homeland, the mother lamented, where he had spent his leisure time outside the house with many friends, in Germany Burhan was confined to the boundary that existed between the public and private sphere by spending most of his free time alone at home. In front of the playstation, smartphone, or television he would consume large amounts of food, sweets, and soft drinks served by his caring mother.

At the beginning of my research, the family's agency was limited with regard to their access to state institutions, which partly resonated with their lack of systemic knowledge and possibly with racialised lines of exclusion. For example, the family accepted the fact that a kindergarten refused to take Bilind because of his disability and did not apply for care benefits, although care was obviously needed. When I called the kindergarten without referring to my status in order to highlight the family's need for an inclusive kindergarten place, it was refused with the statement 'care for these [disabled] children would be too laborious'. Only during my second call, when I identified myself as a university professor, did I receive an appointment with the statement 'of course we can meet personally and see what we can do for him'. It was most likely my status which triggered a process whereby in the end the system provided for the child's needs. One and a half years after arriving in Germany, after appraisals had been initiated (care appraisal, presentation at the Social Paediatric Centre, Sozialpädiatrisches Zentrum [SPZ]), and following intensive discussions with the Job Centre, Social Services, and the statutory health insurance, Bilind was given a place in an inclusive kindergarten at the recommendation of the SPZ. The health insurance's confirmation of cost coverage for outpatient dispensation (via the PEG tube insertion) by a children's care service at the kindergarten was received a further six months after application. This delay occurred because the statutory health insurance only covers nursing care benefits after two years of insurance. Another four months later, after numerous rejections from care providers who were contacted, a care provider agreed to take over Bilind's care service despite the low fee of €10.50 per dispensation. Finally, after a ten-month delay, and 28 months after arriving in Germany, he was given a place in the kindergarten. Bilind could stay at the kindergarten for the whole day, and Leyla could apply for a place on a German language course. She waited a further six months for a place, and from November 2017, three years after arriving in Germany, she learned German three times a week. This was her first opportunity, after fleeing from the war, to do something for herself.

Further examples of the very limited agency of asylum seekers and refugees with regard to state institutions came to the fore in the process of the application for healthcare benefits (the acceptance of a care level) I made with the family. The insurance initially granted a lower care level, which included no financial support, following a 15-minute assessment in the family's home. We objected and a second assessment followed that occurred in my presence and led to a higher care level with annual care support up to €6,192. Again, it was most likely the intervention of a high-status professional German from the other side of the racialised boundary that unlocked access to healthcare entitlements.

After this award, the parents seemed vitalised, empowered, and more self-confident. All in all, the changes in circumstances stimulated the health condition of the entire family. Bilind would use his smartphone only two hours daily, instead of eight, and his gross and fine motor skills were improving. His attention span was longer, and he was beginning to do puzzles and to speak German. Leyla's gendered body was no longer just confined to the private sphere providing care for Bilind. She started learning German with enthusiasm, was intensifying her social contacts, taking part in the weekly Women's Breakfast organised by the primary school in the district and inviting a neighbour to her home. The additional financial support provided by the care benefits seemed to reduce the financial pressure on the family. In addition to his German course, Lahing was beginning to seek advice from the Job Centre about possible work and to plan his future in Germany. These two cases, care level acceptance and arranging a kindergarten place, draw a clear line between positionality, knowledge, and agency and show the ways that new migrants may be excluded from access to resources and benefits which in turn re-enforces racialised social boundaries.

Much later, in 2018, I came to know that the Mohammad family had severe money problems, despite the monthly allowances they received from the Job Centre and the care insurance. For several weeks I had sensed a certain tension in the family and was worried that it had something to do with my research. When I asked what was wrong, Lahing said there was a problem but that he could not tell me. In the following weeks I witnessed how Lahing's brother and sister came around and held long discussions. I did not know what they talked about, but their faces were serious and the usual laughter was missing. Weeks later, Lahing revealed what it all was about, namely the family's high indebtedness as a result of their flight. From the €17,000 they had borrowed they had repaid €7,000 and now the creditor needed the remaining sum all at once, which the family, including the brothers and sisters, was unable to come up with.

On the one hand this vignette demonstrates the level of vulnerability the family is exposed to due to global forces related to war, loss, and exile. On the other it shows how they simultaneously keep their dignity by maintaining a balance of power, or by controlling the ebb and flow of information within our relationship. Throughout the two years I stayed with them, they also rejected my numerous attempts to contribute to the household economy through rental or food payments. Hevidar would even fill my bags with food for my children whenever I returned to my own home. In this our relationship was made reciprocal rather than hierarchical, as they provided home, emotional contact, food, and ethnographic insights for me in exchange for knowledge and action.

Summary of study results and beyond

The results from this ethnographic study along with some results from the RM-VA show that the lack of accessibility of state institutions may negatively affect the health and wellbeing of migrants. Following Fassin

(2011), I showed how borders as external territorial frontiers interrelate with multiple boundaries as internal social categorisations and affect migrants in Hustadt. State institutions create internal boundaries against migrants by not sufficiently accommodating for cultural diversity and partly, by implication, because of racialised exclusison. The culture of the German healthcare system and most of the other public institutions connected to it seem to face a deficiency in terms of outreach structures. They informally exclude all those people who are neither used to asking actively for their rights nor even know which rights to ask for. The Mohammed family and other people in Hustadt lacked information about their basic entitlements to resources such as care insurance, childcare rights, and sometimes the services of family doctors. Many of the institutions our field participants tried to gain access to seemed rather to be designed for the white well-educated, financially secure middle-class used to actively consulting healthcare professionals. People with weaker financial and educational resources and less familiarity with the system have less access and need more support. As mentioned by field participants, certain entitlements to healthcare may not be perceived as a right, but rather as a privilege that was either completely unknown in their previous experience or could only be activated through struggle. In the City Lab, these issues and the barriers created by missing outreach structures and a lack of translation services featured prominently. The fact that the majority of the Hustadt inhabitants are non-white hints of racialised exclusion. Hence, this study also confirms previous studies which indicate that a large proportion of recent migrants (and for sure also marginalised non-migrants) are being disproportionately represented in atypical, low-pay employment structures and by implication suffer from more negative impacts on health compared to people employed in better income employment structures.

In addition to the negative experiences with state institutions with regard to discriminatory practices, respondents spoke about humiliating, time-consuming behaviour in the local institutional landscape. Discriminatory incidents are happening at schools, in kindergardens where members of the domination culture refer to Hustadt people in terms of difference by reminding of their foreign origin. They do so by applying Othering strategies which label them as *Integrationsverweigerer* (integration objecters), 'non-christians' or 'Turks', unwilling to give up their 'Un-European' values and norms. As previous studies have shown, such forms of open or hidden discrimination also negatively affect peoples' health and wellbeing (Krieger and Stephen 1996, Krieger 2005, Krieger et al. 2011).

It was part of the collaborative research design to work against these inequalities. The family ethnography referred to the difficulties they faced in gaining access to healthcare and to the fact that as newcomers to the system they faced informal exclusion due to the lack of information tailored to address their needs. Collaborative research affected the family's level of agency through knowledge transmission, which enabled them to gain access to health-related and educational institutions.

Conclusion

Through collaborative research projects, the City Lab Bochum has created a space for the establishment of new relationships between the university and the city. This relationship helped to illuminate the boundaries existing between the Hustadt community and the rest of Bochum. It also provided insights into the significance of the community with regard to access to healthcare and to the mutual fostering of health and wellbeing within the community through practising healthcare bricolage.

As an ethnographer within the City Lab, I was given insights into the significance of time and involvement in the field as a prerequisite for transcultural communication. This approach balanced hierarchies between me and field participants and enabled us better to listen to and understand each other. However, changes induced for this family were only minor transformations in the overall Hustadt context and in order to dismantle racialised and class-based boundaries and facilitate greater equity, more such projects would be needed. For real changes to occur, we need to go beyond merely filling gaps or applying band-aids and claim wider structural changes that decisively reduce or even put to an end peoples' informal exclusion from healthcare. Moreover, this research enabled us to detect that health-related interventions for people living in precarious contexts should not be limited to the healthcare system but rather address a wider institutional landscape. Current discriminatory practices in the Job Centre and the immigration authorities should be addressed in health-related policymaking, as they directly affect people's health and wellbeing. This needs to go along with a societal awareness that positions diversity as a norm instead of making claims for peoples' assimilation to an imagined European culture.

Returning to De Genova's and Fassin's points introduced at the beginning of this chapter, we have to ask the question: are we dealing with a system that is apparently set up to exclude, deliberately, 'non-white' people? Whatever the answer may be, what we learned from this study is that Germany still does not perceive itself as a place of radical diversity in the Czollekian sense. Hence, the future of the Mohammads' and many other Hustadt families' children is uncertain. In order not to fail they need institutional structures that accommodate their diversity by supporting their mental and physical health and their education. This could be put into action by the following:

- Establishment of multi-lingual outreach services while increasing the number of migrants in public institutions.
- Granting all residents immediate access to full healthcare coverage.
- Developing tools for the inclusion of new migrants into healthcare services and for strengthening health literacy.
- Establishing a cooperative network between policy makers, healthcare, and related social institutions to improve access to healthcare.
- Strengthening a societal awareness for diversity and establishing more anti-discriminatory structures in all spheres of society.
- Establishing new relations between universities and cities and engaging residents in health-related research and interventions.

Alongside these strategies to make our society a place for radical diversity, we need to support those migrant institutions which aim at empowering residents of communities such as Hustadt to stand up for themselves and claim their rights.

Notes

1 Kurdish people in Hustadt originate from different countries such as Turkey, Iraq, Lebanon, Afghanistan, and Syria and identify with different religious groups, the majority as Sunnites but some as Yasidis or Alevites.

2 As mentioned above, the statistical authorities of Bochum do not provide figures for this small-scale area. Therefore, we can only refer to fieldnotes here.

3 This room, the so-called HULab, was set up for all the universities in the region (Hustadt e. V. 2016).

4 The time I actually spent with the family was limited to evenings, nights, and mornings as I was doing this fieldwork after work at the university.

5 Toxic stress is defined as prolonged and continuous stress.

6 This interview was not part of the RM-VA, but held in the context of the academic paper of a student named Mahur Hesamiashrafi. The student belongs to the first generation of Iranian migrants which facilitated her access to the Irani informants.

7 Anonymisation procedures were followed by substituting all names with pseudonyms.

8 (§ 2 AsylbLG, § 48 SGB XII, § 27 ff SGB V). Problems can arise when they want to access benefits of long-term care insurance.

9 According to several lawyers contacted during the course of this study who regularly visit the Job Centre, 50% of the Job Centre decisions are incorrect.

References

Anderson, Bridget (2013) *Us and Them? The Dangerous Politics of Immigration Control*. Oxford: Oxford University Press.

Artiga, S. and P. Ubri (2017) *Living in an Immigrant Family in America: How Fear and Toxic Stress are Affecting Daily Life, Well-Being, & Health*. www.kff.org/disparities-policy/issue-brief/living-in-an-immigrant-family-in-america-how-fear-and-toxic-stress-are-affecting-daily-life-well-being-health/ (accessed 30 June 2020).

Breidenstein, G., S. Hirschauer, H. Kalthoff, and B. Nieswand (2013, eds) *Ethnografie: Die Praxis der Feldforschung*. Konstanz: UVK Verlagsgesellschaft.

Cooper, H.L.F. and M. Fullilove (2016)' Excessive Police Violence as a Public Health Issue', *Journal of Urban Health: Bulletin of the New York Academy of Medicine* 93: doi:10.1007/s11524–016–0040–2.

Czollek, M. (2018) *Desintegrier Euch!* München: Carl Hanser Verlag GmbH Co KG.

De Genova, N. (2016) 'The European Question', *Social Text 128* 34 (3): 75–102.

Deutschlandfunk (2018) www.deutschlandfunk.de/protest-gegen-australische-fluechtlingslagerkein-anderes.1773.de.html?dram:article_id=431340 (accessed 12 September 12).

Deutschlandfunknova (2019) www.deutschlandfunknova.de/beitrag/australien-exterritoriale-fluechtlingslager (accessed 12 September 2019).

Falge, C. (2018) 'The Power of a Professor: Health Care Provision for Deserving Refugees in Germany.' In: E. Speed (ed.) www.cost-ofliving.net/the-power-of-a-professor-health-care-provision-for-deserving-refugees-in-germany (accessed 24 September 2020).

Falge, C. (2019) 'Dynamics of Informal Exclusion. Migrants' Health as Experienced in the City Lab Bochum'. In: K. Kuehlmeyer, C. Klingler, and R. Huxtable (eds) *Ethical, Legal and Social Aspects of Healthcare for Migrants: Perspectives from the UK and Germany*. Oxford: Taylor & Francis, pp. 57–76.

Falge, C. and G. Zimmermann (2014) 'Die Interkulturelle Öffnung im Gesundheitssystem: Ein kritischer Überblick'. In: E. Vanderheiden and C.H. Mayer (eds), *Toolbox! Interkulturelle Öffnungsprozesse in Organisationen Gestalten*. Göttingen: Vandenhoeck & Ruprecht, pp. 325–332.

Falge, C. and H. Dilger (2019) 'Kollaboratives Forschen und Wissen für die Öffentlichkeit: Gesellschaftlicher Interventionen der Medizinethnologie'. In: S. Klocke-Daffa (ed.) *Angewandte Ethnologie – Perspektiven einer Anwendungsorientierten Wissenschaft*. Wiesbaden: Springer-Verlag.

Fassin, D. (2011) 'Policing Borders, Producing Boundaries. The Governmentality of Immigration in Dark Times', *Annual Review of Anthropology* 40: 213–226.

Figgen, M., G. Evers, and A. Van Loocke-Scholz (2012) *Belastung – Auswirkung – Bewältigung. Arbeitsbedingungen in NRW aus Sicht türkeistämmiger Beschäftigter. Transfer 1*. Düsseldorf: Landesinstitut für Arbeitsschutz Nordrhein-Westfalen.

Füsers, F., P. Krauss-Hoffmann, and J-M. Staupe (2018) *Arbeitsschutz in einer kulturell vielfältigen Arbeitswelt. Sicher ist sicher*. Berlin: Erich Schmidt Verlag GmbH & Co. KG.

Hustadt, e.V. (2016) *Hulabor Startet in der Bochumer Hustadt*, 19 October www.huisthu.de/hulabor-startet-in-der-bochumer-hustadt/ (accessed 14 July 2018).

Knipper, M. and Y. Bilgin (2009) *Migration und Gesundheit*. Berlin: Konrad-Adenauer-Stiftung e.V.

Krieger, N.S. and S. Stephen (1996) 'Racial Discrimination and Blood Pressure: The CARDIA Study of Young Black and White Adults', *American Journal of Public Health* 86 (10): 1370–1378.

Krieger, N.S., D. Naishadhamb, C. Hartman, and E.M. Barbeau (2005) 'Experiences of Discrimination: Validity and Reliability of a Self-report Measure for Population Health Research on Racism and Health', *Social Science & Medicine* 61 (7): 1576–1596.

Krieger, N., P.D. Waterman, A. Kosheleva, J.T. Chen, D.R. Carney, K.W. Smith (2011) 'Exposing Racial Discrimination: Implicit and Explicit Measures: the My Body, My Story Study of 1005 US-born Black and White Community Health Center Members', *PloS One* 6 (11): e27636.

Lee, B. (2017) *The Dangerous Case of Donald Trump*. London: Thomas Dunne Books, St. Martin's Publishing Group.

Niewöhner, J. (2014) 'Ökologien der Stadt: Zur Ethnografie Bio-und Geopolitischer Praxis', *Zeitschrift für Volkskunde* 110 (2): 185–214.

Nitt-Drießelmann, D., J. Wedemeier, and J. Schüßler (2015) *HWWI/Berenberg-Städteranking 2015: Die 30 Größten Städte Deutschlands im Vergleich*. Hamburg: Hamburgisches Welt-Wirtschafts-Institut, Berenberg Private Bankiers.

Oldenburg, C., A. Siefer, and B. Beermann (2010) 'Migration als Prädikator für Belastung und Beanspruchung?' In: B. Badura, H. Schröder, J. Klose, and K. Macco (eds) *Fehlzeiten-Report 2010*. Heidelberg: Springer Medizin, pp. 141–151.

Panning, J. (2017) 'Trump Anxiety Disorder'. In: B. Lee (ed.) *The Dangerous Case of Donald Trump*. London: Thomas Dunne Books, St. Martin's Publishing Group.

Razum, O. and A.C. Saß (2015) *Migration und Gesundheit: Interkulturelle Öffnung Bleibt eine Herausforderung*. Berlin: Springer.

Samerski, S. (2019) 'Health Literacy as a Social Practice: Social and Empirical Dimensions of Knowledge on Health and Healthcare', *Social Science & Medicine* 226: 1–8.

Stadt Bochum (2018a) *Menschen. Flüchtlinge in Bochum. Aktuelle Zahlen*. Stand: 4. Juni 2018, www.bochum.de/C125708500379A31/vwContentByKey/W2A5A9RK432BOCMDE (accessed 13 April 2018).

Stadt Bochum (2018b) *Arbeitslose im Städte- und Regionenvergleich*, www.bochum.de/C125708500379A31/vwContentByKey/W27CMHX3113BOLDDE (accessed 4 June 2018).

Tornaghi, C. (2010) *Forschungsethik. Experimenting Action Research in Planning Education – A Reflection*. Retrieved from Wien: Stadtentwicklung Wien. Öffentliche Räume in Favoriten. Playful spatial games. Magistrat der Stadt Wien.

Weissköppel, C. (2015) Interkulturelle Öffnung in einem Sozialamt Einblicke in die Ethnografische Organisationsberatung, *Ethnoscripts* 17: 127–146.

7

Joint struggles for care and social reproduction in Spain: contested boundaries and new solidarities

Sílvia Bofill-Poch

Since the beginning of the 2008 financial crisis, grassroots activism around care has significantly increased in Spain, and particularly in Catalonia. Especially significant has been activism by immigrant women who are fighting to have their rights as domestic workers recognised. Other groups, such as family carers and professionals from the public health and welfare system, have also made themselves heard, organising protests against the cutbacks in social programmes, the precariousness of public services, and the lack of recognition and social appreciation for care work. Under renewed forms of social and political activism, they all have addressed the so-called *crisis of care*, which for decades has been affecting Spain's capacity to meet the care and social reproductive needs of broad sectors of the population (Pérez-Orozco 2006, Zimmerman et al. 2006). The creation of the Care Network in Barcelona (Xarxa de cures), an attempt to bring together claims from different social groups affected by cutbacks and austerity policies, has been particularly interesting. In this chapter, I analyse grassroots activism around care in Spain within the context of a double crisis: the crisis of care, that goes back to the 1990s, and the 2008 financial crisis. This double crisis has brought care and reproductive work issues to the political front. It has also enabled activists to draw together different social demands that had not previously been seen as interrelated. I show how their demands create inclusiveness and social solidarity, challenging the attempts of politicians to address the crisis through half measures.

The current care regime in Spain is based on what Shellee Colen (1995) has called stratified reproduction; that is, a system in which labour and social rights are granted or denied based on gender, class, race, and legal status. This is sustained by a border regime (Fassin 2011) – both in geo-political and conceptual terms – that reinforces, through the legal system, a model of care that is feminised, precarious, and stratified (Pérez-Orozco 2006, see also Pine and Haukanes, Chapter 1, this volume).

Drawing on recent literature on citizenship and border regulation (Fassin 2011, Anderson 2015, Morris 2018), I show how social activists challenge the boundary drawing at play in the stratified system of entitlement (Morris 2018). In revealing the central role that care plays in social reproduction, they contest deservingness frames that exclude carers, both migrant and non-migrant, both paid and unpaid, from being recognised as real workers bearing rights (Chauvin and Garcés 2014, Anderson 2015, Bofill-Poch and Márquez 2020). Their work is an articulated response to what critical feminist theorists have called a new wave of accumulation by dispossession of reproductive work (Hartsock 2006, Ezquerra 2012, Leonard and Fraser 2016). Adopting a critical feminist perspective, I describe how activists respond through their demands and alliances to the logic of value extraction underlying the current care regime in Spain. By doing so, they show its potential to contest the boundaries upon which care rights are granted or denied.

Finally, I highlight the central role that solidarity can play in the politicisation and democratisation of care. The term *democratisation of care* refers to a social organisation of care based on democratic values, both for care receivers and caregivers. It involves four axes of action: promoting the centrality of care and demanding that it be recognised; socialising care responsibilities; distributing care between men and women to eliminate the sexual (mis)division of labour; keeping in mind the rights and demands of care receivers as citizens and not only as consumers (Ezquerra and Mansilla 2018).

I collected the ethnographic data for this chapter during my participation in numerous acts and conferences organised by various groups of immigrant women in Catalonia, over the last five years (2014–2019). I also participated as an academic alongside these groups in numerous working groups about domestic work, organised by the municipal and regional administrations. Additionally, I held informal conversations and conducted more than 20 in-depth interviews with members and representatives of women-led immigration associations, representatives of labour unions, labour mediation agents, lawyers, and members of associations of family carers and other civil platforms. I used a semi-structured interview format that allowed participants to talk about different issues relating to care work, labour regulation, migration, social policies, political mobilisation, and the role of the state. This chapter also emerges from my close collaboration with Women Moving Forward (Mujeres Pa'lante), an association located in Barcelona that promotes the integration of immigrant women, as well as offering legal advice and psychological counselling. One of its main tasks has been to fight for the dignity of domestic workers, and it has become a key political actor in this struggle in Catalonia. Together, we have conducted a collaborative research project that began in 2014 and has resulted in a process of joint creation and reflection from the parameters of a feminist and activist anthropology.

Care regimes, border regimes

Spain's care system has been described as familist (Anttonen and Sippilä 1996, Leitner 2003, Bettio and Plantenga 2004), or, more specifically, as an example of unsupported familism (Saraceno and Keck 2010). Spain shares this pattern with other countries in Southern Europe (see Isaksen, Chapter 8, this volume). In contrast, in (East) Central Europe, familism takes a different form. There, women's role as family carers has been supported and encouraged through family and fiscal policy (see, for example, Hašková and Dudová, Chapter 10, this volume). In Spain, family, and especially women, have formed the backbone of the structure of care (Tobio et al. 2010). Informal carers provide 85% of care. But there is another key element for understanding care in Spain: immigration (Benería 2008, Martínez-Buján 2011). In the 1990s, Spain became an important destination for immigrants. From this moment, care increasingly became commodified and externalised, as families hired foreign women from the global South primarily to care for children and dependent adults. This incorporation into the family of foreign women as paid carers is a consequence of the crisis of care, which marks the end of the prior model of care based on the male breadwinner. It also reflects the fact that in Spain, social policy surrounding dependent care and work–family balance has been sorely inadequate (Pérez-Orozco 2006, Díaz-Gorfinkiel 2008).

Since the late 1990s, Spain has developed policies to address the issue of work–family balance in the form of leave for childcare and the right to request flexible working patterns to care for both small children and dependent adults. These measures have aimed at achieving a better articulation of family, work, and personal life, transferring work time to care time. Although the current Gender Equality Act (OL 3/2007) promotes more equitable measures than the previous Conciliation Law (1999), the policies continue to be insufficient. They fail to promote gender equality in terms of the possibility of making a real choice for men and women to balance work and care, as they tend to reproduce inequalities in the division of labour between men and women. Proximity services and real changes in the organisation of working hours are still needed (Comas d'Argemir 2015).

Public policy in Spain has only recently begun to address clearly the question of long-term care for adults, with the passage of the Act of Personal

Autonomy and Long-Term Care (LAPAD) in 2006 (Comas d'Argemir 2015). The new legislation granted universal access to social services, with eligibility determined by the applicant's degree of dependency. This entailed such a large-scale structural change in the organisation of long-term care that some described it as a fourth pillar of the Spanish welfare state, alongside the health, education, and pension systems of the 1980s (Peña-Longobardo et al. 2016). The law responds to the crisis of care and converges with policies promoted in the European Social Space, which were initiated in the 1980s in the Nordic countries and in the 1990s in countries such as Germany, Austria, and France (Comas d'Argemir 2015). These policies arrived in Spain at a time when the welfare state was contracting.

The LAPAD increased the number of people benefiting from public assistance (Comas d'Argemir 2015, Martínez-Buján and Martínez 2015, Montserrat 2015). Between 2004 and 2010, the number of people receiving home-care services in Barcelona increased six-fold (City Council of Barcelona, cited in Comas d'Argemir 2015: 390). However, the implementation of the Act was marred by insufficient funding and a poorly developed public services network. The situation has strengthened the private sector, especially in Catalonia, whose public administration satisfies the existing demand by partially subsidising services provided by for-profit companies.[1] Also, running counter to the intention of the Act, cash payments have increased, with 50% of all help awarded taking the form of a cash payment to a relative or non-professional carer (Martínez-Buján 2011, Comas d'Argemir 2015). These facets of the law have reinstated the family, and particularly women, as natural carers. They also encouraged commodification through the informal economy, as cash payments are often used to informally employ female immigrant workers (Martínez-Buján 2011, Bofill-Poch 2013). Certainly, the use of a cash benefit can be partly explained by its lower cost, but also by a culture of care that continues to depict the ideal of care as that provided 'at home and by the family' (Moreno-Colom et al. 2016, Bofill-Poch 2018). In her analysis of the impact of public policies on long-term care in Spain, Comas d'Argemir (2015) arrives at three conclusions. Firstly, public policies complement rather than substitute for the role of the family, which continues to have an important role. Secondly, the involvement of the state does not decrease the role of the market. Quite the opposite, in fact: the market for care provision expands in two directions, in the form of the growth of private businesses providing services in the care sector and the hiring of employees in the home. Thirdly, public policies have not changed the gender structure: women remain the principal carers and men are hardly ever involved.

In summary, just a few years after the Act was passed, the lack of funding and political will to implement it has already weakened it. The Royal

Decree-Law 20/2012 on budgetary stability, passed in the context of austerity policies, not only changed the scheduled timeline of its implementation but also substantially altered its spirit, reducing the supply and quality of care and restricting the eligibility criteria for benefits (Montserrat 2015, Peña-Longobardo et al. 2016). In Catalonia, the rollout of the Act suffered severely from the effects of budget cuts. The number of recipients of benefits fell and the fourth pillar of the welfare state broke down completely. Responsibility for care was returned to families, thus reinforcing the pre-existing social and gender inequalities (Deusdad et al. 2016). The severe cutbacks have affected not only long-term care, but also work–life balance (public support for which was already weak in Spain), pensions, healthcare, and social services (Ezquerra 2012).

Given the lack of adequate public policy, more and more families address their care needs by hiring foreign women as domestic workers, who care for their dependent adults and children and clean their homes. We can see this trend not only in mid- and high-income families, but also in low-income families. Because foreign care providers command low wages, hiring them becomes attractive even in households with limited resources and low purchasing power. This explains the rapid growth of the sector in recent years. Between 1995 and 2010 the number of domestic workers more than doubled – increasing from 350,000 to 750,000 (International Labour Organisation [ILO], 2013). According to the ILO, Spain is one of the three countries that generate the most domestic employment in Europe, together with France and Italy, accounting for 5% of occupations in the country. Currently, almost 50% of domestic workers in Spain are foreign women. Approximately 30% of these women work without a permit or without a contract. They come mainly from Latin America, North Africa, the Philippines, and Eastern Europe.

Historically, the domestic employment sector has been particularly unstable. It offers employees fewer protections than those enjoyed by workers in other sectors. Domestic employment is largely unregulated in Spain, and, as a consequence, workers are subject to working conditions and wages that are clearly discriminatory (Martínez-Veiga 1995, García et al. 2014). To remedy this situation, in 2011 and 2012, new regulations for domestic work were approved (Law 27/2011; RD 1620/2011; RD-Law 29/2012) in response to pressure from unions and workers' groups and the international context (in 2011 the ILO approved Convention 189). The goal was to make sure that domestic workers have contracts and decent working conditions. However, the regulations did not end job instability or the informal economy. The new legislation included these workers in the General Social Security Regime, but it did so under a specific contribution plan, which did not include, for example, unemployment benefits or the application of rules about occupational hazards. In general, the reforms fall short. They either ignore or actually reinforce the structural elements that cause inequality and defencelessness among domestic workers. As a result, these reforms have been a major disappointment to women workers' groups. Members of these groups fear that the new regulations will be a 'step backwards' in the fight to have their rights recognised. Several authors have recently pointed out cases in which female workers were subjected to labour exploitation, racism, and the infringement of rights (Nogueira and Zalakain 2015, Offenhenden 2017, Bofill-Poch and Márquez 2020, Márquez and Bofill-Poch forthcoming). In some cases, these workers live under what Anderson (2000) has called 'modern slavery'. This is a particular risk for live-in domestic workers.

Immigration policy (OL 4/2000 and later reforms) has tolerated and even incentivised the hiring of these vulnerable workers. Domestic employment has been practically the only option for such women to enter Spain legally. Because of the unmet demand for domestic workers in Spain, there is a quota system for offering permits to foreign workers to fill these jobs. In addition to being one of the only ways for foreign women to work legally in Spain, domestic work is practically the only option for undocumented women seeking employment. Spain's Foreign Nationals Law has made matters worse. For a foreign national to receive a work permit, she must prove that, among other things, she has been offered a yearlong full-time contract. This high bar means that the situation of these workers becomes chronic: they have little chance to get a work permit, and the lack of a work permit means that they have little chance of upward social mobility. This is especially the case because domestic work is informal, stratified, and highly ethnicised.

These conditions can be explained by the intersection of three government policies: a) Spain has weak policy surrounding dependent care; b) Spain's labour market regulations – and in particular its domestic work regulations – discriminate in how they recognise and protect workers' rights; and c) immigration regulations have contributed to creating a domestic labour niche that is highly ethnicised (Martínez-Buján 2011, León and Pavolini 2014, Nogueira y Zalakain 2015). We see how the governability frames of care in Spain are built on a border regime (Fassin 2011) oriented to providing care that is feminised, precarious, and stratified. The border regime is sufficiently permeable to supplement the care sector with foreign women, mostly illegally. At the same time, it is sufficiently impermeable (through immigration and labour regulations) to keep these women and the work they perform in a prolonged – even chronic – situation of irregularity and informality. In this way, stratified reproduction is perpetuated (Colen 1995).

The financial crisis that began in 2008 and the return of almost the full burden of care to families impoverished by the crisis have only exacerbated this situation, making these female workers even more vulnerable. The new legislation from 2011 and 2012 aimed to improve the working conditions of domestic workers. However, research has shown that the financial crisis has undermined the legislation, supporting a moral economy in which families that have been forced to cut costs feel justified in violating the law and contributing to the poor wages and labour conditions of domestic workers. In the context of a profound and persistent devaluation of care work, the crisis acts as a moral argument – even in families with high purchasing power – for the rights of domestic workers to be overlooked (Briones et al. 2014). Current labour regulations fail to recognise domestic workers' rights, but they do aspire to place domestic work within the contractual framework. However, these regulations do not succeed in challenging current categories and ideas about who does and does not *deserve* to be recognised as a worker bearing rights (Segato 2003, Chauvin and Garcés 2014, Anderson 2015).

Grassroots activism

In this context, grassroots activists have begun engaging in collective action and political mobilisation to denounce the difficulty that people in Spain face in meeting their daily care needs, and the unequal and unjust consequences of this. Key activists have been female immigrant domestic workers, who have led protests and mobilisations for their labour and social rights. In Catalonia, a group that stands out is Sindillar. An inventive compound of the Catalan words 'sindicat' (labour union) and 'llar' (home), Sindillar is the first independent union of home and careworkers in the Spanish state. It was founded in 2011 with the objective of defending the labour rights of female workers, placing special emphasis on the issue of immigration. Associations such as Women Moving Forward (Mujeres Pa'lante), Migrant and Diverse (Migrantes y Diversas), and Dragonfly Group (Grupo Libélulas) are others that have taken on the struggle for the rights of domestic employees as one of their central axes of political action. These workers face precariousness, lack of regulation, informality, and occupational isolation. In response, they have demonstrated in front of Spain's Congress building, made statements in regional parliaments, and protested for immigrants' rights and the appeal of Spain's Foreign National Law. They have urged the government to take measures to support families and to implement the International Labour Organisation's Convention 189 on Decent Work for Domestic Workers. As of the time of writing, the Convention remains unratified.

In March 2016, the Spanish Congress of Deputies approved with modifications the bill introduced by the leftist parliamentary group We Can (Podemos) about the ratification of Convention 189. In that session, We Can stated that 'the recognition of the rights of domestic employees is above all a question of human rights, of the dignity of women and of gender justice'. The party encouraged the Spanish government to ratify 'without further delay' Convention 189 and its Recommendation 201. The governing conservative People's Party (Partido Popular) argued against ratifying the Convention on the grounds that it was incompatible with the Spanish legal system and could have 'possible negative impacts on the employment'. The Socialist Party (Partido Socialista Obrero Español) also has shown no interest in strengthening the rights of domestic workers. In 2018, it supported the proposal by the People's Party to wait until 2024 to give these workers the same treatment as other workers within the General Social Security Regime, enshrining the legislative stagnation of their rights.[2] Although the Socialist Party has justified itself by saying that it intends to ratify Convention 189, a number of associations of domestic workers report that the vast majority of the rights recognised by the Convention are already part of Spanish law but are unenforced (Otxoa 2018). In other parliamentary debates using the same zero-sum logic, the right of women workers to decent work has systematically been pitted against the right of the middle-class people to reconcile family and work life (Peterson 2009: 52–54).[3] More recently, at the 1st Conference on Domestic and Care Work organised by the Network of Fair Domestic Work (Xarxa de Treball de la Llar Just) in Barcelona, a member of the regional government expressed his belief that the struggle for the recognition of the labour rights of careworkers faced serious difficulties, because 'if some win (workers), others lose (employing families)'. According to domestic workers, this statement reflects a logic of class struggle.

While social rights and social programmes contract, domestic workers question the alleged dangers of regulation invoked in the moral economy that make them exploitable, undeserving of being recognised as subjects with full rights. Faced with deservingness frames that they consider unjust and that pit people against each other, the workers demand the creation of an historic political bloc for care:

> Now it seems we have to fight each other for resources. Let's not think that we have to take it out of education to give it to domestic workers; or that we have to fill some holes with others. Let's think much deeper, in terms of what are the logics that are being played out. The question is how do we redistribute wealth. The logic cannot be that some classes fight against other classes. We must come together and recognise more rights so that we can constitute a historical political bloc that places care at the centre of political life. (Spokesperson of Sindillar. Independent Union of domestic workers. 1st Conference of Domestic and Care Work, Barcelona, May 2017)

Another relevant social actor that has recently become mobilised is the family carer. Family carers started by organising local mutual-support associations and only recently have moved into politics, demanding salaries and decent retirement pensions for carers, most of whom are women. The Family Carers Association (Associació de cuidadors familiars) established in 2013 in Barcelona, has played a central role in promoting family carers as political subjects. The association emerged from a workshop held at a primary health centre:

> It was a matter of going to that workshop and there was a before and an after. There I understood for the first time what it means to be a family carer, the value that family carers have. I understood that the family carer exists. It helped empower me; it helped me understand how important it was to have done this work during all these years. And naming all of this helped me a lot. We formed a strong bond among all of us and when they said that the workshop was over, I said, 'It can't be over'. Under no circumstances did I want that group to be lost. I decided to put out a call and create the association. (President of the Family Carers Association. Interview, July 2017)

In recent years, the association has managed to mobilise thousands of people, collect signatures and hold demonstrations in front of public administration offices. They insist on the need for greater public investment, and they demand concrete, tangible, politically committed responses. They make visible the precariousness and vulnerability of families, and in particular of family carers, who bear the full responsibility for care:

> We need real support from the public administrations. We need for family carers to be *visible*. They are people who work 24 hours a day, 365 days a year. They don't get a break. […] My mother-in-law lives with us; her pension is 400 euros a month. Entering a private nursing home costs 2,700 euros a month. If you don't have that money, you have to wait five years for a spot in a public nursing home. In the association, there are people who spend all day with their father or mother who's 90 years old and they can't go outside. They have no salary; they've had to leave their job to be able to take care of their relatives. Tomorrow these people won't have anything, only the clothes on their backs. I think it's totally unfair. Ninety percent are daughters and wives. […] The carer is nobody's responsibility. We're in a no man's land. (President of the Family Carers Association, 1st Conference on Home and Care Work, May 2017)

In June 2017, with the support of the group Popular Movement (Moviment Popular) from Barcelona's Gràcia neighbourhood and many other groups, the Family Carers' Association presented to the city administration 5,000 signatures demanding the construction of a public day centre to be owned and run by the city (in a working-class neighbourhood) and the social recognition of the figure of the family carer. For their indispensable work, they demanded that family carers be able to make social security contributions and receive a salary and a retirement pension.

The association coordinates with other groups also working for the right to decent care, among them the SOS Platform Older People Barcelona – Live with Dignity (Plataforma SOS Gent Gran Barcelona-Viure amb dignitat) launched in 2017 by the Federation of Neighbourhood Associations of Barcelona. The platform opposes the private management of publicly owned nursing homes and the instability in service that this has provoked. In the manifesto 'For nursing homes where older people can live in dignity', they denounce the poor management of companies such as OHL and Clece, a subsidiary of the ACS group. These two corporations – known for their work in the construction sector – are also the two most important corporations in the elder care sector. Under the slogan 'Struggling families: Decent care for our grandmothers and grandfathers', the platform have undertaken protests, signature collections, and meetings with representatives of the municipal government, the regional government (Barcelona Consortium of Social Services) and the Office of the Ombudsman. One of their publications reads as follows:

> This mistreatment began to be reported in 2016, but the situation hasn't improved. During this period, some nursing home residents have died without having their dignity restored. [...] Meanwhile, private companies from the construction sector win most public tenders for nursing home management, and they continue to make a profit with our elderly people. [...] The construction is finished and now they are speculating with the elderly, with the consent of the government. (FAVB, 'Neighborhood coalition demands decent care for older people' – Front veïnal per reclamar atenció digna a la gent gran, *Carrer* 144, June 2017)

Not only the elderly, but also professionals from the public health and welfare system have raised their voices against austerity policies, privatisation, and the shrinking of social programmes. They have organised into several civic associations, including Home-care Service Platform of Catalonia (Plataforma d'atenció domiciliària de Catalunya), State-level Platform of Home-care Service Workers (Plataforma estatal de trabajadores del servicio de ayuda al domicilio), Platform of People Affected by the Catalan Institute of Medical Assessments (Plataforma de persones afectades per l'Institut Català d'Avaluacions Mèdiques), and Primary Health Care Rebellion (Rebel·lió Atenció Primària). Faced with what they consider the unacceptable deterioration of public services and the loss of rights, they have pointed out the negative effects that cutbacks in health and social programmes are having on health, particularly that of the most vulnerable people. They defend the right to be ill with dignity and demand a reversal of austerity policies and health and welfare services that are 100% public.

> In health centres every day, we see overburdened female carers, workers who are sick due to poor working conditions, citizens living in unacceptable situations

> to whom we can't offer the attention that they request and deserve. We see people who expect social and economic benefits that are owed to them and that they will never receive. This condemns them to live in unhealthy, disgraceful conditions. (Manifesto 'The necessary rebellion of doctors' presented by the civil platform Primary Health Care Rebellion to the Ministry of Health of the Government of Catalonia, May 2017)

Particularly interesting is the case of home-care service workers, who have denounced their job instability and the deterioration of home care and have urged the public administration to bring these services back under city control. They invoke both the rights of workers – 93% of whom are women – and the social rights of care recipients.

Care network: contested boundaries and solidarities

Together, these organisations have launched innovative initiatives, such as the Care Network. The Care Network (Xarxa de cures), founded in Barcelona in 2017, is a conglomeration that brings together more than a dozen social organisations to demand changes in the care system. The Network has used the slogan 'Let's recover dignity' to fight against austerity measures and the deterioration of public services. In particular, the Network has built an alliance around the devaluation of care work, whether paid or unpaid, uniting women (particularly, but also people more generally) across race and class boundaries. Using the language of rights and reflecting a very gendered experience of austerity, the Network has presented itself as a tool for mutual support and mobilisation against the exploitation of women's reproductive work. They are fighting for 'full public services and 100% public provision as a tool for the redistribution of wealth and also for building a society that puts life at the centre of the socioeconomic model'.

> We want to create a Care Network to give voice to the most vulnerable people and to denounce the lack of centres and public services for attending to our patients. We emphasise the fact that care tasks are undervalued both socially and politically. These tasks are unpaid or very badly paid and garner little respect from society. We demand that the cutbacks in health and social programmes be reversed. We want high-quality services and centres that are 100% public and accessible to all. And we demand that they offer fair economic and social remuneration and *dignity* to the people upon whom care tasks fall. (Manifesto 'Let's recover dignity' read at Plaça San Miquel in Barcelona, on the occasion of the official presentation of the Care Network, September 2017)

Contrary to official discourses, which tend to pit groups and interests against each other, the Network is committed to mutual concern and solidarity, demanding, from a feminist perspective, that the current social organisation of care be thoroughly overhauled. It proposes a model in which reproductive and care tasks are fully socialised and redistributed, and not assumed almost entirely by women who remain unpaid, or very badly paid, and are still not recognised as real workers. As the Network publicity puts it, 'We are weaving a new society, from the feminist struggle.'

> We can't allow family carers to remain invisible. We can't allow people in home-care services to work in disgraceful conditions. We can't allow female immigrants who care for our relatives to work in subhuman working and economic conditions. We can't allow our elderly people to be in public nursing homes managed by private companies, in deplorable conditions. We ask to be heard, to be seen. We must take a step forward and gradually achieve decent work situations for all and expose a whole socio-economic system that is being enriched at the expense of women, those who carry the burden of care. (Manifesto 'Let's recover dignity', Care Network, September 2017)

In short, the Network has managed to mobilise thousands of people, collect signatures, and organise protests in front of local government offices. In response to what they define as the collapse of the social pact of 1978, they demand that the public administrations provide concrete, tangible, and politically committed responses to reverse the long-term trend of disinvestment in care programmes. In examining their narratives and strategies, I identify three main intersecting demands: proper regulation of domestic work and true equal rights; recognition and political support for informal family carers; and the reversal of public disinvestment in health and welfare programmes, which affects both the labour rights of workers and the social rights of the people they care for.

Activists' alliances dispute the processes of exclusion that sustain the current care system in Spain, and ideologically confront what Lydia Morris (2018) – following Lockwood (1996) – calls civic stratification: a system of inequality rooted in the differential granting or denial of rights by the state. Their demands centre on an inclusive citizenship, affecting people's rights to access care, and particularly affecting women who care.

These demands have mostly fallen on deaf ears in the administration. The Spanish administration has shown little interest in the topic. Only the municipal government, led by mayor Ada Colau from the leftist party Together We Can (En Comú Podem), has shown clear signs of wanting to place the issue of care on the political agenda. Some interesting initiatives in this regard have included a working table with domestic workers and labour unions, from which emerged a joint set of proposals for dignifying domestic work.[4] In 2017, the Commission on Cooperative, Social and Solidary Consumption, along with the Council on Feminisms and LGBTI of the Barcelona City Hall presented the 'Government measure for the democratisation of care

(2017–2010)', which included a series of measures at the municipal level (see Ezquerra and Mansilla 2018). One measure was the creation of a Care space (Espai de cures) in the city, which would provide information about services related to care. Another measure was to promote changes in the management model of home-care service in Barcelona, in favour of the third sector. For now, and despite the political relevance that all of these actions have, most of them have had a mostly symbolic value and have revealed a limited impact in terms of scope and capacity for redistribution.

Conclusion

The social costs of care in Spain are distributed unevenly, in terms of gender, class, race, and legal status. The crisis of care has highlighted the insufficiency of Spain's traditional care regime. The financial crisis and the austerity measures implemented to address it have merely deepened the inequalities of the system. Austerity measures have had severe effects on care, resulting in the contraction of social programmes for long-term care and work–life balance, the privatisation of public services and increasing job insecurity for health professionals. The severe effects that the crisis has had on families' capacity for social reproduction have caused widespread discontent, a sense of injustice, and the perception that society is regressing instead of progressing, as the rights of people who provide and receive care are violated in increasingly egregious ways. As a result, grassroots activism around care has significantly increased.

Until recently, the tendency has been for social demands to be presented in a segmented fashion. That is, domestic workers demanded decent working conditions; older people demanded decent pensions and effective long-term care policies; and health professionals demanded greater public investment in public services and better working conditions. The novelty of the Care Network is that it transcends these boundaries, bringing together the different social groups that are affected by the violation of the right to care and to be cared for with dignity. The Care Network surpasses the traditional boundaries that separate – or even bring into conflict – social groups affected by Spain's care regime.

In the face of public discourses that pit groups against each other (e.g. the right of older people to receive care vs the right of carers to perform their work in decent conditions), the activists offer a systemic view of the crisis of care, by exceeding pre-established social categories and building new solidarities and moral boundaries. The activists point out the need to recognise all the situations of injustice that the current care regime produces, as well as the relationships between them. This perspective is powerful and disruptive. It delegitimates the geo-political and conceptual borders that underpin the stratified denial of rights that sustain the care system: 'Rights for one person', they say, 'should not be obtained at the cost of the rights of another person. Our struggle is the same struggle. We are creating a historic political bloc for care.' Thus, mutual concern and solidarity among social actors and groups emerges as a political tool for ideological and social transformation (see also Falge, Chapter 6, this volume).

Social activism has also become a space of collective empowerment. From this space, activists point out that care is by nature political and therefore falls under political responsibility. Female political engagement makes visible how women cope with and/or resist the crisis, crossing the conceptual boundaries that historically have relegated care to the private sphere (Vaiou 2016). By placing care at the centre of their struggles, these movements show the profoundly gendered nature of this double crisis – the crisis of care and the financial crisis. From a critical feminist perspective, they reveal not only how the current care regime affects women, but also how it is structurally configured by gender, class, and race. They do not present the dispossession of reproductive work (and its unequal and unjust consequences) as merely a short-term collateral effect of the economic crisis. Rather, they view reversing this dispossession as a central step in overcoming the crisis. They express in their own terms what Leonard and Fraser (2016) have called capitalism's inherent drive to subordinate reproduction to production, which in fact appears as the core of today's crisis of social reproduction. The Care Network and its demands reveal the central role that grassroots activists may play in the politicisation and democratisation of care, by showing its potential to contest boundaries of inclusion and exclusion from real citizenship.

Acknowledgements

This chapter presents part of the results of the Research Project 'Popular notions of social justice in the face of the crisis and austerity policies' (2016–2019) [CSO2015-67368-P] directed by Sílvia Bofill-Poch and Mikel Aramburu from the University of Barcelona, and financed by the Spanish Ministry of Economy and Competitiveness [MINECO] and the European Regional Development Fund (ERFD, EU). I thank the associations that participated in the research and particularly Women Moving Forward (Mujeres Pa'lante) for their support. I also want to thank the participants of the Panel on 'Regimes of care, gender and reproduction: solidarities and contestations across borders' (IUAES 2019 Inter-Congress 'World Solidarities', Poznan), coordinated by Frances Pine and Haldis Haukanes, for their stimulating comments and suggestions.

Notes

1 In Catalonia, the number of private nursing homes receiving public funding reached 83.62% in 2011 (Comas d'Argemir 2015).
2 Royal Decree-Law 29/2012 approved by the government of the Popular Party established a transition period until 2018 for the progressive equalisation of these workers within the General Social Security Regime. However, no action was taken during these six years to achieve this goal.
3 See the debates following the appearances of activists from the Association of Domestic Workers of Vizcaya (Asociación de trabajadoras del hogar de Vizcaya) in the Basque regional parliament in December 2013: www.youtube.com/watch?v=qGRH9E9gRUc and March 2016: www.youtube.com/watch?v=uISM9eD0WKs (accessed 15 June 2019).
4 See Consell Municipal d'Immigració de Barcelona (2017) *Propostes per a la Dignificació del treball de la llar i la cura de les persones*. Ajuntament de Barcelona.

References

Act 39/2006, of 14th December, on the Promotion of Personal Autonomy and Care for Dependent Persons (LAPAD) (BOE-A-2006–21990). /www.boe.es/buscar/act.php?id=BOE-A-2006–21990 (accessed October 2018).
Anderson, B. (2000) *Doing the Dirty Work?: The Global Politics of Domestic Labour*. London: Palgrave Macmillan.
Anderson, B. (2015) *Us and Them? The Dangerous Politics of Immigration Control*. Oxford: Oxford University Press.
Anttonen, A. and J. Sippilä (1996) 'European Social Care Services: Is It Possible to Identify Models?', *Journal of European Social Policy* 6 (2): 87–100.
Benería, L. (2008) 'The Crisis of Care, International Migration, and Public Policy', *Feminist Economics* 14 (3): 1–21.
Bettio, F. and J. Plantenga (2004) 'Comparing Care Regimes in Europe', *Feminist Economics* 10 (1): 85–113.
Bofill-Poch, S. (2013) 'Género, cuidado y ciudadanía: la sostenibilidad social y económica de los cuidados desde una perspectiva global'. In: S. Narotzky (ed.) *Economías cotidianas, economías sociales, economías sostenibles*. Barcelona: Icaria, pp. 367–382.
Bofill-Poch, S. (2018) 'Changing Moralities: Rethinking Elderly Care in Spain', *The Australian Journal of Anthropology* 29 (2): 237–249.
Bofill-Poch, S. and R. Márquez (2020) 'Indefensión, injusticia y merecimiento en el colectivo de trabajadoras del hogar: análisis de casos judicializados', *Etnográfica. Revista do Centro em Rede de Investigação em Antropologia* 24 (1): 225–244.

Briones, E., A. Agudelo, M.J. López, C. Vives, F. Ballester, E. Ronda (2014) 'Percepción de las mujeres inmigrantes del servicio doméstico sobre los efectos de la regulación del sector en España', *Gaceta Sanitaria* 28 (2): 109–115.

Care Network (2017) 'Let's recover dignity'. Manifesto read at Plaça San Miquel, Barcelona, September 2017. /www.mareablanca.cat/recuperem-la-dignitat-xarxa-de-cures-es-presenta/ (accessed 20 September 2019).

Chauvin, S. and B. Garcés-Mascareñas (2014) 'Becoming Less Illegal: Deservingness Frames and Undocumented Migrant Incorporation', *Sociology Compass* 8 (4): 422–432.

Colen, S. (1995) '"Like a Mother to Them": Stratified Reproduction and West Indian Childcare Workers and Employers in New York'. In: F. Ginsburg and R. Rapp (eds) *Conceiving the New World Order: The Global Politics of Reproduction*. Berkeley: University of California Press, pp. 78–102.

Comas d'Argemir, D. (2015) 'La atención a los cuidados de larga duración y el cuarto pilar del sistema de bienestar', *Revista de Antropología Social* 24: 173–196.

Consell Municipal d'Immigració de Barcelona (2017) *Propostes per a la Dignificació del treball de la llar i la cura de les persones*. Barcelona: Ajuntament de Barcelona. https://bcnroc.ajuntament.barcelona.cat/jspui/bitstream/11703/108871/1/TreballdelaLlar_CAT_WEB.pdf (accessed October 2019).

Constitutional Act 3/2007 of 22 'March for effective equality between women and men' (BOE-A-2007-6115) www.boe.es/eli/es/lo/2007/03/22/3/con (accessed October 2018).

Deusdad, B., D. Comas d'Argemir, and S. Dziegielewski (2016) 'Restructuring long-term care in Spain: The impact of the economic crisis on social policies and social work practice', *Journal of Social Services Research* 42 (2): 246–262.

Díaz-Gorfinkiel, M. (2008) 'El mercado de trabajo de los cuidados y la creación de las cadenas globales de cuidado: ¿cómo concilian las cuidadoras?', *Cuadernos de Relaciones Laborales* 26 (2): 71–89.

Ezquerra, S. (2012) 'Acumulación por desposesión. Género y crisis en el Estado español', *Revista de Economía Crítica* 14: 124–147.

Ezquerra, S. and E. Mansilla (2018) *Economía de los cuidados y política municipal: hacia una democratización del cuidado en la ciudad de Barcelona*. Barcelona: Ajuntament de Barcelona. http://ajuntament.barcelona.cat/tempsicures/sites/default/files/economia_i_politica_13.pdf (accessed October 2019).

Fassin, D. (2011) 'Policing Borders, Producing Boundaries: the Governmentality of Immigration in Dark Times', *Annual Review of Anthropology* 40: 213–226.

FAVB, Federation of neighborhood associations of Barcelona (2017) 'Neighborhood coalition demands decent care for older people' (Front veïnal per reclamar atenció digna a la gent gran), *Carrer* 144, June 2017. /www.favb.cat/articlescarrer/front-ve%C3%AFnal-reclamar-atenci%C3%B3-digna-la-gent-gran (accessed November 2018).

García, C., M.L. Santos, and N. Valencia (2014) 'La construcción social del mercado laboral doméstico en España a comienzos del siglo XXI', *Cuadernos de Relaciones Laborales* 32 (1): 101–131.

Hartsock, N. (2006) 'Globalization and Primitive Accumulation: The Contributions of David's Harvey Dialectical Marxism'. In: N. Castree and D. Gregori (eds) *David Harvey: A Critical Reader*. New York: Blackwell, pp. 167–190.

International Labour Organization (2013) *Domestic Workers Across the World: Global and Regional Statistics At The Extent Of Legal Protection*. /www.ilo.org/wcmsp5/

groups/public/—dgreports/—dcomm/—publ/documents/publication/wcms_173363.pdf (accessed September 2019).

Law 27/2011, August 1st, for the updating, adaptation and modernization of the social security system (BOE-A-2011–13242). www.boe.es/buscar/doc.php?id=BOE-A-2011–13242 (accessed November 2018).

Leitner, S. (2003) 'Varieties of Familism: The Caring Function of the Family in Comparative Perspective', *European Societies* 5 (4): 353–375.

León, M. and E. Pavolini (2014) '"Social Investment" or Back to "Familism": The Impact of the Economic Crisis on Family and Care Policies in Italy and Spain', *South European Society and Politics* 19 (3): 353–369.

Leonard, S. and N. Fraser (2016) 'Capitalism's crisis of care', *Dissent Magazine*. /www.dissentmagazine.org/article/nancy-fraser-interview-capitalism-crisis-of-care (accessed September 2018).

Lockwood, D. (1996) 'Civic Integration and Class Formation', *British Journal of Sociology* 47 (3): 531–550.

Márquez, R. and S. Bofill-Poch (forthcoming) 'Defenselessness, Offense and Vindication in Legal Disputes Between Employers and Domestic Workers'. In: I. Terradas, R. Márquez, and R. Mazzola, *Vindicatory Justice, beyond Revenge and Law: An Awkward Paradigm for Positive Law*. Zurich: Springer.

Martínez-Buján, R. (2011) 'La reorganización de los cuidados familiares en un contexto de migración internacional', *Cuadernos de Relaciones Laborales* 22 (4): 406–418.

Martínez-Buján, R. and L. Martínez Virto (2015) *La organización social de los cuidados de larga duración en un contexto de austeridad y precariedad*. Gobierno Vasco: Departamento de empleo y políticas sociales.

Martínez-Veiga, U. (1995) *Mujer, trabajo y domicilio. Los orígenes de la discriminación*. Barcelona: Icaria.

Montserrat, J. (2015) 'Impactos de las medidas de estabilidad presupuestaria en el Sistema de Autonomía y Atención a la Dependencia: retos del futuro', *Revista de servicios sociales* 60: 9–30.

Moreno-Colom, S., C. Recio, V. Borràs, and T. Torns (2016) 'Significados e imaginarios de los cuidados de larga duración en España. Una aproximación cualitativa desde los discursos de cuidadoras', *Papeles del CEIC. International Journal on Collective Identity Research* 1: 1–28.

Morris, L. (2018) 'Reconfiguring Rights in Austerity Britain: Boundaries, Behaviours and Contestable Margins', *Journal of Social Policy* 48 (2): 271–291.

Nogueira, J. and J. Zalakain (2015) *La discriminación múltiple de las mujeres inmigrantes trabajadoras en servicios domésticos y de cuidado en la CA de Euskadi*. Emakunde: Instituto Vasco de la Mujer.

Offenhenden, M. (2017) '"Si hay que romperse una, se rompe". El trabajo del hogar y la reproducción social estratificada.' Tesis doctoral. Universitat Rovira i Virgili, Tarragona.

Organic Law 3/2007, of 22 March, on effective equality between men and women (BOE-A-2007-6115). /www.boe.es/eli/es/lo/2007/03/22/3/con (accessed September 2019).

Organic Law 4/2000, of 11 January, regarding the rights and freedoms of foreign nationals living in Spain and their social integration (BOE-A-2000–544). www.boe.es/eli/es/lo/2000/01/11/4/con (accessed September 2019).

Otxoa, I. (2018) 'Con y sin Convenio 189 OIT, todos los derechos para las trabajadoras del hogar', *VientoSur*. /https://vientosur.info/spip.php?article14010 (accessed September 2019).

Peña-Longobardo, L.M., J. Oliva-Moreno, S. García-Armesto, and C. Hernández-Quevedo (2016) 'The Spanish Long-term Care System in Transition: Ten Years since the 2006 Dependency Act', *Health Policy* 120 (10): 1177–1182.

Pérez-Orozco, A. (2006) *Perspectivas feministas en torno a la economía: el caso de los cuidados*. Madrid: Consejo Económico y Social.

Peterson, E. (2009) 'Género y Estado de bienestar en las políticas españolas', *Asparkía* 20: 35–57.

Primary Health Care Rebellion (2017) Manifesto 'The necessary rebellion of doctors', presented to the Ministry of Health of the Government of Catalonia, May 2017. /https://rebelionprimaria.wordpress.com/pagina-de-inicio/ (accessed September 2019).

Royal Decree 1620/2011 November 14th, which regulates the special labour relationship that pertains to service in the family home (BOE-A-2011–17975). /www.boe.es/buscar/doc.php?id=BOE-A-2011–17975 (accessed September 2019).

Royal Decree-Law 29/2012 December 28th, which improves management and social protections in the Special System for Home Employees (BOE-A-2012–15764). /www.boe.es/eli/es/rdl/2012/12/28/29 (accessed September 2019).

Royal Decree-Law 20/2012, July 13th on Measures to Ensure Budgetary Stability and on Encouraging Competitiveness (BOE-A-2012–9364). /www.boe.es/buscar/act.php?id=BOE-A-2012–9364 (accessed 17 April 2018).

Saraceno, C. and W. Keck (2010) 'Can we Identify Intergenerational Policy Regimes in Europe?', *European Societies* 12 (5): 675–696.

Segato, R. (2003) *Las estructuras elementales de la violencia*. Buenos Aires: Universidad Nacional de Quilmes.

Tobio, M., M. Agulló, M. Gómez, and M.T. Martín Palomo (2010) *El cuidado de las personas: un reto para el siglo XXI*. Barcelona: Fundación La Caixa.

Vaiou, D. (2016) 'Tracing Aspects of the Greek Crisis in Athens: Putting Women in the Picture', *European Urban and Regional Studies* 23 (3): 220–230.

Zimmerman, M.K., J.S. Litt, and C.E. Bose (2006) *Global Dimensions of Gender and Carework*. Stanford: Stanford University Press.

8

Migration, gender dynamics, and social reproduction: Polish and Italian mothers in Norway

Lise Widding Isaksen and Elżbieta Czapka

Introduction

This chapter discusses ways that highly educated Polish and Italian women use, experience, and adjust to welfare services related to family and work in Norway. After the EU extension in 2004 and the financial crisis in 2008, the numbers of young, well-educated people leaving the two countries increased; some of these young people settled in Norway.

Based on interviews with two small selections of young Polish and Italian mothers living in Norway, we discuss their adjustments to gender equality-oriented welfare services and the social meanings they attach to their use of the services. The aim of the chapter is to explore how migrant mothers compare, challenge, and combine childcare practices in Norway with similar practices in their home countries, and the meanings migrants attach to their use of public services when balancing work and care in their individual lives.

Poles are currently the largest group of migrants in Norway. According to SSB data (Statistics Norway), there are 103,800 registered Poles in Norway (SSB 2018). After Poland's accession to the European Union, it was primarily men who moved to Norway, due to the demand for manual labour in the Norwegian construction industry. Lately, the number of women has been growing a little faster than the number of men, due to family reunification processes.

An increasing number of Italians arrived in Norway after the financial crisis of 2008. Currently, 5,455 Italians live in Norway (SSB 2018). Both Polish and Italian female migrants in Norway are of relatively young age. As many as 84% of Italian female migrants and 68% of Polish female migrants are found in the age group 20–49 (SSB 2018, our own calculations).

Polish and Italian migrants aged between 25–45 years have grown up in modern welfare regimes. In the Polish case, between the late 1940s until late 1980s, the socialist regime introduced policies promoting gender equality in every sphere: even if policies were not always carried out, they still were present in law (Pine 1992). Since 1989 there has been a 'backlash' when it comes to gender egalitarian policies in Poland (Szelewa 2014). The Italian welfare regime is described as Catholic, conservative, and corporative (Esping-Andersen 1990). This means that conservative family values promoted by the Catholic church influence local cultures. The social norms promoted by Catholicism support a male breadwinner model, and the idea that mothers' occupational activities can be harmful for children is widespread (Esping-Andersen 1996, Emmenegger 2010). During the financial crisis in Italy, several social, economic, and political processes which aimed to support more gender equality in society were halted. Researchers on Italian family politics have described contemporary gender egalitarian processes and politics metaphorically as a 'frozen landscape' (Saraceno 2015).

Polish and Italian women move from societies experiencing changing welfare regimes and processes of stalled gender egalitarian policies to a welfare society actively supporting women's integration in the labour market (Bjørnholt and Stefansen 2018, Isaksen 2019). In Norway, gender egalitarian values are diffused across all social strata, and public services aimed at supporting the involvement of working mothers and fathers in childcare are socially recognised (Ellingsæter, Kitterød, and Lyngstad 2017). Public childcare is universal and is a cornerstone in families' work–family balances.

In the first part of our discussion, we introduce the Norwegian welfare state and its gender orders before a brief presentation of public care arrangements in Poland, Italy, and Norway. Next, we describe the study, our samples, and the research methods we used. In the subsequent parts, we discuss the role of public childcare and local gender regimes in transnational families' lives.

National welfare and migrants as actors

Social norms and cultural values are not a set of shared meanings causing similar types and modes of actions in a given population. They can be better described as 'repertoires' or as a 'toolkit' actors use when constructing actions and social practices (Swidler 2001). In this context, we think of Polish and Italian migrants as 'mobile gender equality-oriented actors' and we focus in particular on their negotiations of work–family balances. Mobile gender equality-oriented actors are migrants who move between national institutional contexts with different gender equality processes and work–family policies helping to reconcile work and care. Their comparative experiences provide important insights into similarities and differences between Norway, Italy, and Poland. Public kindergarten plays a key role in terms of gender equality and working families' childcare strategies. When migrants act as 'mobile gender equality-oriented actors' they combine the different welfare services institutionally available for them. However, local and global institutions which structure individuals' strategies and actions are embedded in historical processes (Giddens 1990). In this case, migrants living in Norwegian contexts are expected to act according to current norms and values embedded in the Norwegian welfare state. The welfare state is described as an institutional structure offering a 'socio-political space' or 'a structure of opportunities' oriented towards the implementation and support of gender egalitarian practices (Ellingsæter 2006). The analysis focuses on migrants' everyday practices and is inspired by perspectives from institutional ethnography. Smith (1987, 2005) argues that institutions adapt to changing social practices, particularly to actors' organisation of everyday social activities during their cooperation or interaction with specific local institutions.

Gender equality models and gender orders

Comparative research on women's conditions in the labour market, the family, and the state across Europe shows a great variety in the ways that these institutions interact. However, there is a significant difference between Nordic welfare state regimes and welfare states in eastern and southern Europe (Addis et al. 2011). The role played by Nordic welfare states when it comes to women's situations and political support for gender equality is crucial in this context. The Norwegian gender equality model is a national construction of a specific 'gender order' (Connell and Pearse 2015). A 'gender order' is closely connected to the idea of norms, understood as collective definitions of socially approved conduct, stated rules, or ideals; gender norms are definitions applied to groups constituted in the gender order, to distinguish between men and women.

The 'gender order' in Norway is expressed in what Ellingsæter, Kitterød, and Lyngstad (2017: 151) define as the 'structure of opportunities' the welfare state offers to cover individual needs, to support gender equality, and to encourage full participation in society. The state supports a dual earner/dual carer family model. A standard work–family model of welfare services for parents of newborn babies is a shared yearlong paid parental leave. Mothers are entitled to stay at home the first three months. Fathers normally stay at home with the mother the first two weeks after birth but in addition they have a 'daddy quota' that currently amounts to one third of the total leave. If fathers do not use their leave, the family loses this time since mothers cannot use time reserved for fathers. For the remaining part of the parental leave, the parents are free to share this between themselves. After the end of the parental leave, children are normally offered a place in a public childcare institution, and both parents return to work fulltime. Fathers and mothers are entitled to leave if they need to stay at home when children are unwell. They receive a monthly, universal child benefit and if parents of children between 1 and 2 years prefer family care to public childcare, they are entitled to a monthly cash allowance of 7500 NOK (ca €700).

In the majority population, a gender egalitarian family life is a socially recognised ideal. Family policies come with normative expectations that both parents participate in the labour market, share housework and care work equally, and contribute to the financial provision of the family (Aarseth 2010). In 2016, 96.8% of children aged between 3 and 5, and 82% of children between 1 and 2, attended a childcare institution (SSB 2017). In the period 1980–2010, fathers of small children increased their participation in housework and care work, and fathers with higher education increased their share more than other fathers (Kitterød and Rønsen 2013a). Mothers of children aged between 0–16 have increased their participation in paid work and spend less time on housework and care work (Kitterød and Rønsen 2013b).

In Poland and Italy, gender orders are different from Norway. Compared to Norway, Italy has a relatively marked distinction between work and family life, and women who have children often have to choose between work and family. For women with children under 3, employment was 54% in 2011, which is among the lowest in Europe (Anxo et al. 2011). On the other hand, Italian women with university education have changed their position in the labour market in a short time, and their participation is now on par with women's participation in northern European regions, and higher than the average for OECD countries, despite lack of welfare services and family policy measures to promote equality (Estevez-Abe 2013). Women in younger generations are less financially dependent on male income, and work hard to find a balance between work and family (Ruspini 2011). In millennial generations, men take greater responsibility for childcare and housework than men in generations before them did (Ruspini 2011).

In Poland, women struggle to reconcile family life and work and are still responsible for most unpaid work in the household. Titkow coined the term 'managerial matriarchy' to describe the situation of the Polish women who are the main organisers of the family life (2007). The current family policy implemented by the state, with its high cost of care and relatively high child benefit payments allowances, does not promote women's participation in paid labour. Still, Polish women aged 24–49 have become more active on the labour market and their labour participation is similar to the EU average (PL: 80%, EU: 79%) (Magda 2020). However, there are differences within that age group regarding labour activity. Women who are less educated, have two or more young children, and live in rural areas or small towns are less likely to participate on the labour market. As in Italy, higher education is positively correlated with women's labour activity: 53% women in the Polish labour market have a university degree (Magda 2020). According to a GEQ study, women's paid employment promotes a more egalitarian family model where both partners work and participate in care giving (Slany 2018)

Despite changing family patterns, the male provider model still has a socially recognised status in both countries. Family care is socially supported as it is generally considered the most beneficial for small children, particularly for children below 3 years of age. There is widespread social and cultural support for stay-at-home mothers in both countries, and the husbands and fathers are normally responsible for the household income.

The World Value Surveys found in 2015 that among Italians, being a housewife is considered 'fulfilling' by 54% of the population (Abertini and Pavolini 2015). There is little childcare available for under-threes, although it is widely available after that (Rondinell et al. 2010). Statistics show that public opinion across all sectors of the population in Italy holds that the mother's absence from home is potentially harmful to a child's development, particularly for the under-threes (Naldini and Jurado 2009). Still, institutional childcare, organised by the national welfare regime and local municipalities, is popular and socially recognised in Italy (Hohnerlein 2009). As indicated above, gender orders are changing and the male breadwinner family model is on the move. On the one hand, most mothers of pre-school children are active in the labour market, although many women risk losing their jobs when they become pregnant. On the other hand, among dual earner couples with small children, time use seems to have changed; compared to older generations, parents spend more time caring for children and doing things together, and less time performing housework (Saraceno 2015).

Attitude changes supportive of gender equalitarian values are also taking place and findings indicate that they are more beneficial for educated women than for other groups in the population (Albertini and Pavolini 2015). In 2013, 28% of women in Italy had tertiary education. These changes in attitude correlate with diverging patterns in family dynamics such as more diverse family forms and individual autonomy (Albertini and Pavolini 2015).

Poland has a higher gender inequality index than Italy. The country experienced an anti-gender backlash after 1989. Before 1989, nurseries and public childcare were widely available in Poland and socially accepted. Moreover, it was socially expected that children would attend public childcare, one reason for this being that these institutions were considered important for cultural adaption to the socialist society (Żółtek and Rozbarska 2004). In addition, kindergartens made it possible for women to contribute to the labour force. However, women's employment did not reduce their domestic labour because the role of women in the family was understood in a very traditional way (Andrejuk 2016).

In Poland, staying at home with pre-school children is socially recognised. About 63% of Poles consider being a housewife equally fulfilling to working for pay and 62% believe that a child is likely to suffer if the mother works (Halman, Sieben, and van Zundert 2011). In the 2013/2014 school year, 84% children aged 3–6 in cities but only 59% in rural areas attended pre-school education (CSO 2014). Year by year there has been an increase in the number of pre-school education institutions, both in the city and in the countryside (CSO 2017). However, there are still few institutions offering care to children under 3 years of age. Between 2005 and 2014, the number of care facilities for children up to age 3 quadrupled, but still, in 2014, less than 5% of children aged 0–3 could benefit from public childcare (CSO 2015). Due to the country's political history, public childcare institutions continue to have a reputation for being 'communist', 'cold', and overcrowded, and they have low social status, particularly among the middle class (Heinen 2006).

Methodology

The empirical data we analyse here come from semi-structured in-depth interviews with 20 Polish and 10 Italian female migrants living in Norway in the period between 2012 and 2015. The interviews with Polish females were conducted in Oslo and Bergen as part of the project 'Polish Female Migrants in Norway: A Study of Care Deficit' (2012–2016). The study covered woman who had elderly parents (65 years old or above) and/or grandparents in Poland. Six of them had children in Norwegian pre-school institutions (Table 1), including three who themselves worked as kindergarten assistants. Three of the participants came to Norway to reunite with their husbands. Others had their own individual aspirations and career plans. The interview included questions on transnational care of senior relatives and children, experiences with Norwegian childcare institutions (pre-school institutions, child welfare institutions), and how it is for mothers to live and work in Norway.

Ten semi-structured interviews with Italian females were part of the project 'Morality, Mobility and Migration: Comparing Cultures of Care in Norway and Italy' (2012–2016). The interviewees were all Italian women who had come to Norway to study, work and/or raise a family in the period between

Table 1 Socio-demographic characteristics of informants*

Name	Nationality	Age	Marital status	Education	Work in Norway	Children
Kasia	Polish	32	Married to a Polish man	University	Welfare adviser	Son and daughter (2 and 4), both attend kindergarten
Dorota	Polish	45	Divorced	University	Nurse at nursing home	3 sons (17, 15, 3), the youngest attends kindergarten
Joanna	Polish	29	Married to a Polish man	University	Kindergarten teacher	Daughter (1) attends kindergarten
Anna	Polish	40	Married to a Polish man	University	Dentist	2 sons (8 and 5), the younger one attends kindergarten
Gosia	Polish	33	Married to a Polish man	University	Kindergarten assistant, psychologist	Daughter and son (1 and 4), both attend kindergarten
Monika	Polish	31	Married to a Polish man	University	Kindergarten assistant	Son (4), attends kindergarten
Anna	Italian	32	Married to a Norwegian man	University	Student	Daughter (18 months), attends kindergarten
Esther	Italian	38	Married to a Norwegian man	University	Financial consultant	3 children (3, 5, 8), Two youngest attend kindergarten
Alena	Italian	36	Living with a Norwegian man	University	Unemployed	Daughter (2), attends kindergarten
Stefania	Italian	42	Living with a Norwegian man	University	Environmental engineer	3 children (4, 7, 9), youngest attends kindergarten
Maria	Italian	33	Married to a Norwegian man	University	Elementary school teacher	Daughter (5), attends kindergarten

*All participants' names are pseudonyms

2008 and 2013. Five became mothers after moving to Norway, and the data presented here come from interviews with them. They all had experiences with children in Norwegian pre-school institutions. Interviews covered migration stories, experiences of work–family balances, mothering experiences, and intergenerational and transnational care arrangements. In particular, conversations aimed to reflect upon subjective experiences with Norwegian welfare services.

We used a qualitative methodology to gain rich insight into the participants' constructions of meaning. The two projects used various routes to recruit participants: language schools, Polish and Italian cultural centres, social media, researchers' social networks, and other. The interviews took place in locations convenient for the participants (cafés, private homes, researcher's office, and parks). They were digitally recorded, transcribed verbatim, and coded. We used thematic analysis to analyse data. All our participants have university education, which may have influenced their experiences with public childcare in Norway. In the Polish sample, the women are married to men from Poland, while in the Italian sample, migrants have Norwegian partners and husbands. However, how living with a partner from the same sender country or from the majority population in Norway might influence migrants' experiences with national welfare services was not a topic discussed in interviews. Access to kindergartens plays a key role in women's work opportunities in Norway as well as in Italy and Poland. An analysis of subjective reflections is important to gain knowledge about the ways that gender egalitarian practices in host countries interact with migrants' comparative constructions of care cultures in the home country and in the host society.

Polish migrants

Polish mothers emphasised the economic security they experience in Norway. They all used available public childcare as well as the opportunity to choose the length of maternity leave. This gave the participants a sense of control over their own lives. They could decide whether to return to work after a few months or to stay with the child at home for a longer period.

Kasia: Flexible work, kindergarten, and transnational family care

Kasia, a welfare advisor, expected to find a job in Norway that would make her satisfied and independent. She needs a stable financial situation to be able to help her family in Poland. Kasia points at more flexible work arrangements in Norway than in Poland; paradoxically, living in Norway makes it easier for her to visit her ageing parents and to fulfil her caring obligations. Kasia is very satisfied with Norwegian public childcare. She knows that in Norway, she can decide herself how long she would like to look after her child at home and she does not have to worry about financial matters. Despite this, she decided she would return to work when the child was 1, like many Norwegians do. Kasia believes that children socialise better when they start kindergarten very early:

> Here, children go to kindergarten relatively early, as soon as they are 1 year old. Thanks to that, they learn social relations. Not everyone likes it. Some psychologists believe that the child will have mental problems later. I do not agree with this. You cannot boil down mental problems to kindergarten. My friend told me that in the USSR there were kindergartens where parents left their children for the whole week to have time for work. This friend is quite a good person though she attended such a kindergarten and she has a great relationship with her mother.

She admits that from time to time, especially when children are ill, she uses her mother's help as a 'flying grandmother'. She emphasises, however, that these are short periods because her 'mother has her own work and her life in Poland'.

According to previous studies, transnational exchanges of intergenerational care are quite common for Polish migrant families (Krzyzowski and Mucha 2014, Kawczynska and Czapka 2016, Bjørnholt and Stefansen 2018). Children provide transnational care to their elderly parents and, at the same time, parents are expected to help in the care of grandchildren.

Kasia, like other Polish participants of our study, believes that well-functioning kindergartens are beneficial for both mothers and children. Moving with children to a new country and a new community generates new socialisation challenges. Childcare institutions constitute one of the most influential agents of socialisation. Describing Norwegian kindergartens and their role in children's socialisation, the Polish mothers emphasise differences between Norwegian and Polish institutions. One of the differences mentioned by the Polish mothers is related to the type of activities performed in kindergarten. In Polish kindergartens, teachers prepare a detailed programme for every day. In Norway, children have more freedom in the choice of activities, and that was highly approved of by most of our participants.

Joanna: Climate challenges and clothing expenses

In Norway, it is considered very important for children to be outside as often as possible, and to be involved in outdoor activities. That way they learn how to deal with a rather demanding climate and how to live a happy life despite the extreme weather conditions (Borge et al. 2003). This is particularly important for immigrant children. A previous study shows that Polish migrants generally support the idea of involving small children in outdoor activities (Ali and Czapka 2016).

Joanna emphasises how important it is for children to be outdoors, regardless of the weather. At the same time, she is aware that proper clothing that allows children to stay warm, dry, and comfortable is quite expensive:

> In Poland, it depends of course on the parents' financial status, but if there was a possibility for the children to have overalls, to have special waterproof boots, this full set of Norwegian clothes and they could go out every day, I see a great advantage in that, actually I see only the benefits of spending time outside ... While inside, where the space is limited by walls or by the toys that are all around, then how children play is less creative.

Joanna implies that compared to Norway, children in Polish kindergartens do not spend enough time outside. The other study participants share the same view. While Joanna pays attention to the connection between space and intellectual development, Kasia emphasises a positive influence of the Norwegian kindergarten on the motor development of young children:

> In any case, I am satisfied with the kindergarten in Norway and that it puts pressure on the motor development of young children is right because small children have primarily to learn to walk and jump. And it is not very important whether children know how to count to 100 at the age of 3 or read or know poets.

Along with other Polish mothers in our study and also those in a previous study (see Ali and Czapka 2016), Joanna stresses the cognitive and physical benefits that kindergartens offer to children. Working mothers use public childcare as a cornerstone in their work–family balances. Earning an independent income demonstrates capacity and motivation to establish gender egalitarian practices. Polish female migrants in our study construct themselves as gender equality actors and as responsible, caring, middle-class mothers. In addition, their social practices receive social recognition not only from the Norwegians but also from their local Polish community in Norway.

Italian migrants

Italian mothers also act as gender equality-oriented actors when using the 'structure of opportunity' (Ellingsæter, Kitterød, and Lyngstad 2017: 151) made available for them to construct their work–family balances.

Alena: Cash-for-care allowance and being a 'proper' mother

One of the Italian mothers, Alena (38) comes from a traditional working-class family. Her mother worked in a factory producing car seats, and both parents worked long hours. When the factory closed, her mother decided to stay home with the three children. Alena has a master's degree in communications from an Italian university. She met her Norwegian husband while working as a tourist guide in Norway. Over the following years they spent some months in Norway and some in Italy, depending on where they found work and income opportunities. When Alena reached her mid-30s, she felt compelled to decide when and where to start a family. In 2011, the situation in Italy was becoming very difficult, and the couple could find neither stable jobs nor any kind of income security. Alena got pregnant, and they decided to move to Norway where the husband quickly found work. Alena herself did not succeed in finding a job before the child was born. She decided to combine being a traditional stay-at-home mother and having her daughter part-time in childcare until the girl reached the age of 3. This was possible because she got a cash-for-care allowance per month since she did not use subsidised public childcare when the child was between 1 and 2 years old. The allowance was reduced by 50% when the child went to kindergarten part-time. Alena described her experiences of being a mother in Norway:

> What I like about my life in Norway is that it is socially convenient to be a mother here. You can stay at home with the child, just being together with her all day, and welfare support gives you an opportunity to stay at home for quite a long period. In Italy, you have to return to work after three months. You can stay home longer, but only with 30% of your normal salary, which is ridiculously little ... Here in Norway you can be a 'proper' mother and stay at home with the child for a whole year and even longer. I think it is very, very important ... I like the idea of public childcare, but for children older than 3 years.

Alena combined traditional family care with a cash-for-care service from the welfare state. She constructed herself as a 'proper' mother, according to traditional motherhood discourses in Italy, staying at home until her daughter was 3. The cash-for care service she received is quite controversial in Norway and in public discourse is often critiqued for being a service aimed to encourage mothers, in particular immigrant mothers, to stay home and withdraw from paid work (Annfelt 2015). Alena adjusted to a social pattern in the general population where 16% of families with children under 3 receive this allowance, 45% of whom are migrant families (Hamre 2016).

Esther: Father's involvement and better everyday logistics

In Italy, opening hours in public childcare are normally from 9.00 to 13.30 or from 9.00 to 16.00. Mothers working in full-time positions often combine institutional childcare with a paid nanny and/or intergenerational help and support. These care practices combine public services, paid care in informal markets, and family care and have a reputation of being quality care for children and families. However, Italian research finds that misbalance between working hours and opening hours in childcare limits the quality and importance of public childcare as a gender equality service since this makes mothers dependent on intergenerational family care (Naldini and Jurado 2009, Rondinelli et al. 2010).

Esther (38) has a PhD in economics. She left Italy in 2010 with her husband and their 3-year-old son when the husband got an interesting job offer in Norway. Later she gave birth to a daughter and another son. After the partners had shared one-year-long parental leaves, Esther returned to fulltime work in public administration. When we met, the two youngest children attended kindergarten. She shared:

> In Italy, when my son was 3 years old, he went to public childcare from nine to four. My working hours were from 9.00 to 18.00, and I had quite a long commute by train between home and work. I took him to the local nanny early in the morning, and she went to the childcare with him. My father picked him up at 16.00. When I came home at about 19.00, he was with my parents. Then I had to shop and cook. My husband came home around 20.00. Here childcare opens at 07.30 and is open until 17.00. I work from 9.00 to 16.00, and there is no stress about reaching the kindergarten on time. It is so much easier to have work family balance here in Norway. You do not need to be dependent on your family ... Just as an example, the kindergarten, it enables you to work and have a family, and when you are at work, it is like normal to take leave if your kid is sick ... even fathers can take leave.

Esther liked the fact that their move to Norway made her husband more involved in childcare. As mentioned above, fathers and mothers have equal right to stay at home with a sick child without losing pay. For her, the most important changes were the improved everyday logistics, independence from family help, and the father's increased involvement in childcare.

Migration, care, and gender egalitarian practices

In our discussion of immigrant mothers, we have conceptualised Polish and Italian mothers as 'mobile gender equality-oriented actors' to capture characteristics of their work–family balances and their use of 'opportunity structures' in the national welfare state. As in the majority population, access to public kindergartens plays a key role in gender equality and in working families' childcare strategies. When migrants act as 'mobile gender equality-oriented actors' they use a mixture of welfare services made institutionally available for them and they do it in a very pragmatic and individual way.

According to Ho (2006), migration can result either in reinforcement or disruption of traditional gender roles. We want to go beyond this either/or schema and pay attention to a process where reinforcement and disruption exist side by side. In the data we present here, we find that Polish and Italian migrant mothers develop their own care practices according to individual preferences, while actively using available opportunities such as parental leave, sick leave, subsidised childcare, and cash allowances. Previous studies have found that local gender regimes can ignore, promote, or prevent the development of more equal gender relations in the family (Santero and Naldini 2016).

Polish and Italian participants come from traditional male breadwinner societies with a cultural veneration of mothers, stereotypically known as 'la mamma' in Italy and the 'matka Polka' in Polish culture. In both societies there is a common idea that mothers' participation in the labour market can be harmful, particularly for children under the age of 3 years.

Italian Alena preferred to stay at home with her daughter until she was 3, and then start working. Polish Kasia was happy to receive traditional support from the children's grandmother. When reflecting on her observation in Norway, she shares: 'It's true that women have a better standard of living here. They work less and have more time for themselves. In Poland, you often see 30-year-old women who are quite devastated. Here, fathers are expected to share childcare with mothers.'

Kasia gave birth to two children in a short period. With both support from her husband and access to public childcare institutions, she felt that she could manage the new situation. Still, help from home was much appreciated. She combines the financial security that access to paid parental leave gives her with traditional grandmother care arriving from Poland. Even if there existed a kind of ambivalence towards public childcare institutions as a leftover memory from the communist past, mothers in this sample approached local public kindergartens when in need of childcare in Norway. Our study shows that some Polish mothers do not fully accept Norwegian food standards in Norwegian kindergartens. They complain about the composition of meals ('too many sausages and too much bread'). The findings are in line with previous studies on Polish mothers' interaction with kindergartens that found that some Polish mothers negotiate with kindergarten staff to get permission to send hot food with their children since Norwegian kindergartens normally only offer bread-based meals to children (Bjørnholt and Stefansen 2018).

Another study among Polish mothers living in Norway pointed to the co-existence of reluctance with recognition. Some did not accept or recognise what they understood as local socialisation norms in childcare (Odden 2016). For example, they thought Norwegian parents were ignorant and careless, instead of assuming that children's dirty clothes were an expression of being active, playful, and happy. For them dirty clothes were related to undisciplined behaviour.

In our sample, Italian participants were quite ambivalent about familial care in traditional male breadwinner families, an attitude reflecting existing ambiguities in an Italian gender contract under pressure (Saraceno 2015). Esther, having been dependent on a combination of public care, paid nanny services, and intergenerational care, pointed out how migration had improved her everyday logistics and allowed her to be independent of family care. Better rights for fathers was another opportunity she appreciated. In contrast to Alena, she supported the idea that children under 3 could benefit from institutional childcare. However, Alena and Esther shared an ambivalence about being dependent on intergenerational care.

Seeing themselves as migrants from societies where gender equality processes, for different reasons, were 'frozen', access to new opportunity structures made it possible to organise work–family balances composed of a mix of new and old norms. Norms regulating interdependency between generations in Italy changed from having been necessary to being a voluntary choice. Transnational family relations in Polish dual earner families in contrast gave preference to traditional care from home. Even if some migrants distanced themselves from parts of existing care models in the home country, some still preferred to combine traditional intergenerational care with gender equality-oriented practices.

In the majority population in general in Norway, well-educated middle-class women more often than working-class women and migrant women support the gender orders embedded in dual earner/dual carer models. As mobile gender equality-oriented actors, well-educated migrant mothers from Poland and Italy use the available opportunity structures in ways that include them in local gender orders. Public childcare services play a key role in the establishment of care practices in the host country. Even if there are some ambivalences, mothers in general expressed an acceptance of public childcare as a part of modern childhood in Norway.

Conclusion

For participants in this study, their migration from Poland and Italy to Norway has opened new gender equality-oriented practices, made available to them as an opportunity structure in the Norwegian welfare state. On the micro-level, Polish and Italian migrants attach meanings to their migrations as implementations of a desired social practice. In their home countries, gender egalitarian policies and processes were 'frozen' due to the financial crises in Italy and due to political and economic changes in postsocialist Poland.

A dualism and ambivalence related to institutional care for children under the age of 3 is present among Italian and Polish mothers. However, Italian mothers come from a social context where universal childcare for all children between 3 and 5 has been available since 1968 (Hohnerlein 2009). Migration to Norway made childcare also available for children aged between 1 and 3 and this is appreciated by some but not all the mothers in our study. Italian Alena preferred family care for her daughter until she was 3, and from then on full-time public childcare. Polish Kasia thought childcare was a good idea for all children from very early ages. Being independent from intergenerational care was another change appreciated by Italian mothers. Transnational care was an issue that was present more among Polish than Italian mothers, but both Polish Kasia and Italian Esther supported fathers' welfare rights and local expectations that fathers should be involved in childcare.

Mobile gender equality-oriented actors can bring norms, social expectations, and ideas on gender equality from one context and implement them in new contexts if the right kind of opportunities are available. The 'gender order' expressed in what Ellingsæter, Kitterød, and Lyngstad (2017) define as the 'structure of opportunities' was a possibility for all families, mothers as well as fathers. Migrants in our samples actively 'used the structure of opportunities' to establish and organise care practices according to their own norms and values. In this sense, they are mobile gender equality-oriented actors.

References

Aarseth, H. (2010) 'Husarbeid i Limbo? Emosjonelle Investeringer i den Husmorløse Familien', *Tidsskrift for kjønnsforskning* 34 (4): 349–365.

Anxo, D., L. Mencarini, A. Pailhé, A. Solaz, M. Tanturri, and L. Flood (2011) 'Gender Differences in Time Use over the Life course in France, Italy, Sweden and the U.S.', *Feminist Economics* 17 (3): 159–195.

Addis, E. (2011) *Gender and Wellbeing. The Role of Institutions*. Farnham: Ashgate.

Albertini, M. and E. Pavolini (2015) 'Care Policies in Italy between a National Frozen Landscape and Local Dynamism'. In: U. Ascoli and E. Pavolini (eds) *The Italian Welfare State in a European Perspective: A Comparative Analysis*. Bristol: Policy Press, pp. 133–156.

Ali, W. and E. Czapka (2016) 'Friluftsliv og Innvandrere. En Undersøkelse av Holdninger og Erfaringer blant Innvandrerfamilier i Oslo', *Nasjonal kompetanse-enhet for migrasjons- og minoritetshelse* (NAKMI), Oslo.

Andrejuk, K. (2016) 'Awans Społeczny Kobiet w Czasach PRL. Dynamika Struktury i Sprawczości', *Przegląd Socjologiczny* 65 (3): 157–179.
Annfelt, T. (2015) 'Et Kolumbi Egg? Au Pairordningen og Diskursen om Kulturutveksling', *Tidsskrift for Kjønnsforskning* 39 (3–4): 185–203.
Bjørnholt, M. and K. Stefansen (2018) 'Same but Different: Polish and Norwegian Parents' Work-Family Adaptions in Norway', *Journal of European Social Policy* 1–13, https://doi.org/10.1177/2F0958928718758824.
Borge, A.I.H., R. Nordhage, and K.K. Lie (2003) 'Children in the Environment: Forest Day-care Centres', *The History of the Family* 8 (4): 605–658.
Connell, R. and R. Pearse (2015) *Gender in World Perspective*, 3rd edition, Cambridge: Polity Press.
CSO (2014) 'Education in 2013/2014 school year', Central Statistical Office, Warsaw.
CSO (2015) 'Social assistance, child and family services in 2014', Central Statistical Office, Warsaw.
CSO (2017) 'Education in School 2016/2017', Central Statistical Office, Warsaw.
Ellingsæter, A.L. (2006) 'The Norwegian Childcare Regime and Its Paradoxes.' In: A.L. Ellingsæter and L. Arnlaug (eds) *Politicising Parenthood in Scandinavia: Gender Relations in Welfare States*. Bristol: Policy Press, pp. 121–144.
Ellingsæter, A.L., R.H. Kitterød, and J. Lyngstad (2017) 'Universalising Childcare, Changing Mothers' Attitudes: Policy Feedback in Norway', *Journal of Social Policy* 46 (1): 149–173.
Emmenegger, P. (2010) 'Catholicism, Job Security Regulations and Female Employment: A Micro-level Analysis of Esping-Andersen's Social Catholicism Thesis', *Social Policy & Administration* 44 (1): 20–39.
Esping-Andersen, G. (1990) *The Three Worlds of Welfare Capitalism*. Cambridge: Polity Press.
Esping-Andersen, G. (1996) 'Welfare States Without Work: The Impasse of Labour Shedding and Familialism in Continental European Social Policy'. In: G. Esping-Andersen (ed.) *Welfare States in Transition*. London: Sage, pp. 66–87.
Estevez-Abe, M. (2013) 'An International Comparison of Gender Equality. Why is the Japanese Gender Gap so Persistent?' *Japanese Labor Review* 13 (2): 82–100.
Giddens, A. (1990) *Consequences of Modernity*. Cambridge: Polity Press.
Halman, L., I. Sieben, and M. van Zundert (2011) *Atlas of European Values: Trends and Traditions at the Turn of the Century*. Leiden, the Netherlands: Brill.
Hamre, K. (2016) *Kontantstøtte blant innvandrere, 2015. Økte forskjeller i kontantsstøttebruk*. Statistics Norway, SSB, Oslo.
Heinen, J. and M. Wator (2006) 'Child Care in Poland Before, During and After the Transition: Still a Women's Business', *Social Politics* 12 (2): 189–216
Ho, Ch. (2006) 'Migration as Feminisation? Chinese Women's Experiences of Work and Family in Australia', *Journal of Ethnic and Migration Studies* 32 (3): 497–514.
Hohnerlein, E.M. (2009) 'The Paradox of Public Preschools in a Familist Welfare Regime: The Italian Case'. In: K. Schweive and H. Willekens (eds) *Child Care and Preschool Development in Europe*. London: Palgrave Macmillan, pp. 88–104.
Isaksen Widding, L. (2019) 'Mobile likestillingsaktører. Fra "Stivnet" til "Villet" Likestilling. Italienske Kvinners Komparative Erfaringer med Arbeid og Familie i Italia og Norge', *Tidsskrift for kjønnsforskning* 43 (1): 26–43.
Kawczynska Z. and E. Czapka (2016, eds) *Opieka nad Dziecmi i Starszymi Rodzicami w Rodzinach Migrujacych Kobiet*. Lublin: Polihymnia.
Kitterød, R.H. and M. Rønsen (2013a) 'Hvem er de Nye Involverte Fedrene?', *Økonomiske analyser*, 5/2013, Statistics Norway (SSB), Oslo.

Kitterød, R.H. and M. Rønsen (2013b) 'Yrkes- og Familiearbeid i Barnefasen. Endring og Variasjon i Foreldres Tidsbruk 1970–2010', *Rapport 44/2013*, Statistics Norway (SSB), Oslo.

Krzyżowski Ł. and J. Mucha (2014) 'Transnational Caregiving in Turbulent times: Polish Migrants in Iceland and their Elderly Parents in Poland', *International Sociology* 29 (1): 22–37.

Magda I. (2020) Jak Zwiększyć Aktywność Zawodową Kobiet w Polsce. Instytut Badań Strukturalnych. Migrations, SSB 2018. www.ssb.no/en/statbank/table/10677/tableViewLayout1/ (accessed 13 October 2018).

Naldini, M. and T. Jurado (2009) 'Families, Markets and Welfare States: The Southern European Model', paper presented at the 7th ESPAnet Conference, Urbino.

Odden, G. (2016) '"They Assume that Dirty Kids are Happy Kids". Polish Female Migrants on Being a Mother in Norway', *Miscellanea Anthropologica* 17 (3): 51–56.

Pine F. (1992) 'Uneven Burdens: Women in Rural Poland'. In: A. Phizacklea, H. Pilkington, and Sh. Rai (eds) *Women in the Face of Change: Soviet Union, Eastern Europe and China*. London: Routledge, pp. 57–75.

Rondinelli, C., A. Aassve, and F. Billari (2010) 'Women's Wages and Childbearing Decisions: Evidence from Italy', *Demographic Research* 22 (19): 549–557.

Ruspini, E. (2011) 'And Yet Something is on the Move: Education for New Forms of Masculinity and Paternity in Italy'. In: K. Pringle, E. Ruspini, and B. Pease (eds) *Men and Masculinities Around the World. Transforming Men's Practices*. London: Palgrave MacMillan.

Santero, A. and Naldini M. (2016) 'Migrant Families in Italy: Gendered Reconciliation Processes Between Social Reproduction and Paid Work', Paper to Third ISA Forum of Sociology, Vienna, July 10–14.

Saraceno, Ch. (2015) 'Trends and Tensions within the Italian Family'. In: E. Jones and G. Pasquino (eds) *The Oxford Handbook of Italian Politics*. Oxford: Oxford University Press DOI: 10.1093/oxfordhb/9780199669745.013.36.

Slany, K. (2018) 'Family Relations and Gender Equality in the Context of Migration'. In: P. Kaczmarczyk, A. White, I. Grabowska-Lusińska, and K. Slany (eds) *The Impact of Migration on Poland*. London: UCL Press, pp. 108–130.

Smith, D. (1987) *The Everyday World as Problematic*. Milton Keynes: Open University Press.

Smith, D. (2005) *Institutional Ethnography: A Sociology for People*. Lanham: AltaMira.

SSB (Statistics Norway) (2017) Higher share of children in kindergarten. www.ssb.no/en/utdanning/artikler-og-publikasjoner/higher-share-of-children-in-kindergarten (accessed 30 January 2019).

SSB (Statistics Norway) (2018) Population and population changes. www.ssb.no/en/statbank/table/11366/tableViewLayout1/ (accessed 13 October 2018).

Swidler, A. (2001) *Talk of Love: How Culture Matters*. Chicago: University of Chicago Press.

Szelewa, D. (2014) 'The Second Wave of Anti-Feminism? Post-Crisis Maternalist Policies and the Attack on the Concept of Gender in Poland', *Gender, Rovné Příležitosti, Výzkum* 15 (2): 33–47.

Titkow, A. (2007) *Tożsamośc Polskich Kobiet: Ciągłość, Zmiana, Konteksty*. Warszawa: Wydawnictwo Instytutu Filozofii i Socjologii PAN.

Żółtek A. and M. Rozbarska (2004) 'Opieka nad Dzieckiem Przedszkolnym w Ujęciu Historycznym', *Nauczyciel i Szkoła* 3–4 (24–25): 286–299.

9

Reproductive rights in migration: politics, values, and in/exclusionary practices in assisted reproduction

Izabella Main

Introduction

This chapter analyses politics, values, and areas of inclusionary/exclusionary practices in reproductive healthcare experienced by Polish migrant women in a few European destinations. The post-2004 Polish migration to EU countries has to a large extent transformed from flexible, temporal sojourns to long-term or permanent settlement[1] (White 2011, Okólski 2012, Slany et al. 2018). This process often coincides with and is reinforced by starting a family in the new place of residence. Female migrants' use of healthcare abroad is frequently related to their reproductive health. Yet, the position of women and their knowledge of reproductive rights depends on their financial resources as well as social and cultural capital. They also have very diverse experiences of access to free or subsidised healthcare in different countries (Czapka and Sagbakken 2016, Main 2018).

Based on ethnographic fieldwork in Berlin and Oslo, conducted among Polish female migrants, I explore women's experiences of access to reproductive healthcare, and especially a few cases of assisted reproductive technologies (ARTs). The chapter starts with methodological and theoretical issues. The next two parts of the chapter discuss reproductive politics in Poland in relation to ARTs and discourses on migration, depopulation, and reproduction. I ask how reproduction is influenced by regulations of changing state and local governments, how the Polish state regulates women's bodies and supports biological reproduction of the nation, and how the state relates to migrating women when they (and their bodies) 'leave the nation' to reside in an another country.

The subsequent parts of the chapter comprise a discussion, based on fieldwork, of how easy or difficult it is access to ARTs abroad, how migrating Polish women think about reproduction in cases of ARTs, and whether they are aware of and influenced by the discourse on moral governmentality promoted by the Catholic church in Poland (Mishtal 2015: 13). Overall, women have more reproductive choices and rights in most other European countries than in Poland. For example, access to contraception and abortion is less limited in all other European countries than in Poland, though it varies between them. ARTs are available in all of the studied contexts, although health insurers require co-payments to different degrees. I am interested in how, in addition to administrative measures and financial means, migrant women's moral convictions affect their decision-making processes, particularly if they might be seen as transgressing social norms and values commonly found in their home context. When it comes to reproductive rights, migration affects the ways women think about reproductive choices and birthing practices. For example, in a different socio-cultural context, reproductive choice taboos might not exist. In some cases, intergenerational perspectives also play a role. Moreover, I am interested in situations of inclusion and exclusion in ARTs-based reproduction experienced by Polish migrant women. Crossing borders within the EU/EEA changes the inclusion/exclusion in local reproductive healthcare with regards to ART and may generate new possibilities of reproductive choices in the countries promoting more liberal policies, ideologies, and ideas. Regulations in the reproductive sphere are linked to moral principles, nationalist, religious, and state ideologies, invoking the notion of moral economy to support claims to regulate bodies and construct 'the body of the nation' (see Pine and Haukanes, Chapter 1, this volume). Increasing mobility and transnational lifestyle may result in challenges in access to local healthcare systems but also create new solutions.[2]

Theoretical and methodological considerations

This chapter analyses a few cases of medical treatments related to ARTs undergone by Polish migrant women in two European localities (Oslo, Berlin).[3] Assisted reproductive technology is a highly specialised medical treatment, developed since 1978. As Sarah Franklin (2013: 12) has argued 'the large-scale transfer of experimental reproductive technology "into man" is epitomised by the rapid routinisation of assisted conception technologies such as IVF – a technology that has become both a worldwide service industry and a new norm of family life'. Over 8 million children have been born as a result of diverse assisted reproductive technologies in the world (Faddy, Gosden, and Gosden 2018), but debates concerning the use of ARTs are continuously taking place in different contexts (ethical, legal, and social) and countries (Fortier 2007, Brezina and Zhao 2012, Franklin 2013, Mishtal

2015, Radkowska-Walkowicz 2018). The debated issues include legal regulations, reporting registries, practice regulations, multiple gestation pregnancies, preimplantation genetic testing, fertility preservation, gamete and embryo donation, surrogacy, and financial aspects (Brezina and Zhao 2012).

It has been argued that women often have major responsibilities for managing both their own and their families' healthcare needs, including their own reproductive health (Salganicoff et al. 2005: 39, Stan 2015). Yet, the position of women (and men) and their knowledge of reproductive rights depends on their financial resources as well as social and cultural capital. Migrating women are forming families in diverse ways: they are migrating with partners or starting a family abroad. In some cases, women and men face difficulties in procreation and need to be referred to medical consultants for treatments, including ARTs. It has been shown in a comparative study of non-immigrant and immigrant populations in Canada using state-funded ARTs that immigrants experience reduced fertility quality of life, implying that cost is not the only barrier to IVF use. The fertility quality of life is the quality of life of people with fertility problems, measured by a particular Fertility Quality of Life questionnaire (Hasson et al. 2017). The reduced fertility quality of life may stem from cross-cultural differences in infertility perception and the immigrant population may be at greater risk of depression and anxiety (Hasson et al. 2017). Difficulties in accessing ARTs are also experienced by 'native' populations – for example, unavailability of treatments for single women, men, or same-sex couples, or of particular procedures, such as egg donation – which have led to fertility tourism (Inhorn and Pasquale 2009, Whittaker and Speier 2010, Bergmann 2011). These issues are, however, beyond the scope of this chapter.

It has been maintained that the politics of reproduction is an example of the ways individual choices and local contexts are being shaped by state policy, power relations between states and individuals, and ideological control of people by institutions imposing regulations and laws (Ginsburg and Rapp 1991: 313, Gal and Kligman 2000: 17). The ways local and individual choices are shaped may be generated by 'moral regimes [which] refer to the privileged standards of morality that are used to govern intimate behaviours, ethical judgements, and their public manifestations' (Morgan and Roberts 2012: 242). Moral regimes are related to reproductive governance, which is based on

> the mechanisms through which different historical configurations of actors – such as state institutions, churches, donor agencies, and non-governmental organisations (NGOs) – use legislative controls, economic inducements, moral injunctions, direct coercion, and ethical incitements to produce, monitor and control reproductive behaviours and practices. (Morgan and Roberts 2012: 234)

As Gal and Kligman argue, referring to the case of postsocialist Europe, 'the laws, regulations, and administrative machinery that the new states are installing will have long-range repercussions for the ways in which women in East Central Europe give birth and how people practice contraception, raise their children, and imagine their own and their children's futures' (Gal and Kligman 2000: 17).

This research utilised the multi-sited ethnographic approach proposed by Marcus (1995) and examines the topic of experiences with local healthcare in different European localities and from diverse angles, including discourses and experiences of reproductive care.[4] The ethnographic research was conducted among Polish female migrants in London, Barcelona, and Berlin between 2008 and 2013, and in Oslo in 2016–2017. The migrants chosen for the interviews and observations had lived abroad for at least a year, although the majority had been abroad for more than five years; their ages varied (22 to 65). They came from very diverse educational and social backgrounds and different family situations: single, with a Polish or a foreign partner, with children, or childless. The selection was made using the snow-ball method and purposeful sampling aimed at interviewing diverse groups in terms of age, education, length of migration stay, and family situation. The interviews examined the reasons for and trajectories of migration, respondents' access to and experiences with local, Polish, and other healthcare systems, and changes to their health-related practices and beliefs. The situation of medical travel for ART treatments, undertaken from Barcelona to Poland, has been analysed elsewhere (Main 2014). This text analyses a few cases of Polish migrant women who underwent assisted reproductive technologies when living abroad. In particular I focus on two cases in Oslo and two cases in Berlin, exemplifying inclusion and exclusion of migrants in the reproductive sphere of the Norwegian and German healthcare systems. The four women whose experiences are analysed had lived in Germany and Norway for between 5 and 20 years (at the time of interviews) and planned to stay there permanently. Two had Polish and two local (Norwegian and German) partners. Their treatment took place between one and eight years before our meeting.

Reproductive rights in Poland

After the political change of 1989, reproductive rights in Poland became an increasingly contested matter. According to WHO 'Reproductive rights rest on the recognition of basic rights of all couples and individuals to decide freely and responsibly on the number, spacing and timing of their children and to have the information and means to do so, and the right to attain the highest standard of sexual and reproductive health' (Cottingham et al. 2010). There are a number of controversial procedures and practices within the field of reproduction, such as abortion, assisted reproduction, prenatal testing, and sterilisation.

In Poland the most heated debates concern abortion – the Polish law was first changed in 1990, when access to abortion was made very difficult. In 1993, the law was further tightened and abortions became legally obtainable only in cases of serious threat to the life or health of the pregnant woman, rape or incest, or when the foetus was seriously and irreversibly damaged. Furthermore, access to abortion in these cases has been limited by administrative measures and the conscience clause, introduced in 1996 (Kramer 2007, Różyńska 2008, Zielińska 2010, Wejbert-Wąsiewicz 2012). The restrictive law on abortion remains in place today; moreover anti-abortion groups fought to ban abortion completely in 2011 and 2016 respectively, which led to dramatic and widespread social protests in Poland. Medical personnel in a majority of local hospitals across Poland have signed the 'conscience clause' and refuse to perform abortion even in legally possible situations as result of their own ideological positions and pressures exerted by anti-abortion movements.

Restricted access to abortion is linked to limited access to prenatal testing, contraception, and sterilisation in Poland (Kramer 2010, Mishtal 2012, see also Kościańska, Chapter 12, this volume). These developments have happened as a result of the strong position of religious and political groups and organisations supported by the Catholic church in Poland. It can thus be argued that political alliances between right-wing parties, activists, and the Catholic hierarchy form the core of Poland's system of reproductive governance, attempting to control reproductive practices and behaviour in a number of different ways.

Due to ideological disagreements, ARTs in Poland were not regulated by specific legislation until 2015. ART was also not considered to be an important topic in public debate; rather, it was confined to a number of private clinics and state hospitals (where patients had to cover most of the costs). In 2007, an announcement was made that the cost of such treatments would be covered by the state budget. It was only after this announcement that ARTs became a political matter. Still, until 2015, assisted reproduction was primarily regulated by the demands of the market, as well as by the competences and traditions of Polish reproductive medicine. Once the law on infertility treatment was enacted, however, the political discussions accelerated. This stimulated new areas of debate; for example, about in vitro fertilisation – whether it should be allowed in Poland at all, and if so, for whom and how? (Radkowska-Walkowicz 2018: 979).

Public support for ARTs is high: public opinion polls in 2015 showed that 76% of Poles supported its use for married couples, 62% for unregistered relationships, and 44% for single women; 42% stated that it should be financed by the state (CBOS 2015). The issue of state (co)financing ARTs was a matter of heated debate and changing policies. In mid 2013, the sitting government, established by the centre-right parties Civic Platform (*Platforma Obywatelska*) and Polish People's Party (*Polskie Stronnictwo Ludowe*), decided to introduce a state-(co)sponsored ARTs programme for infertile couples. This programme was cancelled in 2016 as result of political change. In October 2015, the Law and Justice party (*Prawo i Sprawiedliwość*) won the elections and formed a right-wing government which introduced financing of a 'governmental program of naprotechnology'[5] in the place of ARTs. Since then, several local city councils have decided to cover partial costs of ARTs for their residents. In some cities, councils refuse to participate in such cost-sharing and the citizens have to cover the costs of treatments themselves (Szczerbiak 2018). Financing in vitro treatment by local governments was even addressed by politicians in the mid-2018 election campaign (Szczerbiak 2018). For example, Patryk Jaki – representing the conservative Law and Justice (PiS) party – a candidate for the position of city's mayor (*prezydent*) in Warsaw, mentioned that he planned to cancel the city's program of co-financing ARTs. Rafał Trzaskowski (representing Civic Platform), who actually won the election, supported the city's programme of co-financing ARTs.

Reproductive care regulations in Poland reflect ideological arguments and political alliances, yet directly influence the situation of infertile couples. A change of the party in power – from a more liberal party to a right wing one strongly under the influence of Catholic doctrine – led to immediate cancellation of the government's programme to assist infertile couples, yet the issue remains highly contested and representatives of other political options (on regional or local level) continue to support financing ARTs. Thus, reproductive governance is constantly renegotiated by political actors.

Migration (de)population and reproduction

I argue that there is an ideological link between discourse on the future of the nation expressed in reproductive politics and discourse on recent migration of Poles. Migration, and especially migration of women and families as well as long-term migration leading to settlement abroad (Burrell 2009), is an axis upon which questions of demographic stability, reproduction of families, and the nation's future are raised, albeit in a more subtle way. There is public and political discourse about the process of de-population of Poland, and the necessity to maintain the strong social and economic bonds migrants have with Poland and to stimulate their return (Odrowąż-Coates et al. 2014, www.powroty.gov.pl). Scenarios of a depopulated country are described by demographers and sociologists (Iglicka 2011) and reported by mass media (see Andrejuk 2013: 7–9). The estimates of post-2004 emigration from Poland are around 2.5–3 million people. The statistics are not fixed because there is constant migration and mobility and EU countries have no strategic interest in declaring smaller populations since the compensatory subsidies for less developed areas depend on the numbers of inhabitants (also on a local level) (Święchowicz 2017).

During a visit to Cambridge University in January 2017, the Polish Prime Minister Mateusz Morawiecki appealed to Poles in Great Britain: 'All young families with children come back to us, please. It will be good for Poland and not bad for Great Britain.'[6] The comment about families with children refers to the opinion common in the media that Poles abroad have more children than Poles in Poland. Such views were particularly present in the media in 2014–2015, referring to birth statistics in the UK, where Poles were the second-largest migrant group after the Pakistanis in terms of the number of newborns (Iglicka-Okólska 2014, Wielowieyska 2014). The government in Poland has also introduced family allowances to boost fertility rates in Poland (Family 500+ programme, giving a monthly allowance of 500 złoty (about €125) per child) since 2015.

There are a few studies of the reproductive behaviour of Polish migrants. One is a study of the reproductive situation of Polish migrant women in Ireland by Węgrzynowska, who pointed out that their expectations of the medicalisation of birth were derived from their healthcare knowledge in Poland (Węgrzynowska 2016). In another study, Polish female migrants in Berlin described their experiences with local healthcare as positive; they emphasised that this was thanks to the local healthcare system giving space to personal agency and decision-making power (Main 2015).

A comparative study of reproductive behaviour of Poles in Germany, Sweden, and the UK showed that different factors play a role in how they come to arrange their lives in relation to reproduction. In Germany 'the importance of childbearing norms and patterns in the migrants' countries of origin for their childbearing behaviour' was noted, while in Sweden an established position on the labour market also played a role (Janta 2013: 68–69). The post-accession migration to the UK resulted in a rapid increase of births to Polish mothers as a consequence of the large number of Polish migrants being in a highly reproductive age group (Janta 2013: 85).

'Abortion tourism' from Poland was explored by Ewa Hirvonen, who showed that accessibility of the service, responsiveness of personnel, and opinions on the internet were more important than price, distance, language skills, and transportation. There was no mention of facilitation of abortion tourism by Polish migrants living in destination countries (Hirvonen 2017: 24); nevertheless, the topic of abortion tourism is regularly mentioned in mass media and internet forums in Poland (Święchowicz 2014, Snochowska-Gonzalez 2016, Naleśnik 2017, Bielaszyn 2018). The term abortion tourism, or medical tourism (compare Cohen 2014, Connell 2011), is commonly used, though as Beth Kangas (2010) showed, it is highly problematic. Kangas proposed the term 'medical travels' since tourism might imply travels combining treatment, tourism, and leisure while medical travels to other countries are sometimes the only way to access medical care (also in the case of life-threatening diseases). Andreas Whittaker and Amy Speier (2010) used the term 'reproductive travel' when writing about care, commodification, and stratification in cross-border reproductive travel.

Inclusion in the reproductive sphere and changing values

Reproductive policies are formulated at the national level for citizens of EU/EEA states. As a result of the right to move between European countries, Poles have the opportunity of access to medical treatment, including reproductive treatment, in less restrictive countries. For the majority of Polish women in my study, migration from Poland to other EU/EEA states led to an improvement in reproductive rights because they gained access to practices and programmes which are not available, or are available only to a limited extent, in present-day Poland. Overall, women have more reproductive choices and rights in the countries of this study – i.e. Germany, Norway, Spain, the UK – than in Poland. For example, access to contraception and abortion is less limited abroad than in Poland, though it varies between countries. During pregnancy and birth, women have more rights in choosing which and how treatments will be implemented. ARTs are available in all contexts and health insurers cover their costs to different degrees. I argue that in addition to administrative measures and financial means, migrant women's personal experiences and social position play a large role. I now move on to describe cases of Polish women who underwent assisted reproductive treatments in Germany and Norway.

Anna

Anna moved to Berlin to join her partner Tomasz, also Polish, who had been living there for more than 15 years. She had two teenage children from a previous relationship and now the couple wanted to have a child together. It soon become clear that there was a medical problem and the GP referred them to a specialised hospital. Tomasz had a low sperm count so the procedure of ICSI[7] was advised and carried out. The couple was insured by a private German medical insurance company [*Krankenkasse*] so actually they got four treatments covered, in two different hospitals. Anna said that she was well prepared, she had read a lot on internet fora and joined a Polish support forum Our Stork [*Nasz bocian*][8] which she often consulted about her situation. In the first cycle she received a lot of hormones and produced many eggs but the transfer did not result in pregnancy and there were no embryos to freeze. She believed that financially it was better for the hospital to start a new cycle than to freeze embryos. It became very stressful for the couple because for each procedure they had to get agreement from the insurer that it would cover the costs. They wrote letters, met and discussed the available options, then waited for decisions. The second cycle also did not result in pregnancy. Anna and Tomasz once again visited the insurer's office and received permission to change the clinic and try one more time. She remembered that she was very pushy in the clinic, immediately stressing that she wanted a different kind of protocol since she believed it would work better: 'I was a terrible and irritating patient. I often went and said that I want this or that ... even if it made no sense, ... more scans, more things. Tomasz tried stopping me but it was really hard. They – the insurers and the doctors – did everything but we failed once again.'

Anna stressed a few times during the interview that she got very good treatment, and she had influence on how it was carried out, although she was not convinced at the very end that her ideas and suggestions made sense. She emphasised that she felt listened to. She also underlined that such treatment would not have been possible for her in Poland where the couple would have had to pay for it, whereas her insurer in Germany covered most of the costs. At the time of the treatment and afterwards, Anna was active on the internet forum Our Stork, especially in a group for Polish infertile women and couples living abroad, and compared the ART options in different countries. She showed appreciation of the treatments accessible to her in Germany.

On a larger scale, Anna saw many changes in herself as a result of migration – in her own words she became braver, she did not feel such pressure to conform to certain values as she had in Poland, she was able to do more and change more than if she had lived in Poland.

For Anna, moving to Germany meant crossing many borders, not only political and administrative, but also cultural. She encountered cultural differences and new understanding regarding social roles as well as areas of freedom and taboos. She mentioned that in Poland she went to church and sent her children to religious classes and first communion ceremonies because she did not question these values. She was not interested in what religious norms actually meant. Undergoing ART treatments in Germany was one example where she realised that she was transgressing religious norms of the Catholic church, that the church disapproved of her medical treatment. After a few years of living in Germany, when she learnt about the need for ARTs, she realised how far she had moved from Catholic norms. She learnt about the church's teaching in relation to ARTs and completely rejected this position. The Catholic church's position on ARTs became unacceptable for her, turned her into a religiously ambivalent person, and this in turn led her to antagonise a few family members in Poland. In recent years, Anna had been involved in political activity in defence of reproductive rights and democratic values in Poland. I asked her in a follow-up interview (in May 2018) how she explains her involvement:

> when I lived in Poland, I did not notice changes to the detriment of women, we all agreed to them, women agreed, I did not protest … I was afraid of stigmatisation, I was afraid to stand out. I would decide differently now but it was so hard for me to stand out, to confront, to say what I think, lay out my views. Here, in Germany, people have rights, it is easier for me to protest against [recent] changes in Poland, because I am not there.

During the first years after Anna moved to Germany, she had to learn the German language, work, and take care of her children. The next years in her life were devoted to attempting to have another child. This coincided with a period of heated debate in Poland about IVF and disapproval of ART treatments by the Catholic church and some political actors (Radkowska-Walkowicz 2018), which triggered Anna's involvement in protests against changes in reproductive rights in Poland. After the electoral victory of the Law and Justice party in 2015, Anna co-organised and joined protests against the disruption of the democratic system, organised in Germany and Poland. Her involvement in these activities was not supported by her family members who feared for her life priorities and even security due to her public visibility.

Ela

I met Ela in Oslo where she had moved in 2009 to join her Polish partner whose company had transferred him from Poland to work as an IT specialist. Ela learnt Norwegian quite quickly and soon started working in her profession as well. The couple had wanted to become parents when still living in Poland and had realised that it was not going to be easy, but they did not start treatment because of other financial priorities. After moving to Norway and a few months of unsuccessful attempts to conceive, they started medical treatment and were referred to a specialist clinic. As a result of IVF procedures in Norway the couple have two daughters aged 5 and 1 (at the time I spoke to Ela). Ela noticed that

> it was not difficult to arrange the treatment. There was a short waiting list and the waiting time was used for consultations and tests. The cost was mostly covered by the insurer, we paid just a tiny part for some medicines and tests. Overall we spent maybe even less than my monthly salary which was almost nothing. If compared to the Polish situation where people take loans for years to cover the costs, it was nothing.

Financial availability of the ART treatment was very important for Ela. I asked her if she faced any difficulties during the treatment, regarding language understanding or family circumstances.

> We [the couple] managed using Norwegian. We did not ask for an interpreter because it would make it longer and less efficient. They [medical personnel] understood that they were talking with foreigners so chose easier words, and talked in such a way that we understood. They also had experience in talking to people who do not speak Norwegian language fluently. And [they] got lots of aids – pictures and boards – showing them to us when describing the procedure.

On the other hand, Ela found communication with family in Poland about the IVF treatment in Norway difficult; she felt it was a taboo topic, contested by society. Her family asked her not to talk openly about it because it might antagonise people. Again, the Catholic church teaching was mentioned by her relatives as the reason for contestation in Poland. She admitted to being really happy to live in Norway where there is 'a practical approach to the treatment', nobody 'makes a fuss about it' and 'I feel normal'. For Ela and her husband migration meant moving to a country where ART treatment not only was much more available from a financial point of view but also was generally approved by society and state policies. At the same time, it is worth noting that there has also been debate about ART treatment in Norway: in the 1980s when the first IVF procedure took place, or more recently about homosexual couples' access to the treatment (Sundby 2010, Birkvad 2017). Norwegian law and regulations have until very recently not allowed egg and gamete donation, thus prior to the change in law[9] Norwegian couples might travel to other countries for treatment, and since surrogacy is permitted in Poland (Präg and Mills 2017), they might actually decide to go there for treatment.

Wiola

Another woman, Wiola, moved to Germany as a teenager with her parents, started studies in pedagogy and worked as an office manager in Berlin.

When she met Klaus she already had a baby from a previous relationship. After a few years, Wiola and Klaus decided to have a child together, but he was diagnosed with medical problems. Wiola had public insurance while Klaus' was private, which made a significant difference during their medical treatment. Wiola said:

> If it had been my problem, we would have had to pay, the insurance company would not have covered it but since the problem was related to Klaus, they had to pay. We were so lucky. It cost something like about 7000 ... so expensive. Some people even decided to go to Poland for a private treatment. But we got this good combination of insurance systems. For me to pay for private insurance would have been really expensive since I have problems with my spine and other issues, thus the public insurance is much cheaper and I went for it ... We were directed to a really good clinic and just started visits at a good moment of the [menstruation] cycle so all went really well, I got pregnant and our daughter was born.

Wiola's case shows that access to free or highly-subsidised assisted reproductive treatment was not influenced by the fact that she was a migrant but instead by the kind of health insurance she had in the German healthcare system. At the same time, she was aware that women living in Poland had to cover all costs of such treatments.[10] She noted that she would have considered ART treatment in Poland – as she believed in its high standard – if she had been obliged to pay for it in Germany. Wiola's parents also lived in Germany and approved of ART treatment.

Anna, Ela, and Wiola were open about their treatments, and they all stressed that it was not a taboo topic in Germany and Norway, and neither was it a controversial medical treatment. These women were surprised that it was a topic of political discussion in Poland. Ela and Wiola stated that they were not religious and had no interest in the negative attitude of the Catholic church to ARTs. They both saw it as an opportunity opened up through technological improvements, but had no moral hesitations about it. Still, Ela's family in Poland was negative about her treatment and referred to Catholic values to explain their position. Ela was only made aware of such negative opinions when she tried openly to speak about her treatment; it was not something that she had encountered earlier. For Anna, who before ART treatment had seen herself as a 'regular Catholic' – not very devout but still attending church and participating in religious practice – undergoing ARTs made her rethink her position in relation to the church and religion in her life. She stopped attending church and became involved in the women's movement. Anna, Ela, and Wiola emphasised that they had access to financially affordable treatment which would not have been possible had they remained in Poland. The differences between them resulted from differences between the German and Norwegian healthcare insurance systems.

Wiola and Anna, who actually used private health insurance in Germany, had to go through a process of seeking permission; Ela's access to state-funded treatment was very easy.

Migration and exclusion in reproductive rights

The case of Lena, another Polish female migrant living in Oslo, shows that migration to a country with accessible ART treatment might not preclude difficulties in this sphere. Lena lived in Norway with her Norwegian partner for a number of years before she was diagnosed with breast cancer; she was in a high risk group since her mother also had been treated for it a few years before. She was 32 years old at the time of diagnosis and was committed to preserving her fertility in case she wanted to have children in the future.[11] After a mastectomy and before chemotherapy, Lena had a brief time window to undergo stimulation and egg collection and she was offered the chance to take part in a specific procedure within a particular research programme in a hospital in Oslo. Yet Lena, who was educated in social sciences, had become concerned about ethical issues of the programme and her situation.

> I did not want to be a guinea pig. I wanted the best treatment. My cousin was working in an IVF clinic in the US at the time and I consulted with him about the available options. He worked in a lab but sought the advice of consultants during informal dinners about my case and the best treatment. And this mini-stimulation – the best option – was not offered in Norway. I found out that there was such possibility in Sweden. In Oslo they only proposed to me a full stimulation that previously was not recommended by a consultant in chemotherapy unit in another hospital. So I called my cousin and had him online during the decisive meeting with the doctors in the research programme. We asked many questions but they had no clue [about this mini-stimulation]. I was really a titbit for them: how many young women with such a condition are in Norway? So I opposed and applied for permission to go to Stockholm and have mini-stimulation but it was denied. I sat and cried … And later we wrote a complaint. So we went to Sweden and paid for it privately.

Lena was angry that men in Norway had the right to receive fertility preservation procedures but women did not, unless they were enrolled in a particular research scheme that was not using the most advanced methods based on scientific evidence. Her husband, actually a GP, was not able to get them access to anything better. The couple decided that they had no choice but to borrow money from family members and undergo the procedure of mini-stimulation in Sweden. As a result, Lena has frozen eggs in a Swedish clinic.

Lena was also angry that she was approached by a Polish doctor, a trainee, during the decisive meeting about her participation in the research programme in the clinic in Oslo. She said to me 'from a patient's perspective it was all not fair. I have a feeling of great injustice. The doctor was not prepared to answer my questions, and why? Because I was from Poland? Why did they think that a Polish trainee would be a better option? It was really a trauma for me.' Lena expected a professional approach. However, she believed she suffered discrimination as a Polish national. She was consulted by a Polish trainee doctor even though there was no such need regarding language. This doctor was neither in charge of important decisions nor had sufficient knowledge. It proved to be very difficult within the Norwegian healthcare system because the procedure available was not what she wanted. However, Lena had international links to medical professionals in the US and used these to learn about possible treatments. She and her husband read a lot of scholarly works and searched for the best options. Having social capital related to the medical and in particular the reproductive sphere put her in a privileged position, even in relation to Norwegian women in need of fertility preservation. Being an immigrant with an international framework and opportunity to travel contributed to her willingness to have treatment elsewhere.

Conclusion

In the case of Polish migrant women, there are aspects of power and agency in both inclusionary and exclusionary situations of regulation of their reproductive bodies. I argue that migration leads to dynamic situations, ambiguities, and constraints in gendered reproductive rights and related ideologies. Migrant women seek the best practices and use diversified strategies to receive the best healthcare.

For the Polish migrant women living in Berlin and Oslo whom I interviewed, using assisted reproductive technologies was an obvious choice in relation to difficulties in becoming pregnant or the necessity – in the case of Lena – to preserve fertility after a cancer diagnosis. They had no ethical concerns about using ARTs. Anna and Wiola were not aware of disputes concerning in vitro fertilisation in Poland before they learnt about the necessity of treatment and underwent it abroad. They already lived abroad when the regulations were passed in Poland in 2015. Ela considered IVF in Poland and was aware of the debates but these were not important for her since she postponed treatment until later. For Lena – attempting to preserve her fertility – these debates were also insignificant.

When seeking in vitro fertilisation some of the women were confronted with negative attitudes to ART not only in Polish society but also from family members in Poland. This made some of the women like Anna, who was a practising Catholic before moving to Germany, question their position and change their attitude towards the Catholic church and the values promoted by it. As migrants in Germany and Norway, they noticed the absence of debate, and the negative views about ARTs, which characterised the situation in Poland. These three women had the opportunity to receive financial support for their treatment, which was appreciated by them. Both the ideological and financial aspects shown made them feel included in local societies and they enjoyed recognition of their reproductive rights.

The experiences of Lena, who required fertility preservation in Norway, were very different. Not only was she refused when she applied for state financing for a more advanced and safer medical procedure available in Sweden, but she also experienced discrimination in a Norwegian clinic. She was offered consultation with a Polish doctor because it was assumed, incorrectly, that she needed it. Yet Lena's case also shows that as a migrant she was able to gather information on the best medical treatments as a result of her international links with medical professionals. Her perseverance, language and communication skills, and agency made her someone that could be called 'a global patient'. This in itself is an interesting development taking into account the fact that reproductive rights are increasingly limited in Poland.

Reproductive governance is applied in different national and global contexts, with regulation of reproductive rights in terms of access to diverse treatments, or offering or limiting financial support. In Poland there are continuous attempts to limit reproductive rights – including availability of ARTs – both from a legal and financial perspective. The experiences of some Polish migrant women in Germany and Norway show that there were various regulations and limitations, not always clearly expressed, which they faced when attempting to use ARTs, reflecting different systems of reproductive governance and different opportunity situations. Still, as Polish migrants living in EU/EEA countries, they face a much less restrictive system than the one imposed by the present conservative government in Poland and its allies. Their individual experience with ARTs is shaped by the reproductive policies in the country of settlement, as well as by public debates in Poland, as a result of transnational connections, social networks, and family ties. The ability to cross borders is thus also an ability to escape gendered boundaries imposed by a particular kind of moral regime, yet they also experience challenges of different kinds when using ART while living outside Poland.

Acknowledgements

This chapter is based on research financed by the National Science Centre in Poland, entitled 'Mobile Lives, Immobile Realms? Female Mobility between Poland and Norway' [2014/14/M/HS3/00842].

Notes

1 Since migration is a contextual and processual phenomenon, such changes as Brexit in the UK or family policies in Poland might lead to a revision of migration plans and trajectories.
2 Some migrants experience difficulties in learning about local healthcare. For example, they find it difficult to receive free pregnancy care when they live and work in different countries due to state regulations limiting health insurance to one EU country. My fieldwork with migrant women also shows lack of trust in the healthcare systems of foreign countries and a certain level of misunderstanding about reproductive rights and prenatal care, resulting in searches for private healthcare in the countries of residence and in Poland. For example, when Polish women used private care in the UK or Norway, they preferred clinics providing medical consultations and tests in Polish by doctors and nurses either commuting from Poland or living there.
3 More than 120 people, mostly migrant women, but also officials, activists, and nurses, were interviewed, some a few times over longer period of time. Observations at homes, playing grounds, and institutions were also conducted.
4 In previous texts I have focused on experiences of birth, medical travels, and patients' perspective on biomedical practices (Main 2014, 2015, 2018).
5 Naprotechnology is a modified version of Creighton model of fertility, based on natural family planning.
6 'Wszystkie młode rodziny z dziećmi proszę: wróćcie do nas; to będzie dobre dla Polski, a niekoniecznie złe dla Wielkiej Brytanii' [All young families with children come back to us, please. It will be good for Poland and not bad for Great Britain] (Święchowicz 2017).
7 Intracytoplasmic Sperm Injection ICSI is very similar to conventional IVF in that gametes (eggs and sperm) are collected from each partner. The difference between the two procedures is the method of achieving fertilisation. ICSI is the laboratory procedure where a single sperm is picked up with a fine glass needle and is injected directly into each egg. Very few sperm are required and the ability of the sperm to penetrate the egg is no longer important as this has been assisted by the ICSI technique. (www.sims.ie/treatments/intracytoplasmic-sperm-injection-icsi.1040.html (accessed 2 June 2018).
8 Nasz bocian (in English 'Our Stork') Stowarzyszenie na Rzecz Leczenia Niepłodności i Wspierania Adopcji (Association for the Treatment of Infertility and Support for Adoption) was founded in 2002 as a support group with most

of its activity on internet forum www.nasz-bocian.pl/stowarzyszenie (accessed 10 September 2018).

9 A new law on biotechnology which permits egg donation (applying from 1 January 2021), was passed in the Norwegian parliament on 8 June 2020, see: www.regjeringen.no/no/aktuelt/endringer-i-bioteknologiloven-fra-1.-juli/id2721705/ and www.bioteknologiradet.no/2020/06/bioteknologiloven-hva-ble-endret/ (accessed 20 August 2020).

10 The costs of ART in Poland varies between 10000 and 20000 Polish zlotys (€2500–5000), see www.chcemybycrodzicami.pl/ile-kosztuje-in-vitro-w-polsce-cennik-vs-rzeczywistosc/ (accessed 10 September 2018). As mentioned earlier, there are places where co-financing is offered by local governments for some couples.

11 Fertility preservation for individuals afflicted with cancer is needed because 'often the chemotherapeutic agents used to treat cancer are toxic to the ovary and result in diminished ovarian reserve and reduced fertility' (Brezina and Zhao 2012).

References

Andrejuk, K. (2013) 'Mobilni Europejczycy czy Powracający Patrioci? Dyskursy o Migrantach Powrotnych w Internetowych Serwisach Informacyjnych', *Młoda Polska Emigracja w UE jako Przedmiot Badań Psychologicznych, Socjologicznych i Kulturowych*. Konferencja EuroEmigranci.PL, Kraków 23–24.IX.2013 r.

Bergman, S. (2011) 'Fertility Tourism: Circumventive Routes That Enable Access to Reproductive Technologies and Substances', *Signs: Journal of Women in Culture and Society* 36 (2): 280–289.

Bielaszyn, W. (2018) 'Paczka z Tabletkami czy Wyjazd do Berlina? O Aborcji w Warszawie', *Gazeta Wyborcza*, 9 March 2018. http://warszawa.wyborcza.pl/warszawa/7,54420,23119961,paczka-z-tabletkami-czy-wyjazd-do-berlina.html (accessed 10 August 2018).

Birkvad, I.R. (2017) 'Assisted Fertilisation Has Become Natural', *Kilden. The Journal of Gender Research* http://kjonnsforskning.no/en/2017/01/assisted-fertilisation-has-become-natural (accessed 24 May 2020).

Brezina, P.R. and Y. Zhao (2012) 'The Ethical, Legal, and Social Issues Impacted by Modern Assisted Reproductive Technologies', *Obstetrics and Gynecology International*, Article ID 686253, https://doi.org/10.1155/2012/686253.

Burrell, K. (2009, ed.) *Polish Migration to the UK in the 'New' European Union: After 2004*. Farnham: Ashgate.

CBOS (2015) '76 proc. Polaków Akceptuje in Vitro dla Małżeństw' https://wiadomosci.wp.pl/cbos-76-proc-polakow-akceptuje-in-vitro-dla-malzenstw-6027750510257281a (accessed 1 September 2018).

Cohen, I.G. (2014) *Patients with Passports: Medical Tourism, Law, and Ethics*. Oxford Scholarship Online.

Connell, J. (2011) *Medical Tourism*. Cambridge, MA: CABI.

Cottingham, J., E. Kismodi, A.M. Hilber, et al. (2010),'Using Human Rights for Sexual and Reproductive Health: Improving Legal and Regulatory Frameworks',

Bulletin of the World Health Organization, 88: 551–555. www.who.int/bulletin/volumes/88/7/09–063412/en/ (accessed 21 August 2018).

Czapka, E.A. and M. Sagbakken (2016) '"Where to Find Those Doctors?" A Qualitative Study on Barriers and Facilitators in Access to and Utilization of Health Care Services by Polish Migrants in Norway', *BMC Health Services Research* 16: 1–14.

Faddy, M.J., M.D. Gosden, and R.G. Gosden (2018) 'A Demographic Projection of the Contribution of Assisted Reproductive Technologies to World Population Growth', *Reproductive Biomedicine Online* 36: 455–458.

Fortier, C. (2007) 'Blood, Sperm and the Embryo in Sunni Islam and in Mauritania: Milk Kinship, Descent and Medically Assisted Procreation', *Body & Society* 13 (3): 15–36.

Franklin, S. (2013) 'In Vitro Anthropos: New Conception Models for a Recursive Anthropology?' *Cambridge Anthropology* 31 (1): 3–32.

Gal, S. and G. Kligman (2000, eds) *Reproducing Gender: Politics, Publics, and Everyday Life After Socialism*. Princeton: Princeton University Press.

Ginsburg, F. and R. Rapp (1991) 'The Politics of Reproduction', *Annual Review of Anthropology* 20: 311–343.

Hasson, J., T. Tulandi, T. Shavit, T. Shaulov, E. Seccareccia, and J. Takefman (2017) 'Quality of Life of Immigrant and Non-Immigrant Infertile Patients in a Publicly Funded in Vitro Fertilisation Program: A Cross-Sectional Study', *BJOG* 124 (12): 1841–1847.

Hirvonen, E. (2017) 'Polish Abortion Tourism'. Laurea University of Applied Sciences (Masters thesis).

Iglicka, K. (2011) 'Migracje długookresowe i osiedleńcze z Polski po 2004 roku – przykład Wielkiej Brytanii. Wyzwania dla statystyki i demografii państwa', *Raporty i analizy*. Centrum Stosunków Międzynarodowych 5 1–19.

Iglicka-Okólska, K. (2014) 'Jak dzieci, to tylko na emigracji', *Rzeczpospolita* 14 March 2014. https://archiwum.rp.pl/artykul/1235839-Jak-dzieci-to-tylko-na-emigracji.html (accessed 1 September 2018).

Inhorn, M. and P. Pasquale (2009) 'Rethinking Reproductive "Tourism" as Reproductive "Exile"', *Fertility and Sterility* 92 (3): 904–906.

Janta, B. (2013) 'Polish Migrants' Reproductive Behaviour in the United Kingdom', *Studia Migracyjne – Przegląd Polonijny* 39 (3): 63–96.

Kangas, B. (2010) 'Traveling for Medical Care in a Global World', *Medical Anthropology: Cross-Cultural Studies in Health and Illness* 29 (4): 344–362.

Kramer, A.-M. (2007) 'The Abortion Debate in Poland: Opinion Polls, Ideological Politics, Citizenship and the Erasure of Gender as a Category of Analysis'. In: J.E. Johnson and J.C. Robinson (eds) *Living Gender after Communism*. Bloomington: Indiana University Press, pp. 63–79.

Kramer, A.-M. (2010) 'Defending Biomedical Authority and Regulating the Womb as Social Space: Prenatal Testing in the Polish Press', *European Journal of Women's Studies* 17 (1): 43–59.

Main, I. (2014) 'Medical Travels of Polish Female Migrants in Europe', *Sociologický časopis/Czech Sociological Review* 50 (6): 897–918.

Main, I. (2015) 'Giving Birth in Berlin: Reproductive Experiences of Polish Migrant Women'. In: H. Cervinkova, M. Buchowski, and Z. Uherek (eds) *Rethinking Ethnography in Central Europe*. New York: Palgrave Macmillan, pp. 89–111.

Main, I. (2018) *Lepsze Światy Medyczne? Zdrowie, Choroba i Leczenie Polskich Migrantek w Perspektywie Antropologicznej*. Warszawa: Wydawnictwo Naukowe Scholar.

Marcus, G. (1995) 'Ethnography in/of the World System: The Emergence of Multi-Sited Ethnography', *Annual Review of Anthropology* 24: 95–117.

Mishtal, J. (2012) 'Irrational Non-Reproduction? The 'Dying Nation' and the Post-socialist Logics of Declining Motherhood in Poland', *Anthropology & Medicine* 19 (2): 153–169.

Mishtal, J. (2015) *The Politics of Morality. The Church, the State, and Reproductive Rights in Postsocialist Poland*. Athens, GA: Ohio University Press.

Morgan, L.M. and E.F.S. Roberts (2012) 'Reproductive Governance in Latin America', *Anthropology & Medicine* 19 (2): 241–254.

Naleśnik, M. (2017) 'Bóg się Rodził, a Polki Jechały za Granicę Usuwać Ciążę. Byliśmy tam z Ukrytą Kamerą' https://wiadomosci.wp.pl/bog-sie-rodzil-a-polki-jechaly-za-granice-usuwac-ciaze-bylismy-tam-z-ukryta-kamera-6200713765967489a (accessed 1 September 2018).

Odrowąż-Coates, A., M. Kwiatkowski, and M. Korczyński (2014) 'The Advantages and Drawbacks of Polish Migration Post Poland's Accession to the EU – Diversity, Social Trust and Learning Curve', *Kultura i polityka* 15: 32–47.

Okólski, M. (2012) *European Immigrations: Trends, Structures and Policy Implications*. Amsterdam: Amsterdam University Press.

Präg, P. and M.C. Mills (2017) 'Assisted Reproductive Technology in Europe: Usage and Regulation in the Context of Cross-Border Reproductive Care'. In: M. Kreyenfeld and D. Konietzka (eds) *Childlessness in Europe: Contexts, Causes, and Consequences*. Cham: Springer International Publishing, pp. 289–309.

Radkowska-Walkowicz, M. (2018) 'How the Political Becomes Private: In Vitro Fertilization and the Catholic Church in Poland', *Journal of Religion and Health* 57 (3): 979–993.

Różyńska, J. (2008) *Od Zygoty do Osoby. Potencjalność, Identyczność i Przerywanie Ciąży*. Gdańsk: wydawnictwo słowo/obraz terytoria.

Salganicoff, A., R. Usha, and R. Wyn (2005) *Women and Health Care: A National Profile. Key Findings From Kaiser Women's Health Survey*. Washington, DC: Kaiser Family Foundation.

Slany, K., M. Ślusarczyk, P. Pustułka, and E. Guribye (2018, eds) *Transnational Polish Families in Norway. Social Capital, Integration, Institutions and Care*. Peter Lang: Frankfurt am Main.

Snochowska-Gonzalez, C. (2016) 'Pociągiem po Aborcję: Ciocia Basia Pomoże w Zorganizowaniu Bezpiecznego Zabiegu w Berlinie', *Wysokie obcasy*, 24 July 2016. www.wysokieobcasy.pl/wysokie-obcasy/1,114757,20432960,pociagiem-po-aborcje-kazdy-moze-zadzwonic-do-cioci-basi-i-uzyskac.html (accessed 21 August 2018).

Stan, S. (2015) 'Transnational Healthcare Practices of Romanian Migrants in Ireland: Inequalities of Access and the Privatisation of Healthcare Services in Europe', *Social Science and Medicine* 124: 346–355.

Sundby, J. (2010) 'Infertility in public health: the case of Norway', Facts, Views & Vision, *ObGyn* 2 (3): 177–181.

Szczerbiak, A. (2018) 'Już 10 Miast i Jedno Województwo Refunduje w Polsce Zabiegi in Vitro', *Polityka*, 2 July 2018. /www.polityka.pl/tygodnikpolityka/twojemiasto/1754466,1,juz-10-miast-i-jedno-wojewodztwo-refunduje-w-polsce-zabiegi-in-vitro.read (accessed 21 August 2018).

Święchowicz, M. (2014) 'Turystyka Aborcyjna Kwitnie. Polki Masowo Przerywają Ciążę za Granicą', *Newsweek*, 28 January 2014. www.newsweek.pl/polska/aborcja-za-granica-dlaczego-polki-przerywaja-ciaze-za-granica-,artykuly,278162,1.html (accessed 21 August 2018).

Święchowicz, M. (2017) 'W najnowszym „Newsweeku". Bezpowrotni. Wrócili z Emigracji do Polski, ale Szybko Ponownie Wyjechali, bo to Już nie Był ich Kraj', *Newsweek*, 15 October 2017. ww.newsweek.pl/polska/spoleczenstwo/emigracja-z-polski-liczba-polakow-wracajacych-do-kraju-,artykuly,417513,1.html (accessed 21 August 2018).

Wejbert-Wąsiewicz, E. (2012) *Aborcja w Dyskursie Publicznym. Monografia Zjawiska.* Łódź: Wydawnictwo Uniwersytetu Łódzkiego.

Węgrzynowska, M. (2016) 'Transnational Healthcare Practices in the Enlarged Europe: The Case of Polish Migrant Women in Ireland and Their Pregnancy and Childbirth Practices'. Dublin City University (doctoral dissertation).

White, A. (2011) *Polish Families and Migration since EU Accession.* Bristol: The Policy Press.

Whittaker, A. and A. Speier (2010) '"Cycling Overseas": Care, Commodification and Stratification in Cross-border Reproductive Travel', *Medical Anthropology: Cross-cultural Studies in Health and Illness* 29 (4): 363–383.

Wielowieyska, D. (2014) 'Polki na Wyspach Chętniej Rodzą Dzieci niż w Kraju? To mit. Ale są Najdzietniejsze Spośród Imigrantek', *Gazeta Wyborcza*, 6 February 2014. http://wyborcza.pl/1,76842,15413232,Polki_na_Wyspach_chetniej_rodza_dzieci_niz_w_kraju_.html (accessed 21 August 2018).

Zielińska, E. (2010) 'Between Ideology, Politics, and Common Sense: The Discourse of Reproductive Rights in Poland'. In: S. Gal and G. Kligman (eds) *Reproducing Gender. Politics, Publics, and Everyday Life after Socialism.* Princeton: Princeton University Press, pp. 23–57.

Webpages

www.sims.ie/treatments/intracytoplasmic-sperm-injection-icsi.1040.html (accessed 8 October 2020)

www.nasz-bocian.pl/stowarzyszenie (accessed 8 October 2020)

www.chcemybycrodzicami.pl/ile-kosztuje-in-vitro-w-polsce-cennik-vs-rzeczywistosc/ (accessed 8 October 2020)

www.powroty.gov.pl (accessed 8 October 2020)

Part III

Shifting gendered policies: reproduction and care in national and historical perspectives

10

Children of the state? The role of pronatalism in the development of Czech childcare and reproductive health policies

Hana Hašková and Radka Dudová

Introduction

Human reproduction has been discussed by experts and policymakers in Czechoslovakia since its foundation as an independent state in 1918. Despite the continuity of policy and expert discourse (Rákosník and Šustrová 2016), the period following 1948, when the Communist Party became the leading party, differed from the previous era. After the Second World War and the expulsion of ethnic Germans from Czechoslovakia in 1945 and 1946, Czechoslovakia's total population decreased by more than three million. In this context, consideration was given to taking policy steps to support increased reproduction rates. However, only a limited range of actors were permitted to speak, and only some arguments could be used; not everyone was considered to constitute the nation and its 'quality population'. This chapter highlights the role of the pronatalist framing in policy formation and argues that since the 1950s, this framing has been constantly activated to increase the salience of the problems and thus carry out policy changes. While the pronatalist framing has sometimes been instrumental in achieving certain feminist goals, it has also strengthened the heteronormative norm to reproduce. We show how, in conjunction with nationalism, heteronormativity, and belief in the biological basis of separate gender roles, the norm to reproduce has never been applied universally; it has been used to categorise 'others' whose reproduction is labelled 'undesirable'.

In this chapter, we analyse three important Czech debates from both a historical and present-day perspective: the debate on abortion, the debate on childcare, and the debate on assisted reproductive technologies (ARTs). We trace the framings that were used at different points in time by different actors in public debates, paying special attention to pronatalist framing. We understand framing as a way in which information or an issue is presented in the public discourse to promote a certain problem, definition, or solution. We investigate how the pronatalist framing has been used in policy debates and how it has affected the bodily and sexual citizenship of various women, non-heterosexual people, and persons with 'other' nationalities or ethnicities. In the context of this book (see Pine and Haukanes, Chapter 1, this volume), we seek to shed light on the practices of bordering and boundary work within a particular care regime and a moral economy to contribute to the understanding of gendered and sexualised classifications and the ordering of space and relations through which deserving persons, practices, and ways of life are defined.

Theoretical background: biopower, biopolitics, and population concerns

Michel Foucault developed the concept of 'biopower' (Foucault 2004), linking it to the rise of nation-states in the eighteenth century. States developed a vested interest in the bodies of their citizens for demographic, military, public health, and eugenic reasons. Biopower is a normalising power; its objective is to ensure the preservation and reinforcement of a social system against 'non-normal' or potentially dangerous individuals (see Outshoorn et al. 2015). It is concerned with the species-body that is affected by various interventions and regulatory controls, which Foucault summarily refers to as the 'biopolitics of the population' (Foucault 1980: 139). Biopolitics and its instruments have been present in all types of regimes since the end of the eighteenth century, and significant continuity in the policies have occurred from one regime to the next. However, the limited discursive field and the ever-present coercive power have made aspects of biopower particularly visible in state-socialist systems (Heitlinger 1987, Dudová 2012).

Most instruments of biopolitics (including regulations, campaigns, and the attention of experts) have targeted women and their bodies. The fact that women are considered responsible for the reproduction of the national body legitimated their exclusion from many rights, such as the right to control one's body and sexuality (Orloff 1993).

Pronatalism can be defined as an ideological and political project that aims to encourage childbearing by some or all female members of a collectivity. It is based on the assumption of insufficient population size or growth that is putting the population at risk. Studies focusing on pronatalism from a historical perspective (e.g. Hoffmann 2000, Camiscioli 2001, Brown and Ferree 2005) point to its connection with nationalist ideology, in which the objective is to support the fertility rate among members of a particular national community (defined by the borders of the state, a shared culture/

language or origin), usually on the foundation of traditional patriarchal ideology (Yuval-Davis 1998). Pronatalism is often advanced in response to fears of immigration, especially of ethnically different migrants. The national body is perceived as endangered because it is not sufficiently reproducing itself and is thus 'dying out' or at risk of being engulfed by those who are 'different'. As it is women who give birth to children, women are viewed as responsible for the nation's biological reproduction; therefore, it is they who are the targets of pronatalist policies. These policies usually include allowances for maternity leave and care facilities, the availability of contraception (and encouragement of its use), access to abortion, clinics that provide infertility treatment, and, sometimes, forced sterilisation (Yuval-Davis 1998). However, these policies are not applied to all women in the same way. There are differences according to women's membership in different racial, ethnic, and national collectivities (Yuval-Davis 1998: 27). 'Arguments about who is entitled to reproduce the group and how that is to be done express conflict over what the authentic group is, who can claim membership, and what its future will be' (Brown and Ferree 2005: 8).

While the relationship between nationalism and pronatalism is evident, the relationship between feminism and pronatalism is rather ambivalent. As Jessica A. Brown and Myra Marx Ferree put it, on the one hand, feminism rejects the conflation of a woman's personhood with motherhood and calls for a wider range of options in women's lives. On the other hand, feminist support for women who are struggling to raise children in difficult conditions may welcome some pronatalist policies as being 'pro-woman'. 'When and how pronatalism is good for women remains an open question' (Brown and Ferree 2005: 5). Pronatalist programmes are relevant to women, as they often include measures to limit or expand access to contraceptives or abortion, affect women's economic status through care allowances and subsidised childcare, influence gender roles by promoting particular family forms, and influence women's access to ARTs.

Reproductive and care policies are the results of debates and negotiations among many actors who use various framings and discourses aimed at promoting their own definitions of problems and ways of solving such problems. The state is not a 'unitary character' with 'rational planning and coherent intentions' (Rivkin-Fish 2010). Change or continuity in institutions and policies can be explained by the ways in which ideas are generated by policy actors and communicated to the public (Schmidt 2010: 15).

Policy debates emerge out of certain discourses; thus, they have certain framings. According to Fairclough (1992: 28), discourse can be defined as 'language in use, whether speech or writing, seen as a type of social practice'. Data and information in a particular discourse are grouped together under the heading of one subsuming category, a larger 'frame' that provides them with a recognisable structure and meaning. This frame works as a guide for what is to be understood in the discourse. Once a frame is elicited, data or elements that are difficult to fit will be adapted or selectively excluded. Framing is understood as the activity of selecting some aspects of a perceived reality and making them more salient in a communicating text in such a way as to promote a particular problem definition, causal interpretation, moral evaluation, and/or treatment recommendation (Entman 1993: 52).

Our aim is to examine the role of pronatalism and concerns about low fertility in the development of Czech childcare and reproductive health policies. For this purpose, we need to uncover the discourse that has accompanied the development of these policies in Czechia since 1955 and show which frames were used in the public debates and how they competed or allied. In order to do this, we use the approach described by Paolo R. Donati (1992) as *political discourse analysis* and by Snow and Bedford (1988) as *framing analysis*. In our previous studies (Hašková, Maříková, and Uhde 2009, Dudová 2010, 2012, Hašková and Saxonberg 2016, Hašková and Dudová 2017), we analysed documents dating from the 1950s that are related to abortion and childcare. For the purpose of this study, we also focus on artificial reproductive technologies (see also Hašková and Sloboda 2018). The empirical base included laws and legal regulations; parliamentary debates; newspaper and journal articles; interviews with stakeholders; social science articles (demographic, sociological, and psychological); medical materials and articles; feminist and women's groups' materials; and other interest groups' materials. The arguments used in the texts were identified, coded, and grouped into categories through comparisons on multiple levels (intratextual and intertextual comparisons, comparisons of different types of texts, comparisons of texts of different authors, etc.) until several 'systems' of argumentation (i.e. framings) emerged. We specified each framing's main characteristics and arguments, and we checked by whom they were used. We also paid attention to the relationships between framings – for instance, their alignments and resonance (with other framings within the same text and the framings of other actors).

The Czech history of pronatalism in reproductive and care policies

During the nineteenth and twentieth centuries, concerns about nations 'dying out' could be found in the United States as well as every country in Europe. From the very founding of Czechoslovakia in 1918, experts emphasised the need to create a population plan, of which the objectives were to limit 'the (excess) procreation of less valuable individuals' and combat 'genetic degeneration' (Rákosník and Šustrová 2016: 18). Specific measures, however, were only taken after 1948 when the Communist Party seized power and especially in the second half of the 1950s. In 1957, the State Population Commission in Czechoslovakia was established to address the problem of low fertility, as the fertility rate had begun to decline. Resolving the problem of insufficient population growth was also intended to tackle the 'population explosion' among inhabitants of so-called Gypsy origin (Rákosník and Šustrová 2016: 142). Alongside these debates, concern was voiced over the degree to which the high employment rate among women of reproductive age was preventing demographic growth. Below, we focus on three areas of state policy related to reproduction and analyse the framings that accompany them. We are especially interested in the relationship between the pronatalist framing and the women's rights framing. We seek to show the degree to which these two framings were allied and where they came into conflict, as well as the consequences that the continued presence and emphasis of a pronatalist framing have on the formation of reproductive and care policies in Czech context today. We also look at those who were and continue to be excluded from these policies and the boundaries that such exclusions reinforce or create.

The issue of abortion

In 1957, abortion was legalised in Czechoslovakia under specific conditions (including social reasons), and special commissions were endowed with the authority to decide whether or not to grant women permission to have abortions. This permission depended on whether the reasons given by the woman were in accordance with the conditions stipulated by the law. The commission consisted of the hospital director, one doctor-gynaecologist, and an 'experienced woman enjoying confidence and reputation of the people'. In the public discussion leading up to the adoption of the act on the induced termination of pregnancy in 1957, the main participants were doctors – primarily gynaecologists – and most of the arguments used were medical (Dudová 2010).

Paradoxically, the legalisation of abortion was interpreted as a pro-population measure; the reproductive health of women would be saved by legal, hospital-performed abortions so that those women would be able to have children later in life. Legal and safe abortion was considered to be justified for women in difficult social situations that prevented them from caring properly for children. The 'healthier motherhood' frame resonated strongly with other frames, in particular the 'population' frame advanced by demographers, planners, and politicians (see also Dudová 2010). This 'population' frame encompassed concerns about both quantity and 'quality'.

It was assumed that not only would the law improve the 'quality' of the population (as women would have only those children they would be able to care for properly), but in the end it would also lead to further population growth, as safe abortions would improve the reproductive health of women. This is conveyed through the following quote: 'criminal law is not the right and appropriate measure for population growth, but on the contrary, it acts quite the opposite and drives pregnant women into the hands of bunglers and horse doctors, who by force of unskilled and unhygienic interventions induce serious injuries on the health of our women' (Šťastná, a member of Parliament, in parliamentary debate about the law 68/1957 on 19 December 1957; authors' translation). Abortion was therefore not presented as a means of women's emancipation (even though a few small voices tried to put it this way); rather, it served to bind women even more tightly to their 'natural vocation' of motherhood (Dudová 2010).

Over the next 30 years, the legislation did not change significantly; however, it was repeatedly amended by the Ministry of Health, depending on Czechoslovakia's demographic and economic situation. When fertility rates declined in the 1960s, the access of married women with fewer than two children to abortion was restricted. Abortion regulations were tightened again in 1973, reflecting the societal atmosphere after the invasion by Warsaw Pact troops in 1968 to stop democratisation forces in the country. Recommendations were issued that abortion commissions be stricter in their decisions, especially in cases of women without children or with just one child who requested an abortion for social reasons. This move was justified in the media as a measure to improve population quantity and 'quality'. A more liberal attitude was recommended in the decision-making regarding abortion for parents suffering from some genetic disease or of foetuses with some kind of malformation 'in order to prevent the formation of a "low quality" population' (Zajíček 1973: 20).

By the end of the 1970s, the abortion commissions were facing considerable criticism. This was due to two events. The first was the invention of early uterine evacuation, which involves a vacuum extraction of the inside of the uterus in the early pregnancy stage (up to 6–8 weeks of pregnancy). The negative health consequences of this abortion method are minimal. The second event was the publication of a study of 'unwanted' children, which confirmed the psychological damage of an unwanted pregnancy on children born out of such a pregnancy (see Matějček, Dytrych, and Schüller 1976). The following debate, led by experts in gynaecology and obstetrics, psychology, psychiatry, and demography, led to the introduction of a new act on induced termination of pregnancy in July 1987. After this legislation was introduced, abortion could be granted in response to a written request by the pregnant woman as long as the duration of the pregnancy did not exceed 12 weeks. This legislation still applies today.

The doctors argued that early uterine evacuation was a significantly better option for the preservation of the woman's reproductive health; however, the long process of approving applications for abortion meant that this safer and lower-cost method could not be used. Moreover, with the popularisation of the study of unwanted children, it became clear that children from unwanted pregnancies do not necessarily fit the definition of a 'healthy and "quality" population'. The interests of the children and their psychological wellbeing were presented together with the best interests of society (which was equated with a healthy and 'quality' population) (e.g. Birgus 1979).

In expert discourse, women were objects of care and control, not subjects. While some women (young, majority population, and married, with fewer than three children) were discouraged from having an abortion, in the case of others, abortion was considered the best solution. These were mothers who lived in poverty and were unable to care properly for their children. Roma mothers were explicitly mentioned in a number of texts and associated with these characteristics. Ján Sojka (1966), in an article in the popular journal *Vlasta*, enumerated the issues connected with Roma families, concluding, 'Socialist solution of this issue is not suppression of the so-called unclean race, but respecting current knowledge in genetics, biology and social sciences, and trying ... to create such conditions that physically and mentally healthy individuals are born, capable of full, free and active participation in the life' (authors' translation).

After 1970, the focus shifted from attempting to 're-educate' Roma mothers to influencing their fertility. The methods used for this ranged from information campaigns about contraception, via the granting of financial subsidies to Roma women who decided to undergo sterilisation and facilitation of Roma women's access to abortion, to performing sterilisation without the woman's consent or obtaining consent by threatening the woman and/or providing her with incomplete information (Dudová 2012).

After 1989, with the emergence of civil society, space opened up for framing abortion in feminist discourse as a basic right for women; however, space also opened up for the rejection of abortion on religious grounds. Despite several post-1989 religiously grounded attacks, the law from 1986 is still valid in 2019. The petition drawn up by Czech feminist NGOs[1] as a reaction to proposed restrictive legislation in 2003 did not use any feminist arguments. It pointed out the health risks of illegal abortion and argued that banning abortion would not lead to a higher fertility rate. It suggested educating people on reproductive rights and responsibilities and introducing work–life balance policies and family support instead.

Thus, abortion was still prevailingly framed in medical terms; emphasis was placed on the health of mothers, combined with a focus on the 'quality' and quantity of the population. Given that abortion in the Czech context has never been framed and interpreted in terms of human or women's rights, it proved impossible to widen the discussion about abortion to encompass the rights of all women, not only those whose future reproductive health required protection to serve the country. This became manifest in a discussion in late 2008 about extending the right to abortion to 'foreigners'. Women without permanent residence status remain excluded from access to abortion, which limits the rights of the most vulnerable immigrants (Dudová 2010).

The issue of childcare

Pronatalism has also played a significant role in the development of childcare policies in Czechoslovakia. Childcare facilities and other family measures were originally introduced for children from poor families in the nineteenth century. In the 1950s, they were intended to restructure the Czechoslovak economy by increasing the number of employed women due to the acute postwar need for labour and the ideology of women's emancipation through their economic independence from men. From the 1960s to the end of the state-socialist period, however, family measures primarily sought to promote fertility (Hašková, Maříková, and Uhde 2009).

In the 1960s, the economies throughout the Soviet bloc stagnated, fertility continued to decline much more quickly than in the West, and criticism of the 1950s family policies increased. Psychologists and paediatricians debated the low quality of care and the high illness rates in overcrowded nurseries (e.g. Damborská 1957, Langmeier and Matějček 1963, Dunovský and Suchá 1963, 1967, Dunovský 1971).

According to one study:

> the costs of a single place in a nursery are high and sometimes exceed the contribution of the woman-mother of a child in such a facility ... There is growing distrust in the real purpose of these facilities. Criticism of them is strengthening, annoyance increasing, and a completely disapproving view of the entire concept of such facilities is taking shape (Srb and Kučera 1959: 115; authors' translation).

> One of the main problems children face in nurseries is a higher illness rate than children cared for at home. (Bařinová 1965: 11; authors' translation)

> The average length of time a child spends in a nursery is almost 9 hours a day. With the 12 hours of sleep they need and an average of 40 (2 × 20) minutes commuting, precious little time is left for the family. (Dunovský and Suchá 1967: 20; authors' translation)

Demographers became alarmed at the declining birth rates, which they claimed resulted from the economic difficulties and the burden on mother-workers (Bartošová 1978). Consequently, in the early 1960s, the State

Population Commission proposed measures to increase fertility and improve the quality of childcare. However, most of these measures were not introduced until the 1970s. At that time, in the name of increasing fertility and the 'quality' of the population, many gender-specific promaternity provisions were introduced that cemented the role of women as mothers (Havelková 2014). During the 1970s and 1980s, among other measures introduced in Czechoslovakia, a maternity allowance for full-time mothers was introduced, and the so-called extended maternity leave was expanded to two and then three years. It was assumed that despite the decline in women's employment this measure was expected to bring, it would benefit Czechoslovakia both demographically and economically because mothers would be less burdened and thus opt to have more children, children would be healthier, the unmet demand on nurseries would be lower, and mothers' sudden absences from their workplaces due to sick children would be a less common occurrence (Hašková, Maříková, and Uhde 2009). Because the maternity allowance was originally intended for families who had at least two dependent children, this measure was intended to motivate mothers to quickly give birth to a second child (Hašková, Maříková, and Uhde 2009).

Fears of a decreasing and 'since childhood psychologically deprived' population increased the salience of problems defined by psychologists, paediatricians, and economists. Their arguments resonated with each other in terms of the proposed solution to these problems. That solution was the introduction of extended maternity leave, accompanied by maternity allowance payments. This solution also resonated well with the gender conservative attitudes of the population (Hašková and Dudová 2017). Extended maternity leave was introduced in the 1960s, and the payment of maternity allowance up to a child's first birthday was introduced in the early 1970s, when fertility in Czechoslovakia was low compared to Western countries (and among the lowest in the socialist states). The further extension of leave and allowance until a child reached the age of 3 was brought in at a time when fertility in Czechoslovakia was higher than that in most other European countries. Since fertility increased in the 1970s, it was argued that additional paid extended maternity leave would further support the quantity and wellbeing of the future population (Hašková, Maříková, and Uhde 2009).

After 1989, Czech childcare policy exhibited a great deal of continuity (Hašková and Saxonberg 2016). Although the 1990s saw a drop in fertility from almost two children per woman to fewer than 1.2 children per woman (i.e. the lowest fertility rate that the country had ever experienced), interestingly (and in contrast to other postsocialist countries), the pronatalist framing was not reactivated (Hašková and Dudová 2017). Instead, the post-1989 drop in fertility was interpreted as the 'free choice' of young people to postpone parenthood in order to invest in their career and personal pursuits that their parents had been denied. The postponement of childbearing to a later age was interpreted as a sign of responsibility (supported by an increase in the use of modern contraception and a decrease in the number of abortions on request) and alignment with Western European 'mental structures' (Rabušic 2001).

It was only in the new millennium that the parental allowance (previously 'maternity allowance') was made more flexible so that there were fewer disincentives to returning to work or having another child before the (previous) child was 3 years old. However, this flexibility, introduced in 2008, was only opened to families in which the mother or father earned an income exceeding the threshold of 16 500 Kč per month, representing approximately 80% of the median of wages in the Czech Republic. This separated those who should be supported to have more children (and work–life balance opportunities) from those who remained excluded from this flexible option, namely the poor and unemployed. In Czechia, this primarily meant solo and Roma mothers (e.g. Pulkrábková 2009, Czech Statistical Office 2019).

The pronatalist framing of childcare policies surfaced again in the negotiations over the Family Policy Strategy adopted in 2017, which defines the direction that family policy should take over the next few years. This strategy was introduced by a minister who is a feminist herself. During the governmental negotiations, the gender equality framing and even measures in support of gender equality were reduced to achieve consensus across the coalition parties.[2] Instead, the investment-economic framing and the pronatalist framing gained importance. While gender equality was no longer among the main goals of the strategy, higher birth rates did remain one of its main goals. A number of legislative proposals that feminist organisations had long been calling for were included in the strategy and supported by pronatalist arguments, which resonated better with the views in the government coalition. For example, a proposed three-month gender equality bonus in parental leave, which was intended to support both parents sharing parental leave, was argued for on the grounds that it would 'have a positive effect on increasing birth rates'.[3] Additionally, a set of proposals to increase the availability and affordability of childcare for children aged 0–6 years was presented as a remedy against 'low birth rates, and the decreasing number of second or more children in families'.[4]

The issues of ARTs and prenatal screening

Prenatal screening represents a set of medical procedures that have been widely accessible to Czech women since the 1970s. The concern with a 'quality population', expressed in the politics of abortion and childcare, grew stronger with the advances made in genetics, which fuelled eugenic thinking in state-socialist Czechoslovakia (Prajerová 2018b). The prenatal screening of genetic problems (and abortion in cases of positive results) was to be used in the state-socialist period as a tool to 'improve the gene pool of the population' (Černý 1971: 120) and to minimise the number of children that would be born with a life-incompatible defect and thus negatively influence perinatal mortality statistics. In 1971, demographer Miloš Černý called for 'the registration of families with the incidence of unwanted genetically determined indices and the use of the methods of fertility regulation', the 'identification of carriers' and the introduction of the 'choice for a healthy child' (Černý 1971: 118) method, a label for terminating a pregnancy when the foetus is not completely healthy. Even today, undergoing prenatal screening is typically the norm in Czechia, and women who decide not to do so face negative reactions from others (Hasmanová Marhánková 2008).

ARTs represent another type of scientific knowledge applied to (mainly women's) bodies. Assisted reproduction (AR) empowers individuals by increasing the range of reproductive options available to them, but it also increases women's moral responsibility to become mothers (Nash 2014). In 1971, Miloš Černý was already suggesting in the journal *Czechoslovak Gynecology* that AR should be used as a means of 'increasing the fertility of healthy families' (Černý 1971: 120).

The earliest regulation for ARTs in the Czech context was introduced in 1982. This initial measure was concerned with in vitro fertilisation (IVF) using the semen of the woman's husband or a donor. The procedure could only be performed at the request of both spouses. IVF was allowed only for health reasons, which included infertility or a genetic disease. The treatment was recommended for women up to the age of 35. A fee of 500 Czechoslovak Crowns was to be paid by the couple, which was a large expense for low-income families.[5] The next regulation, which was not enacted until 1997, stipulated that the treatment (three cycles with embryo transfer) was to be covered by the national health insurance system for women aged 18–38 years.

Discussions began for a more complex project to regulate AR in 2008; this project aimed to reform the healthcare sector. It assumed the right of single women to request IVF. This feature sparked extremely negative reactions, mainly from the conservative Christian-Democratic Party. Another version of this law was passed in 2011; however, provisions to allow women without a male partner to have access to AR were not included. This means that all women with a heterosexual partner (only married couples until 2006) have access to AR, and the first three cycles of IVF treatment are partly covered by health insurance for women aged under 39. The maximum age limit for treatment is 49 years, and women without a male partner are denied treatment completely.

The discussion on allowing women without a male partner access to AR was revived with discussions about the Family Policy Strategy adopted in 2017. In addition to granting single women access to AR, the strategy proposed raising the limit for women to receive AR cycles partially covered by health insurance up to 43 years of age and to increase the number of IVF cycles covered to four cycles per wanted child (not per woman).[6] Since AR was one of the most contested issues during the coalition government negotiations about the Family Policy Strategy, this set of proposals did not make it into the final version of the strategy.[7]

Advocates for increasing the age limit until which women can use AR covered by health insurance and increasing the number of insured IVF cycles, argued that the majority of Czech families favour having two children, but the current age and insurance limits mean that they are not able to do so. The pronatalist framing was thus activated. Emphasis was placed on the low fertility rate, population ageing, and unfulfilled reproductive plans. Those who proposed allowing women without a male partner to use ART also stressed that this measure would support fertility: 'Granting women access to assisted reproduction without the consent of a partner would rank the Czech Republic in the group of European countries that … have issued a positive signal in support of fertility' (authors' translation).[8] The issue of people travelling from abroad to Czech clinics for AR, contributing to stratified reproduction, did not appear in the debate.

While the strategy proposed expanding access to AR as one road to increasing fertility, the following statements illustrate opinions that were behind the opposition to the strategy's proposals:

> measures that involve raising the age to 43 years will not in any way support fertility … but will on the contrary encourage couples to put off natural conception (or AR) to an age at which they have minimal chances of carrying a healthy child to term. (authors' translation)[9]

> While older women can conceive and give birth at increased risk, they may not be able to take care of the child. (authors' translation)[10]

Those who opposed allowing women without a male partner to use ART also underlined the risks to the child's development and the creation of dysfunctional (read: non-heteronormative) families. They warned against encouraging 'the emergence of (poor) single-parent families' and 'eliminating men from reproduction' while stressing the importance of both a mother and a father in a family for the healthy development of children and thus for a 'quality' self-reproducing population.[11] Within this heteronormative ideology, the use of AR is defined as helping nature in cases of infertile heterosexual couples; however, it is considered to contradict 'nature' in cases of single individuals and non-heterosexual couples.

Discussion and conclusion

Our analysis has explored the ways in which pronatalism has influenced the formation of reproductive and care policies in Czechia. The pronatalist framing was activated in the construction of reproductive and care policies regardless of whether it was during the formation of Czechoslovakia between the two world wars, during the state-socialist regime, or after 1989.

We have shown that the pronatalist framing has been selective and nationalistic. In the case of abortion policy, policies regulating the use of ART, and care policies, pronatalist framing divides people into those whose reproduction is defined as desirable for the state and who thus deserve support from public sources (the young, able-bodied, heterosexual, coupled, and sufficiently educated) and others, referred to by Prajerová (2018a: 192) as the 'bio-underclass'. These 'others' are defined by their lack of such attributes, their foreign nationality (lack of citizenship status), or their unsatisfactory hygiene, health, or lifestyle, the latter often acting as a proxy for Roma ethnicity. The 'bio-underclass' (partly) corresponds to 'dangerous classes', a concept that Pine and Haukanes refer to in Chapter 1 when highlighting the interconnectedness of the practices of rebuilding geographic, political, and symbolic borders through the processes of exclusion, inclusion, and regulation of persons – especially migrants and particular types of 'failed' citizens.

Through its emphasis on the quantity and 'quality' of the population, pronatalism has always defended support for fertility while defining the limits of that support (and thus has always been selective). The main motivation for these limits has not been for the rational allocation of public resources but the interest in protecting society's dominant values – mainly heteronormativity, ethnic and national belonging, and norms of reproduction. Reproductive and care policies formulated within the pronatalist framing have thus been used both to support the reproduction of 'valuable citizens' and to limit the reproduction of 'the less valued', via the same tools – abortion, childcare support, preventive prenatal screening, and access to ART.

Abortion was made legal for women in Czechoslovakia to advance the goal of responsible motherhood and a 'quality' future population. It was intended to protect the reproductive health of young women so that they could go on to become responsible mothers (and produce 'better citizens') several years later when their partnership or socio-economic situation conformed more closely to the normative idea of a responsible parent. At the same time, abortions were recommended and sometimes forced in an authoritarian manner on an ethnically defined group of women who did not correspond to the normative idea of responsible parenthood and a 'quality' population.

Similarly, maternity allowance for families with at least two dependent children was introduced in the 1970s as one measure taken in an explicitly pronatalist programme to increase fertility and the 'quality' of the population by providing an incentive to have a second child (or more children) soon after the first. The allowance would work by postponing the point at which children started attending the increasingly criticised nursery and by not awarding support to parents with only one child. The recent increase in the flexibility of the parental allowance supports the earlier birth of a second child and more opportunities to combine work and care (explicitly in order to support fertility by making the conditions for being a parent easier) only to those with higher incomes; however, Roma and solo mothers remain implicitly excluded from this support. Childcare benefits and services thus delineate how many children one should have, and when, and how a gendered person should care for them.

The introduction of prenatal screening and AR was also framed as a means of improving the population and enhancing the fertility of some groups of citizens – heterosexual, coupled, and within a certain age range (not only because ART success rates decline with increasing age but also explicitly in order to ensure quality childcare).

Pronatalism is applied to enhance the demographic and economic sustainability of a community, nation, or state by means of its internal reproduction and control. Control is imposed by policy measures, welfare monetary support, and legal limits, but also by expert knowledge appropriated by popular media promoting 'responsible parenthood'. The objectives of the pronatalist framing are self-disciplined, gendered, and sexualised citizens who make responsible reproductive choices and 'perfect babies' who will grow into able-bodied, heterosexual, coupled, and educated people who will also make responsible reproductive choices.

The pronatalist framing presents itself as resting on statistical evidence of decreasing, low, or insufficiently rising fertility. Our analysis, however, showed that how the situation at a given time is defined has been more important for determining policies than the actual birth rate (trend) itself. Childcare policies were reformulated in the name of increasing fertility in the 1970s when fertility was high in Czechoslovakia. In contrast, when fertility fell to a historical minimum in Czechia in the 1990s, this did not have the effect of activating the pronatalist framing because it was overruled by the freedom of choice frame, which resonated with the transformation of society after 1989. The freedom of choice frame was backed by expert knowledge that defined low fertility as the result of the postponement of parenthood to a later age. Experts did not define such postponement as a result of socio-economic problems but rather as caused by increased study, work, and travel opportunities and increased access to quality contraceptives. This shows that although the actual birth rate plays a role in (re)shaping policies, the framing of the situation in the discourse is even more important for directing policies.

The development of abortion, childcare, and AR policies also revealed how a pronatalist framing can be employed to increase fertility in order to assert policies that have very different consequences for women, men, and gender equality. We have shown that a pronatalist framing was chosen not only to oppose expanding AR but also to argue for extending the right to AR beyond heterosexual couples. It was used to introduce measures to support mothers in staying out of the labour market longer as well as measures to help them return to paid employment earlier. Moreover, it was used when arguing for the need to establish abortion committees and when arguing for their discontinuation. This leads us to argue that the pronatalist framing was often used to increase the salience of the problem and the need for a measure to solve it, defined within other frames. However, the pronatalist framing also brought new meanings to the definition of the problem. While it has sometimes been instrumental in promoting certain measures advocated by feminists, it has always built on the gendered obligation to reproduce. Instead of gender equality, the goal is to increase birth rates by utilising women's bodies to serve the demographic and economic objectives of the state.

The high visibility of the pronatalist framing and the low visibility of the rights and equality framing in the formation of reproductive and care policies is not surprising in the state-socialist era, especially after the explicitly pronatalist programme was introduced to increase the quantity and 'quality' of the population. However, even after 1989, pronatalism has been strategically used as an ally of newly formed women's groups in the formation of reproductive and care policies, owing to the need to find a consensus across the spectrum of political actors. Our analysis showed that despite its strategic use, the pronatalist framing remains incompatible with women's full bodily citizenship. Although it has sometimes been used instrumentally to accommodate certain feminist goals, its application in policy debates has been conservative, exclusionary, and implicitly nationalist. At the end of the day, the pronatalist framing used in the debates on reproductive and care policies has intruded on the bodily and sexual citizenship of some women, LGBTQI people, and persons of marginalised ethnicities and nationalities, and it has buttressed the current limitations of human rights.

Acknowledgement

This research was funded by the Czech Science Foundation (grant number 17-04465S) and by institutional support RVO: 68378025.

Notes

1 See www.feminismus.cz/fulltext.shtml?x=162657 (accessed 12 January 2020).
2 Comparing the first version of the Family Policy Strategy from 12 October 2015 and the adopted version from 4 September 2017, published at www.mpsv.cz/strategicke-dokumenty-v-oblasti-podpory-rodiny (accessed 12 January 2020). See also Hašková and Sloboda (2018).
3 Family Policy Strategy, adopted version from 4 September 2017, p. 42.
4 Family Policy Strategy, adopted version from 4 September 2017, p. 32.
5 The average gross monthly salary as of 1982 being 2,765 Czechoslovak Crowns.
6 Family Policy Strategy, version 4.6. from 8 April 2016, p. 29.
7 Family Policy Strategy, adopted version from 4 September 2017, p. 53.
8 Family Policy Strategy, adopted version from 4 September 2017, p. 53.
9 An unpublished document titled 'An evaluation of the interdepartmental comments process' addressing the comments on the material titled *Family Policy Strategy*. This document addresses the comments on the strategy that was distributed for interdepartmental comments on 23 December 2016, see pp. 186–187.
10 See the document titled 'An evaluation of the interdepartmental comments process', p. 96.
11 See the document titled 'An evaluation of the interdepartmental comments process' (e.g. pp. 96 and 172).

References

Bartošová, M. (1978) *Populační Politika v ČSSR 1945–1975*. Prague: SPEV.
Bařinová, M. (1965) 'Rozvoj Počtu Míst v Jeslích v ČSSR', *Zprávy Státní populační komise* 1: 11.
Birgus, J. (1979) 'Několik Připomínek Porodníka k Problému Nechtěných Těhotenství', *Československá gynekologie* 44 (1): 69–76.
Brown, J.A. and M. Marx Ferree (2005) 'Close Your Eyes and Think of England: Pronatalism in the British Print Media', *Gender & Society* 19 (1): 5–24.
Camiscioli, E. (2001) 'Producing Citizens, Reproducing the "French Race": Immigration, Demography, and Pronatalism in Early Twentieth Century France', *Gender and History* 13 (3): 593–621.
Czech Statistical Office (2019) *Příjmy a Životní Podmínky Domácností*. Prague: Czech Statistical Office.
Černý, M. (1971) 'Perspektivy Uplatnění Genetiky v Populační Politice', *Demografie* 13 (2): 109–120.

Damborská, M. (1957) 'Rozdíly mezi Dětmi Vychovávanými v Rodině, v Jeslích a v Ůstavu během Jednoho Roku', Čs. *Pediatrie* (12): 980–982.

Donati, P.R. (1992) 'Political Discourse Analysis'. In: M. Diani and R. Eyerman (eds) *Studying Collective Action.* London: Sage, pp. 136–167.

Dudová, R. (2010) 'The Framing of Abortion in the Czech Republic: How the Continuity of Discourse Prevents Institutional Change', *Czech Sociological Review* 46 (6): 945–975.

Dudová, R. (2012) 'Regulation of Abortion as State-Socialist Governmentality: The Case of Czechoslovakia', *Politics & Gender* 8 (1): 123–144.

Dunovský, J. (1971) 'Mateřství Zaměstnaných Žen a Problémy Péče o jejich Děti v Nejútlejším Věku', *Sociologicky časopis* 7 (2): 153–156.

Dunovský, J. and M. Suchá (1967) 'Charakteristika Sociálních Poměrů Dětí v Jeslích', *Zprávy Státní populační komise* (6): 27P.

Entman, R.M. (1993) 'Framing: Toward Clarification of a Fractured paradigm', *Journal of Communication* 43 (4): 51–58.

Fairclough, N. (1992) 'Introduction'. In: N. Fairclough (ed.) *Critical Language Awareness.* London: Longman, pp. 1–29.

Foucault, M. (1980) *The History of Sexuality. Volume I: An Introduction.* New York: Vintage Books.

Foucault, M. (2004) *Naissance de La Biopolitique: Cours Au Collège de France. 1978–1979.* Paris: Gallimard, Hautes Études.

Hasmanová Marhánková, J. (2008) 'Konstrukce Normality, Rizika a Vědění o Těle v Těhotenství: Příklad Prenatálních Screeningů', *Biograf* 15 (47): www.biograf.org/clanky/clanek.php?clanek=v4702 (accessed 14 October 2018).

Hašková, H. and S. Saxonberg. (2016) 'The Revenge of History – The Institutional Roots of Post-Communist Family Policy in the Czech Republic, Hungary and Poland', *Social Policy and Administration* 50 (5): 559–579.

Hašková, H. and R. Dudová (2017) 'Institutions and Discourses on Childcare for Children Under the Age of Three in a Comparative French-Czech Perspective', *Sociological Research Online* 22 (3): 120–142.

Hašková, H., H. Maříková, and Z. Uhde (2009) 'Leaves, Allowances and Facilities: Childcare Past and Present'. In: H. Hašková and Z. Uhde (eds) *Women and Social Citizenship in Czech Society: Continuity and Change.* Prague: Institute of Sociology, pp. 77–127.

Hašková, H. and Z. Sloboda (2018) 'Negotiating Access to Assisted Reproduction Technologies in a Post-Socialist Heteronormative Context', *Journal of International Women's Studies* 20 (1): 53–67.

Havelková, B. (2014) 'The Three Stages of Gender in Law'. In: L. Oates-Indruchová and H. Havelková (eds) *The Politics of Gender Culture under State Socialism: An Expropriated Voice.* New York: Routledge, pp. 31–56.

Heitlinger, A. (1987) *Reproduction, Medicine and the Socialist State.* London: Macmillan Press.

Hoffmann, D.L. (2000) 'Mothers in the Motherland: Stalinist Pronatalism in Its Pan-European Context', *Journal of Social History* 34 (1): 35–54.

Langmeier, J. and Z. Matějček (1963) *Psychická Deprivace v Dětství.* Prague: Státní pedagogické nakladatelství.

Matějček, Z., Z. Dytrych, and V. Schüller (1976) 'Pražská Studie o Dětech z Nechtěného Těhotenství', *Psychológia a Patopsychológia Dieťaťa* 10 (3): 229–246.

Nash, M. (2014) 'Introduction: Conceiving of Postmodern Reproduction'. In: M. Nash (ed.) *Reframing Reproduction. Conceiving Gendered Experiences.* Basingstoke: Palgrave Macmillan, pp. 1–19.

Orloff, A.S. (1993) 'Gender and the Social Rights of Citizenship: The Comparative Analysis of Gender Relations and Welfare States', *American Sociological Review* 58 (3): 303–328.

Outshoorn, J., R. Dudová, A. Prata, and L. Freidenvall (2015) *European Women's Movements and Body Politics The Struggle for Autonomy*. London: Palgrave Maxmillan.

Prajerová, A. (2018a) 'Biopolitics without Borders: An Intersectional Re-Reading of the Abortion Debate in (Un)democratic Czechoslovakia (1920–1986).' https://ruor.uottawa.ca/bitstream/10393/37415/1/Prajerova_Andrea_2018_thesis.pdf. (accessed 15 October 2018).

Prajerová, A. (2018b) 'The Ideology of Choice: Abortion (Bio-) Politics, Prenatal Screenings and Women's Liberation', *Pulse: the Journal of Science and Culture* 3: 145–160.

Pulkrábková, K. (2009) 'The Roma Minority: Changing definitions of Their Status'. In: H. Hašková and Z. Uhde (eds) *Women and Social Citizenship in Czech Society: Continuity and Change*. Prague: Institute of Sociology, Czech Academy of Sciences, pp. 171–210.

Rabušic, L. (2001) *Kde ty Všechny Děti Jsou? Porodnost v Sociologické Perspektivě*. Praha: Sociologické nakladatelství.

Rákosník, J. and R. Šustrová (2016) *Rodina v Zájmu Státu. Populační Růst a Instituce Manželství v Českých Zemích 1918–1989*. Prague: Nakladatelství Lidové noviny.

Rivkin-Fish, M. (2010) 'Pronatalism, Gender Politics, and the Renewal of Family Support in Russia: Toward a Feminist Anthropology of "Maternity Capital"', *Slavic Review* 69: 701–724.

Schmidt, V.A. (2010) 'Taking Ideas and Discourse Seriously: Explaining Change through Discursive Institutionalism as the Fourth "New Institutionalism"', *European Political Science Review* 2 (1): 1–25.

Snow, D.A. and R.D. Benford (1988) 'Ideology, Frame Resonance, and Participant Mobilisation'. In: B. Klandermans, H. Kriesi, and S. Tarrow (eds) *From Structure to Action: Comparing Social Movement Research Across Cultures*, Vol. 1. London: Jai Press inc., pp. 197–217.

Sojka, J. (1966) 'Problém Nejen Populační', *Vlasta* 20 (45): 6.

Srb, V. and M. Kučera (1959) *Výzkum o rodičovství 1956*. Prague: State Statistical Office.

Yuval-Davis, N. (1998) 'Gender and Nation'. In: R. Wilford and R.L. Miller (eds) *Women, Ethnicity and Nationalism*. London: Routledge, pp. 21–31.

Zajíček, K. (1973) 'Přes Sto Tisíc Zmařených Životů. Jaké Změny v Povolování Interrupcí', *Vlasta* 27 (19): 20.

11

Absorbing care through precarious labour: the shifting boundaries of politics in Norwegian healthcare

Anette Fagertun

Introduction

This chapter explores how labour and labour relations in the Norwegian municipal healthcare sector are enacted and shaped within a specific socio-historical institutional ecology, and it argues that shifting boundaries of politics have contributed to a debasing of (care) work and to the emergence of precarious (contingent) labour situations in care. The chapter aims to analyse imaginaries arising from depoliticisation, and effects on labour realities in the public healthcare services, by mobilising theoretical literature on the 'post-political' and on the anthropology of labour (Mouffe 2013, 2019, Chhachhi 2014, Kalb 2014, Brown 2015, 2019, Carbonella and Kasmir 2015, Wilson and Swyngedouw 2015, Harvey 2017, Postero and Elinoff 2019). The concept of 'boundary' is used analytically to identify conceptual or ideological constructions, or imaginaries that contribute to the acknowledgement of some issues or categories as political 'problems' within a particular policy frame, and to the masking or non-recognition of others (see Pine and Haukanes, Chapter 1, this volume). The current overall and consensual political framing of the welfare state as in 'crisis' is understood as constituting a hegemonic narrative, and representing a critical juncture that creates a 'window of opportunity' for radical change in public welfare (see also Vabø 2015). At this juncture, labour conditions and employment arrangements in the municipal healthcare sector seem to fall outside most policy frames, something that is indicative of a non-recognition of labour as a political category in this context as well as of a change in the boundaries of politics that opens up a space of precarity in labour. Following Roitman (2014: 8) I do not judge the 'crisis' as 'true' or 'false' but rather explore the ways it has become a 'mover' of change.

In Norway, the provision of care for dependent members of society is largely considered a responsibility of the state (Pine and Haukanes, Chapter 1 this volume; Isaksen and Czapka, Chapter 8 this volume). Furthermore, the provision of care services is decentralised to the municipalities. The municipal healthcare services are labour intensive and have steadily grown in scale and in full-time equivalents (FTEs) over the last decades. Women dominate the workforce (80%), many holding part-time positions, and refugees and immigrants are increasingly recruited as workers accounting for 17% of all FTEs in 2017 (SSB 2018). The inclusion and involvement of immigrant labour to meet the increasing recruitment problems in the municipal healthcare sector is commonly viewed as a 'win-win' situation for immigrants, municipalities, and the state in terms of successful inclusion in labour and active participation and integration in society. However, the rise of immigrant labour in this sector has developed alongside increasing precarious employment and we now observe an emergence of a new division of labour and new hierarchy of employment (Tingvold and Fagertun 2020). Norway is commonly characterised as an egalitarian and inclusive society with a broad coverage of collective arrangements and generous unemployment benefits. Debates on precarious labour and the working poor have received some attention in political and academic debates on 'social dumping', often tied to work migration related to the construction industry or the private services sector in Norway. Development in the labour market over the last decade, spurred by migration, new policy framings, and (de)regulation, has nevertheless changed the institutional conditions of labour and labour relations beyond the construction and private sector, and this chapter seeks to contribute to the debate by including the public service sector as a subject of scrutiny. Precarious or contingent elements are increasingly (re)inforced or introduced to labour, to create what is often conceived of in positive terms as a more 'flexible labour market' (Breman and Linden 2014, Standing 2014, Bergene and Hansen 2016, Moen 2018).

The chapter is based on data from fieldwork in three Norwegian municipalities, and on analysis of discourse emerging through white and green papers on healthcare. It aims to show how changing boundaries of politics create a 'shifting institutional ecology' which opens up the way for precarity. Fieldwork was conducted at nursing homes (NHs) in three municipalities from 2016 to 2018. Data was collected through both observations and semi-structured interviews with leaders and staff (both individual interviews and focus group discussions). The gathering of data was ethically approved by the NSD (the Norwegian centre for research data). The analysis of discourses (policy) focuses on the ways calls for transformation of the public healthcare services are framed and on the implications of this framing for labour in the municipal healthcare sector. A discourse is a socio-historically situated social phenomenon identifiable through the grouping of unambiguous ways of talking about, understanding, framing, and relating to a particular subject within a specific context (Bacchi 2005, Fagertun 2017). While discourse analysis often emphasises policy in fluid terms, frame analysis 'assumes that policies communicate a rather coherent and singular frame of the policy problem' (Dekker 2017: 127). Frames are therefore tools used to solve ambiguities in social reality and to simplify complex social 'problems'. The analysis below aims to identify the framing of 'the problem', the ambiguities of the frame, and its consequences for labour.

The 'institutional ecology' in Norway – the labour market

The concept of 'institution' may be vague. Here I follow a conventional understanding of it as 'macro regulation of social behaviours by organizations, groups and individuals. Institutions are based on formal elements such as legislation, bureaucratic regulations or large scale agreements' (Engelstad and Hauglund 2015: 6). The concept of institution refers to a lower level of analysis than the concept of society. Even so, it refers to what is commonly termed the 'macro level'. I understand the labour market, long-term policy engagements in healthcare and labour, and the municipal healthcare sector to be institutions. Like Vike (2018), I see institutions as emergent phenomena, and my interest is in the ways institutions 'work on work'.

The tripartite Norwegian model – the collective basic agreement and wage bargaining arrangement between state, employer associations, and trade union federations – facilitates a highly organised labour market of which this partnership is the cornerstone. The tripartite model is considered as a key to maintain equality and inclusion in labour as well as a base for the welfare state (Engelstad and Hauglund 2015: 11, Moen 2018: 216). There is substantial legal regulation and centralised collective bargaining in the labour markets in the Nordic countries. This is in contrast to the situation in many other countries in Europe. Minimum wages in the Nordic countries are regulated and determined through collective agreements between unions and employer organisations. Union membership rates are high, but have decreased over the last 15 years as part of an international trend (Bhattacharya 2014: 942, Friberg et al. 2014, Bergene and Hansen 2016). Norway has the highest wage level of the Nordic countries and large sections of the labour market are therefore exposed to low-wage competition. Union rates in Norway are the lowest of all the Nordic countries, and the institutional basis for collective bargaining is therefore weaker (Friberg et al. 2014). This has been counteracted by two government actions against social dumping, resulting in increased state involvement in wage regulation ('ad hoc universalism') (Friberg et al. 2014: 43). The part of the labour market that is regulated in Norway is characterised by regulations termed as 'soft measures' (voluntary). 'Hard measures' are introduced to parts of the labour market that are less regulated, such as the cleaning industry where statutory regulations with little discretion and flexibility are used (Nicolaisen and Trygstad 2015: 182). The model of labour relations in Norway therefore consists of regulations through collective voluntary agreements and statutory regulations that combine both soft and hard measures.

Recent labour and welfare reforms aim to integrate more people into the labour force, while at the same time providing employers with more flexibility. This has increased non-standard, or atypical, employment in Norway as elsewhere in Europe, and has been accompanied by an increasing tendency to normalise such employment forms (Hipp, Bernhardt, and Allmendinger 2015: 352, Moen 2018: 208). In Norway, changes in the regulation of labour over the last decade, implying a change in the labour–capital power balance weakening the labour side, have been politically desired and have led to increased tension between the left and right (Moen 2018: 206, 209). Atypical labour in Norway occurs and is increasing in both the private and public sectors (Moen 2018: 210). Hence, Norway seems to follow the same labour market development path as other European countries. Parts of private sector services are becoming 'arenas where the hollowing out of the standard employment relationship have come furthest' (Nicolaisen and Trygstad 2015: 180).

Labour in the municipal healthcare sector

The municipal healthcare sector is one of several sectors that make up the 'institutional ecology' of the service-intense Norwegian welfare state. Primary care services, such as long-term elderly care, are highly decentralised and we might therefore understand the municipalities to be the 'institutional backbone of the state' (Vike 2018: 22). The institutional order of 'municipalising' welfare state service provision has historically given shape to strong local autonomy and limited state control, creating a diversified landscape of local prioritisation. The municipal healthcare sector is the largest of the municipal sectors in terms of FTEs, with 43% of municipality employees working in this sector. It is a labour-intensive sector which has steadily grown in scale and in FTEs in recent decades. Women dominate the workforce (80%), and the sector is riddled with part-time and zero-hour contract employment.

One out of six of the total 142,000 FTEs in all municipalities was held by immigrants in 2017 (17%) (SSB 2018). These FTEs were, furthermore, shared by in total 217,000 workers, many of them employed in part-time positions (Ingstad and Hedlund 2017, Fagertun and Tingvold 2018, SSB 2017). The number of FTEs held by immigrants in the municipal care services has, since 2009, increased by 11,000 which is an increase of 80%. This increase is accounted for by two immigrant groups: Asians and east Europeans. There was, at the same time, a significant decrease in the number of FTEs held by workers from the Nordic countries. Workers from Asia held a third of all immigrant FTEs in 2017, the Philippines and Thailand being the two major countries of origin of these workers. Large geographical variations occur, however, as we can see in the municipality of Oslo, Norway's capital. Oslo's share of immigrant workers in the sector was 44%, while the equivalent share in the county of North Trøndelag in mid-Norway was 8%. Immigrant workers in the county of Hordaland on the west coast of Norway, where the municipality of Bergen (the second largest city of Norway) is located, account for 15% of FTEs in care services (SSB 2018).

The care workforce and 'part-time culture'

Another characteristic of the municipal healthcare sector is that it is highly 'absorbent'. This means that the workforce has a high capacity to deal with increasing demands from both national and local policies and regulations aiming to improve the equal access to services of equal quality (Vike 2018). The sector, due to this capacity, is very flexible, but is challenged by increasing workloads (Vike 2018: 139, 149). One could, of course, rightfully argue that the municipal healthcare sector has been flexible ever since the inclusion of care services into the public welfare regime in the 1960s. Back then, 'flexibility' was the means that both authorities and employers used in order to facilitate women's entry into paid labour through part-time work (Wærness 2010). Today, however, this flexibility is problematic. Non-voluntary part-time work is now recognised as being contingent labour and as constituting a major challenge to the ability of workers to earn a 'living wage' and obtain a decent pension (Hipp, Bernhardt, and Allmendinger 2015, Ingstad and Hedlund 2017). The aim in this section is to describe work–life experiences of both minority and majority workers at Norwegian nursing homes (NH), and to show that part-time work is abundant and an issue for both minority and majority workers.

During fieldwork in the period 2016–2018, I interviewed all categories of workers at three NHs about their work arrangements and working environments. The main categories of workers at Norwegian NHs are registered nurses, ward managers, healthcare workers, and assistants, of which healthcare workers represent the largest share of staff. One of the

NH is a large urban-based institution, while the other two are of relatively average size (between 75–100 residents), located in smaller and more rural locations. At the large NH there are about 200 FTEs distributed amongst 400 employees, and there is a relatively high number of immigrant employees. An employee of Asian origin worked as a healthcare worker in an 80% position at a ward here. She had held a zero-hour contract assistant position for many years before gaining a position as a certified healthcare worker. 'It was very easy to get a job here as someone they could call when they needed extras or when staff were home from work because of illness or sick-leave' she said. It took her many years to get her Norwegian certification as a healthcare worker as this certification required both theoretical training and a number of work hours (5,000) at the NH. She had to struggle hard to get enough hours, so she tried to make herself available always in order to 'collect hours'. She was now happy with an 80% position, as she has a child and her husband has a good job. However, she could easily manage a full-time position but said that 'this is difficult to get here, and I think I am not next in line'. Another employee at this NH was a young majority healthcare worker who held a 75% position. She liked working with the elderly, and would love to continue in this job, but said 'I didn't know what to study or do ... so, I chose the same as my sister, to become a healthcare worker. I was tired of school. I work 75%, but in a job with such a low wage, I have to work full time. I hope to get another job soon. I have already started to think about a new education. I am young; I have the time to find a new direction.'

A young majority registered nurse who held a full-time position at this large NH told me that:

> I won't be working for 30 years in this sector. If I stay I will become burnt out. I see this in some of my colleagues ... they are tired, and I want a better future for myself. I have to deal with the part-time and substitute hiring of workers almost everyday – very often I have new people 'on the floor' and they need to be guided and told what to do – and sometimes I do not have enough people, so other staff have to take on more tasks ... and they get frustrated.

She felt that because of the extended use of part-time and on-call substitutes, she became the one who had to handle this by taking the lead 'on the floor'. She wished for a stronger leadership focus on staffing, and said she was puzzled by the lack of attention to this issue both at her place of work and at the national level.

In an informal interview with a ward manager at the large NH, I found that she was in the process of hiring new staff. She told me that she was very reluctant to hire someone who did not have command of the Norwegian language, and that the positions she had available were from 75 to 100% positions.

> I am hiring new staff but I won't hire someone who does not speak Norwegian. For me, the most important thing is that my staff is able to talk with the patients, to take part in conversations, and that they have skills to interpret what the patients are trying to say. Many of the patients have little language left so then it becomes even more important to be able to understand the few words they utter. However, there are few registered nurses who apply for a job here and the positions are often vacant for long periods. This is a problem. So, I oftentimes use assistants and substitutes, and in such cases I cannot afford to be so insistent on language competence.

A registered majority nurse with a 100% position at this ward told me that she was concerned about the development at the NH.

> there are a lot of foreigners working at this place. I am a bit concerned about this development. Many of the immigrants are assistants with little or no training in nursing or healthcare professions. I see that many of them try to qualify as healthcare workers but that takes time and they often have lower positions. I am often alone as a nurse at a shift, and sometimes the only 'Norwegian'. It is tiresome because I feel lonely in a sense ... and I also miss discussing nursing. Sometimes I think seriously about finding a new job ... wonder how it would be like to be still working here in ten years ... I probably will not be around for so long.

Two common and connected themes that emerged from all NHs were the experience of 'work-overload', of not being able to finish all assigned asks, and the problematic high degree of part-time and zero-hour contract employment and the impact this had on the working environment. The overload theme was commonly tied to unsatisfactory employment arrangements, such as there being too few staff, and the feeling of 'having to run all day', which made them tired. The part-time issue was often tied to the exhausting activity of always making oneself available for extra shifts, or not being able to earn a 'decent wage', or being the one responsible for substitutes and part-time employees.

At one of the other NHs, I found that they were running a project they called 'full-time culture'. This 'full time culture' project signifies that there was a recognition that the 'part-time culture' was causing a range of problems, relating to working environment, recruitment, and quality of care. This NH had 75 FTEs distributed among a total of 130 employees. The NH implemented concrete measures to ensure that staff who held less than 50% positions were offered higher percentages or full-time positions. One of the measures was to cut the substitute/temporary staff-budget and include it in the budget for regular operation. This meant that more employees gained full-time employment, but that the possibility of calling in a substitute in case of illness was lost. This situation created frustration among the staff, and several of the workers I interviewed told me that they sometimes had sole responsibility for a whole ward on a shift. Even so, they appreciated the new focus on full time, as most of the workers wanted this kind of employment. An exception was two elderly and experienced healthcare workers. They said that the work at the NH had become extremely stressful, and that they preferred to work in 60 and 70% positions because, as one said, 'I simply can't handle working more than I do now, because of the stressful situation at work. I understand that the younger nurses want full time employment because of pay. But I fortunately don't need this because my children are grown up and my husband has a good salary.'

I found that part-time and zero-hour contracts were not an issue for the leaders at the two other NHs, but that they were an issue for the staff who in many cases wanted full-time positions and who constantly were 'shopping shifts' (taking extra shifts). At these two NHs, the leader-group acknowledged that they used part-time and substitute hiring extensively. 'It gives us the flexibility we need for operating this 24/7 organisation', one of them explained, and added that in her experience many of the workers actually wanted part-time positions. Part-time was, thus, framed more in a narrative of flexibility for both employer and employee, presented as something positive for both parts and not associated to the same degree with recruitment problems or quality of care services. Part-time working occurred both amongst majority and minority workers, although more minority workers had such working arrangements, and minority workers dominated the category of assistants on-call or part-time.

Many migrants experience precarious employment situations in the Nordic countries, not only in the healthcare sector but also in other service occupations (Pyrhönen, Leinonen, and Martikainen 2017: 29). The opening of the municipal care sector to immigrant labour may pave the way for inclusion and integration of immigrants in important social arenas. However, we can also scrutinise the integrative potential of inclusion in unskilled, low-paid, and highly flexible labour (see also Fagertun and Tingvold 2018). Inclusion of immigrants into low-skilled labour also takes place in other service sectors, such as in the cleaning and fishing industry in the private sector, where the proportion of immigrant workers has dramatically increased in the last two decades (Nicolaysen and Trygstad 2015: 186, Friberg and Midtbøen 2019, Orupabo and Nadim 2019).

Part-time employment, defined as employment of less than 30 hours a week (Hipp, Bernhardt, and Allmendinger 2015), is also a highly gendered phenomenon. In Europe, women are two to four times more likely than men to work part time. The Norwegian welfare model supports women's participation in wage labour and Norway has a higher female employment rate than elsewhere in Europe. Yet, labour markets are characterised by strong occupational and gender segregation, and part-time work is common amongst women (Ingstad and Hedlund 2017, Orupabo and Nadim 2019). In 2015, 28% of all employed women worked part time and many of these in the health and social services fields (Hipp, Bernhardt, and Allmendinger 2015, Ingstad and Hedlund 2017: 74, 76). There are many institutional factors that may influence the prevalence of part-time employment. These include legal regulations (working hours, equal rights for part-time workers), the income taxation system (joint taxation of spouses acting as an incentive for the lowest salaried, often the woman, working part time), social policies (unemployment benefits, available and affordable childcare, sick leave arrangements) and union strength (Hipp, Bernhardt, and Allmendinger 2015). Part-time work is most prominent in the service sector, a sector that is growing fast. Municipal healthcare services provision is part of the public service sector – a sector that as I have shown above is riddled with a 'part-time culture'.

Precarity – and the debasing of labour

Labour is one of the key pillars of the foundation of modern society, and the labour market is a key institution in any industrial society. Today we see a global wave of precarious labour (Chhachhi 2014, Standing 2014, Carbonella and Kasmir 2015, Evans and Tilly 2016, Harvey 2017). This mode of labour takes many forms. The concept of 'precariousness' in general refers to uncertainty, insecurity, and contingency in labour and livelihood. The concept 'is particularly useful ... in the Global North ... where "standard" work makes up (or at least made up until recently) the bulk of employment' (Evans and Tilly 2016: 657). Precarious labour always contains elements such as marginal part-time contracts, zero-hour contracts, casual and undeclared self-employment, or work via digital platforms. These are all forms of employment that are accompanied by low/insecure pay, fewer rights, less protection and access to social security, less representation, and fewer prospects for advancement. The ways labour is 'categorized, differentiated, or unified (and how those configurations change over time and with the intercessions of states and other institutions) is a political question' (Gill and Kasmir 2016: 90). What follows from my understanding of labour as a political formation/category (Carbonella and Kasmir 2015: 43) is therefore that shifts in labour 'are primarily driven by politics and the power of capital' (Evans and Tilly 2016: 652).

In Norway, public debates on precarious labour commonly relate to the issue of 'social dumping' in the wake of the opening of the labour market to EU migrants (in 2004 and 2009). Such discussions have mostly focused on labour conditions in private sectors, such as construction, fish processing, agriculture, and cleaning. Social dumping commonly refers to a situation where a group of workers, for example migrants, receive lower wages than other employees who carry out the same type of work. This issue arises as a problem where employers want to reduce labour costs by recruiting workers from countries with lower living conditions and paying them less than the established standards. Another way of putting this is that employers increasingly hire 'cheap labour' to reduce production costs and produce higher surpluses. This issue is, in Norway, regulated by law and every work migrant must receive a salary that is equal to that of the core worker group. Recent political discussions, for example on the maritime sector, may, however, open up changes in the regulation in this area. One example is the recent discussion on changing the legalisation of the hiring of foreign seafarers on ships sailing Norwegian waters. As of today, what is often called 'cheap labour' is only permitted on Norwegian ships that sail through international waters. Debates on social dumping have revolved around a concern for native workers and the sustainability of the welfare state. I bring this issue in here because the debates have not yet focused on work in the public healthcare sector. I think these discussions are relevant in light of the extended use of part-time positions in the municipal sector – denying workers the possibility to earn a living wage. They are also relevant in light of the recent trend discussed above of recruiting work migrants and immigrants and their long journeys towards qualification as healthcare workers, and, finally, because the debates may indicate ways that labour increasingly is depoliticised and 'debased'.

'The political', politics, and post-politics

The overall argument of this chapter is that the boundaries of politics are changing and that this has implications for labour within a changing institutional landscape in Norway. Thus, we need to address the issue of politics. A common way of conceptualising the political field in current political theory builds on Chantal Mouffe's differentiation between 'the political' and 'politics' (Mouffe 2005, 2013, Dzenovska and De Genova 2018). Mouffe (2013: 4) holds that 'the political' refers to a public space of competing perspectives which is concerned with collective forms of identification, with the antagonisms of 'us' and 'them', and it thus refers to a wide field of struggles. 'The political' refers to antagonisms that can take many forms, but most importantly 'is a dimension that can never be eradicated' (Mouffe 2013: 2). In this also lies a dimension of solidarity and empathy that always will emerge alongside antagonisms (Postero and Elinoff 2019: 6). 'The political' also has a symbolic or discursive nature, and types of ideologies that do not recognise its contingency, but are based in technical necessity and consensus, will therefore foreclose the space of the political and through this deny the possibility of radical politics.

The concept of 'politics' encompasses the many practices and institutions that establish order and organise human coexistence 'in conditions which are always potentially conflicting, since they are affected by the dimension of "the political"' (Mouffe 2013: 3). Mouffe (2013: 17) holds that what characterises politics is 'the confrontation between conflicting hegemonic projects, a confrontation with no possibility of final reconciliation'. Thus, 'politics' is a narrower concept than 'the political'. It refers to established hegemonic orders/regimes and is, from Mouffe's perspective, closely tied to the state, hegemony, and the institutional order. I understand 'policy' as being a subcategory of politics that refers to a specific way of thinking, problematising, and governing a certain conceived, but simultaneously constructed, societal 'problem'. Implicit in the notion and purpose of policy is that something needs to be changed, and solutions need to be suggested. However, the 'problem', or what is in need of change, does not always become explicit in government policies (see Fagertun 2017). 'The problem' may, through policies, also be given shape as problematisations, rather than being 'addressed' by the policies (Bacchi 2009). Healthcare policies, as part of a larger assemblage of knowledge, are thus not solely about finding solutions to conceived 'problems', but also about ways in which problems are constructed through sets of statements and a certain framing 'that brings social objects into being' (Shaw and Greenhalgh 2008: 2508). Policy as a tool of governance therefore both produces and is produced by discourses (Christensen and Fluge 2016: 265, Fagertun 2017).

European societies have, in the last decade, experienced a narrowing of the political and a rise in expert-rule (Kalb 2014). This process of depoliticisation is commonly conceptualised as a transition to 'post-politics', in which neo-liberal capitalism plays a key part by flattening political questions and turning them into the hands of administrative powers. We thus see a move towards a post-political mode of governing – that is, 'a situation in which the political … is increasingly colonised by politics' (Wilson and Swyngedouw 2015: 6, see also Brown 2015, 2019, Dzenovska and De Genova 2018: 3). The key characteristic of this situation is that the modes of 'good governance' 'ensure that the framework for debate and decision-making does not question or disrupt the existing state of the neo-liberal political-economic configuration' (Wilson and Swyngedouw 2015: 5). Following Mouffe's (2019) understanding,

I see the post-political as characterised by a situation in which the antagonistic dimension is blocked or repressed. The process of post-politicisation involves a weakening of the public sphere, through which political space is encompassed by 'a consensual mode of governance' (Wilson and Swyngedouw 2015: 5). Consensus, rejection of (political) conflicts, and all-round cooperation thus emerge as tropes of post-politics. 'In institutional terms, post-politics is defined by the reduction of the political to the economic … This subordination is not purely ideological, but is embodied in concrete institutional forms' (Wilson and Swyngedouw 2015: 8).

The policy field of public healthcare and its normative foundation

Healthcare is a strongly politicised field in every European society. However, I argue that there are also strong tendencies of depoliticising as part of a more general global trend of post-politics (Brown 2015, 2019, Wilson and Swyngedouw 2015, Fagertun 2017, Mouffe 2019). Public healthcare services are portrayed throughout Europe, including in Norway, as being in constant 'crisis' due to an ageing population and decreased public revenues. This creates a frame for policy in which the concept of 'crisis' is active, and a 'futurology' that both shapes and legitimises 'problems' and reforms. The complex healthcare system reforms implemented in response to this 'crisis' are interventions intended to transform the public sector, handle austerity, and create sustainable systems and services for the future. These reforms may have different effects on local governance in different countries. Common aspects are, however, the goal of reducing state expenditure, the devolution of authority, the further development of a care market, and reform as a signifier of a government's capacity to act in times of 'crisis'. The political depiction of 'crisis' in the public sector is part of the more general portrayal of Western societies as being in constant crisis, and 'crisis' has become a powerful tool in the politicians' toolbox (Roitman 2014, Masco 2017: 65, Hansen, forthcoming). Thus, as Blythe et al. (2018: 1208) argue, in this framework the normative premise is 'that fundamental change … is essential to support desirable futures'.

In Norway, the 'Coordination Reform' (Norwegian Ministry of Health and Care Services 2008–2009) unlocked an era of rapid policy intervention in the healthcare sector. The reform was introduced to combat fragmentation in the complex sector and to promote collaboration between providers of public services, through this securing integrated care. The concepts of 'coordination' and 'integration' became political and organisational answers to different kinds of pressures and challenges in the public welfare services, and functioned as tools to frame the 'problems' in the sector. In current

Norwegian healthcare policy, the state envisions the participation of a plurality of actors in the production of healthcare service; patients, their relatives, friends, neighbours, voluntary organisations, NGOs, private market actors, and local communities all being 'invited' to take part as contributors (Askheim 2017, Fagertun 2017). In the recent white paper 'A full life – all your life' (Norwegian Ministry of Health and Care Services 2017–2018), the concepts of 'co-production' and 'co-creation' are introduced as ideal-type models for healthcare service provision, while the concepts of 'unwarranted variation' and 'undesirable priorities' are used to describe a municipal reality that challenges the aim of universal access to public healthcare services of the same quality. These concepts are normative, not neutral, as they point towards something that is bad or wrong, as well as to something that provides 'a benchmark against which to assess actions, events, or states of affairs' (Frega 2019: 2). They are thus recently politicised concepts that become tools in policy to create a specific change in the direction of standardisation through norm compliance and centralisation of the welfare state. This in turn embodies a change in the institutional order (Vike 2018: 17). Thus, these concepts collectively shape *the political framing* of the healthcare sector and they function as directives for municipalities when they choose solutions or methods in their search for 'smarter' services. One key element of this search involves the modernist belief in technology as a form of 'salvation'. Solutions to 'innovative services' in the municipalities often also entail flexible forms of labour and/or the downscaling of FTEs. Moreover, the call for a complexity of actors producing care services indirectly articulates that 'anyone' can provide such services and, as such, represents a debasing of care work as labour. Current 'utopian accounts of how the new technological configurations ... are bringing us to a brave new world ... ignore entirely the dehumanizing alienation of the residual and disposable labour processes that result' (Harvey 2017: 195). Fluctuating institutional conditions produced by shifting boundaries of politics have an effect on the shape of municipal healthcare services provision and on the conditions for labour in this sector.

Vike (2018: 154) has recently argued that the Norwegian welfare state is structurally dependent on women's traditional adaptation to the labour market to reproduce its institutional care regime. For this reason, he states, important challenges in the sector have been labelled as being 'the problem of women', while the core of the problems of flexibility, absorption, and de-skilling have been left 'non-politicised' (Vike 2018: 154). I support Vike's argument, but I hold that this structural dependency should be understood as anti-politics rather than non-politics and that we today may add the flexible adaptation to the labour market by immigrants. Importantly, labour is not visible as a political category in healthcare policy except for a recognition of the fact that in the future the public healthcare services will need more workers and the workers must work 'smarter'. Labour as such is also not visible when it comes to services production, other than in terms of cooperation amongst different actors of services provision, and the services are in a sense represented as being produced by invisible bodies. As shown above, these 'bodies' are increasingly those of immigrants working as care service providers in the lower tier of the sector (see Pine and Haukanes, Chapter 1; Fedyuk Chapter 2; Bofill-Poch, Chapter 7; all this volume). Thus, the labour question is not included in the policy frame of healthcare issues, at least not in the form of recognising the conditions for labour in this sector or the prevalent employment situation of part-time work. The rise of precarious employment in the municipal healthcare sector is therefore not (yet) acknowledged, and this issue may thus be said to be located beyond the boundary, and outside the frame, of healthcare policy in Norway.

Recently, there has been some focus in the media on working conditions in the municipal healthcare sector. In Oslo, for example, which is the largest municipality in Norway, there are about 200,000 employees in the healthcare sector. In 2018, over 70% of the advertised healthcare worker positions, and over 50% of the registered nurse positions, were part-time (Klassekampen 2019). Oslo municipality, through its city council, has declared a 'part-time crisis' and decided politically to establish 'full-time culture' in the healthcare services as they acknowledge that full-time and permanent positions create both job security and more continuity in the services (Klassekampen 2019). This is a move in the direction of making labour a political category and an acknowledgement of the consequences of atypical labour. The case described above on 'full-time culture' was a project at the organisational level of one NH – and the Oslo case is an example of policy at the local 'statehood' level. These cases might represent a kind of radical micro-politics, or a form of resistance, that potentially could spur a re-politicisation of labour in the municipal healthcare services. This also applies to the different forms of grassroot mobilisations observed during the Covid-19 pandemic, as the pandemic exposed structural problems in the care sector that now may gain political focus and thus become part of new policy frames.

Concluding discussion: absorbing care through precarious labour

The overall argument of this chapter has been that the dialectical relation between new exploitative relations in neo-liberal capitalist production and a shifting institutional ecology transforms boundaries in both labour and politics in Norwegian society. My aim was to show how the master narrative of 'crisis' constitutes a critical juncture which opens a 'window of opportunity' for institutional change, and that this has opened a space for precarious labour in the municipal healthcare sector. Changes in working life in Europe are commonly characterised as a shift towards dualisation, the latter referring to a polarised process in which fragmentation and individualisation of labour relations is emerging more obviously in the private service sector and where union membership that ensures collective bargaining is more heavily concentrated in the public sector (Nicolaisen and Trygstad 2015: 179). Dualist regimes will typically secure strong rights for a skilled 'core' workforce, while offering poor conditions on the periphery. This is a fair description of Norwegian working life. However, in this chapter I have shown that the feminised and increasingly culturally diversified workforce of the public municipal care sector represents a 'grey area' in this dualist picture.

A common view in critical political theory today is that the main challenge to labour and labour rights 'comes from the neo-liberal labour reform discourse' (Bhattacharya 2014: 943). The neo-liberal labour reform discourse emphasises flexibility, rejects labour (law) rigidity, and poses labour rights as a 'luxury' both in the global South and North (Bhattacharya 2014: 944). Global competition is fronted as a process that 'demands' low labour costs and strong labour rights and institutions therefore become 'major stumbling blocks to economic growth' (Bhattacharya 2014: 944; see also Brown 2015, 2019). The result is a fundamental debasement of labour (Bhattacharya 2014: 944). In Norway, labour has historically played a key role in the political imaginary of an egalitarian, inclusive, and just welfare society. Labour is still conceived as the main 'tool' for integration in society, a tool with broad political endorsement and one which has a strong ideological force (Rugkåsa 2012: 49). In healthcare policy, labour or labour relations is a subject that falls outside the frame and thus remains outside the boundary of policy (see also Pine and Haukanes, Chapter1, this volume). The focus is on the receiver of services and on the importance of change. This is perhaps appropriate. However, if labour is mentioned, it is always in terms of the ways labour must change – become smarter and technologised – yet the concept of 'labour saving technology' is never used. Evans and Tilly (2016: 665) claim that precarity 'is held in place by political institutions as well as the structure of production'. What follows is that precarity is a social construct, made through both policy and capitalist production, and therefore it can also be *re-made*. I have addressed the question of how labour is construed as a political category and the way it increasingly *is not*, and argued that the current master narrative of 'welfare state crisis' seems to conceal labour as a political category, thereby making labour invisible as part of the 'problem'. There is currently, therefore, a paradoxical labour situation in Norway. On the one hand, labour plays a key role in the imagining of an equal society and it is the main tool for inclusion and integration of citizens into society. Yet labour as a tool for inclusion has changed content and moved from being focused on citizens' rights to make a decent living, to their duties to contribute to state revenues by paying taxes and by not being costly, dependent members of society. On the other hand, labour is debased as a political category and pushed beyond the boundaries of hegemonic policy. Changing labour relations furthermore produce an emerging precariate of careworkers.

I recognise the 'pessimism' underpinning some post-political scholarship and acknowledge the value of focusing on micro-politics and mobilisation (Scott 2012: 113, Mocca and Osborne 2018: 4, Li 2019, Mouffe 2019, Postero and Elinoff 2019). Recent critique of the notion of the post-political has maintained that a consensus driven post-political world does not exist empirically, and that evidence for this is found in various forms of mobilisations, social movements, and micro-politics (Postero and Elinoff 2019: 4). In line with Mouffe (2019: 79), I recognise that grassroot mobilisation may represent potent radical politics from below which may contribute to processes of re-politicisation. However, I hope I have conveyed a nuanced picture. Movements from below do not necessarily negate the occurrence of depoliticisation at the institutional level.

References

Askheim, O.P. (2017) 'Brukermedvirkningsdiskurser i den Norske Velferdspolitikken', *Tidsskrift for Velferdsforskning* 20 (2): 134–149.

Bacchi, C. (2005) 'Discourse, Discourse Everywhere: Subject "Agency" in Feminist Discourse Methodology', *NORA – Nordic Journal of Feminist and Gender Research* 13 (3): 198–209.

Bacchi, C. (2009) *Analysing Policy: What's the Problem Represented To Be?* French Forest: Pearson Australia.

Bergene, A.C. and P.B. Hansen (2016) 'A Historical Legacy Untouched by Time and Space? The Hollowing-out of the Norwegian Model of Industrial Relations', *Nordic Journal of Working Life Studies* 6 (1): 5–24.

Bhattacharya, S. (2014) 'Is Labour Still a Relevant Category for Praxis? Critical Reflections on some Contemporary Discourses on Work and Labour in Capitalism', *Development and Change* 45 (5): 941–962.

Blythe, J., J. Silver, L. Evans, D. Armitage, N.J. Bennett, Michele-Lee Moore, Tiffany H. Morrison, Katrina Brown (2018) 'The Dark Side of Transformation: Latent Risks in Contemporary Sustainability Discourse', *Antipode* 50 (5): 1206–1223.

Breman, J. and M. van der Linden (2014). 'Informalizing the Economy: The Return of the Social Question at a Global Level', *Development and Change* 45 (5): 920–940.

Brown, W. (2015) *Undoing the Demos. Neoliberalism's Stealth Revolution.* New York: Zone Books.

Brown, W. (2019) *In the Ruins of Neoliberalism. The Rise of Antidemocratic Politics in the West.* New York: Columbia University Press.

Carbonella, A. and S. Kasmir (2015) 'Dispossession, Disorganization and the Anthropology of Labor.' In: James G. Carrier and Don Kalb (eds) *Anthropologies of Class. Power, Practices and Inequality*. Cambridge: Cambridge University Press, pp. 41–52.

Chhachhi, A. (2014) 'Introduction: The 'Labour Question' in Contemporary Capitalism', *Development and Change* 45 (5): 895–919.

Christensen, K. and S. Fluge (2016) 'Brukermedvirkning i Norsk Eldreomsorgpolitikk – Om Utviklingen av Retorikken om Individuelt Medansvar', *Velferdsforskning* 19 (3): 261–277.

Dekker, R. (2017) 'Frame Ambiguity in Policy Controversies: Critical Frame Analysis of Migrant Integration Policies in Antwerp and Rotterdam', *Critical Policy Studies* 11 (2): 127–145.

Dzenovska, D. and N. De Genova (2018) 'Introduction. Desire for the Political in the Aftermath of the Cold War', *Focaal – Journal of Global and Historical Anthropology* 80: 1–15.

Engelstad, F. and A. Hauglund (2015) 'Introduction: Institutional Change in Neo-Corporatist Society'. In: F. Engelstad and A. Hauglund (eds) *Conflict and Cooperation the Nordic Way. Work, Welfare, and Institutional Change in Scandinavia*. Warsaw, Berlin: De Gruyter Open Ltd, pp. 1–16

Evans, P. and C. Tilly (2016) 'The Future of Work: Escaping the Current Dystopian Trajectory and Building Better Alternatives'. In: E. Stephen, H. Gottfried, and E. Granter (eds) *The Sage Handbook of the Sociology of Work and Employment*. London: SAGE, pp. 651–671.

Fagertun, A. (2017) 'The Anti-politics of Healthcare Policy and its Blurring Effects on Care Work in Norway', *International Practice Development Journal* 7 (2): 1–11.

Fagertun, Anette and Laila Tingvold (2018) Omsorgsarbeid, kjønn og etnisitet. Flerkulturelle arbeidsfellesskap i norske sykehjem i møte med institusjonelle endringer. In: J. Debesay and C. Tschudi-Madsen (eds) *Migrasjon, Helse og profesjon*. Oslo: Gyldendal Akademisk, 173–193.

Frega, Roberto (2019) The normativity of democracy. *European Journal of Political Theory* 18 (3): 1–22. DOI: 10.1177/1474885116684760.

Friberg, J.H, J. Arnholtz, L. Eldring, N.W. Hansen, and F. Thorarins (2014) 'Nordic Labour Market Institutions and New Migrant Workers: Polish Migrants in Oslo, Copenhagen and Reykjarvik', *European Journal of Industrial Relations* 20 (1): 37–53.

Friberg, J.H. and A.H. Midtbøen (2019) 'The Making of Immigrant Niches in an Affluent Welfare State', *International Migration Review* 53 (2): 322–345.

Gill, L. and S. Kasmir (2016) 'History, Politics, Space, Labor: On Unevenness as an Anthropological Concept', *Dialectical Anthropology* 40: 87–102.

Hansen, Roar (forthcoming 2021) 'Velferdsstaten smelter. Innovasjon, teknologi og kapitalisering av kommunalt omsorgsarbeid..' PhD dissertation, University of Bergen, Norway.

Harvey, D. (2017) *Marx, Capital and the Madness of Economic Reason*. London: Profile Books Ltd.

Hipp, L., J. Bernhardt and J. Allmendinger (2015) 'Institutions and the Prevalence of Nonstandard Employment', *Socio-Economic Review* 13 (2): 351–377.

Ingstad, K. and M. Hedlund (2017) 'Part-time of Full-time Employment: Choices and Constraints'. *Nordic Journal of Working Life Studies* 7 (4): 73–89.

Kalb, D. (2014) '"Worthless Poles" and Other Dispossessions: Toward an Anthropology of Labor in Post-Communist Central Eastern Europe'. In: S. Kasmir and

A. Carbonella (eds) *Blood and Fire. Toward a Global Anthropology of Labor.* London: Berghahn Books, pp. 651–671.
Klassekampen (20 January 2019) (Norwegian left-wing daily newspaper).
Li, T.M. (2019) 'Politics interrupted', *Anthropological Theory* 19 (1): 29–53.
Mocca, L.E. and S. Osborne (2018) '"Solidarity is our Weapon": Social Mobilisation in Scotland in the Contest of the Post-Political Condition', *Antipode* 51 (2): 1–22.
Moen, E. (2018) 'Går vi mot en Kjosifisering av Arbeidslivet'? *Nytt Norsk Tidsskrift* 35 (3–4): 206–218.
Mouffe, C. (2005) *On the Political.* Brooklyn, New York: Verso Books.
Mouffe, C. (2013) *Agonistics. Thinking the World Politically.* London and New York: Verso.
Mouffe, C. (2019) *For a Left Populism.* London, New York: Verso.
Nicolaisen, H. and S.C. Trygstad (2015) 'Preventing Dualization the Hard Way. Regulating the Norwegian Labour Market'. In: F. Engelstad and A. Hauglund (eds) *Conflict and Cooperation the Nordic Way. Work, Welfare, and Institutional Change in Scandinavia.* Warsaw, Berlin: De Gruyter Open Ltd., pp. 180–200.
Norwegian Ministry of Health and Care Services. White paper. St. meld. 15 (2017–2018), 'Leve hele livet — En kvalitetsreform for eldre' (A full life – all your life – a quality reform for the elderly).
Norwegian Ministry of Health and Care Services (2008–2009). White paper, Report No. 47 to The Parliament, 'The Coordination Reform — Proper treatment – at the right place and right time'. Oslo, Norway.
Orupabo, J. and M. Nadim (2019) 'Men doing Women's Dirty Work: Desegregation, Immigrants and Employer Preferences in the Cleaning Industry in Norway', *Gender, Work & Organization* 27 (3): 1–15. https://doi.org/10.1111/gwao.12378.
Postero, N. and E. Elinoff (2019) 'Introduction: A Return to Politics', *Anthropological Theory* 19 (1): 3–28.
Pyrhönen, N., J. Leinonen, and T. Martikainen (2017) 'Nordic Migration and Integration Research: Overview and Future Prospects'. *Policy Paper* 3/2017, NordForsk.
Roitman, J. (2014) *Anti-Crisis.* Durham, NC: Duke University Press.
Rugkåsa, M. (2012) *Likhetens Dilemma: om Sivilisering og Integrasjon i den Velferdsambisiøse Norske Stat.* Oslo: Gyldendal akademisk.
Scott, J. (2012) 'Infrapolitics and Mobilizations: A Response by James C. Scott', *Revue Francaise d'ètudes Americaines* 131 (1): 112–117.
Shaw, Sara E. and Trisha Greenhalgh (2008) 'Best Research - For What? Best Health – For Whom? A Critical Exploration of Primary Care Research Using Discourse Analysis', *Social Science & Medicine* 66: 2506–2519.
Standing, G. (2014) 'Understanding the Precariate through Labour and Work', *Development and Change* 45 (5): 963–980.
Statistics Norway (SSB) (2017) 'Innvandrere i og Utenfor Arbeidsmarkedet'. SSB informasjonstjeneste, november 2017. https://www.ssb.no/arbeid-og-lonn/artikler-og-publikasjoner/innvandrere-i-og-utenfor-arbeidsmarkedet (accessed 29 November 2018).
Statistics Norway (SSB) (2018) 'Innvandrere stod for 1 av 6 Årsverk innen Omsorg. SSB's Informasjonstjeneste', 5.juli 2018 (accessed 1 October 2020).
Tingvold, L. and A. Fagertun (2020) 'Between Privileged and Oppressed? Immigrants Labour Trajectories in Norwegian Long-term Care', *Sustainability* 12: 1–17. doi:10.3390/su12114777.
Vabø, M. (2015) 'Changing Welfare Institutions as Sites of Contestation.' In: F. Engelstad and A. Hauglund (eds) *Conflict and Cooperation the Nordic Way.*

Work, Welfare, and Institutional Change in Scandinavia. Warsaw, Berlin: De Gruyter Open Ltd, pp. 242–260.

Vike, H. (2018) *Politics and Bureaucracy in the Norwegian Welfare State*. London: Palgrave MacMillan.

Wilson, J. and E. Swyngedouw (2015) 'Seeds of Dystopia: Post-Politics and the Return of the Political'. In: J. Wilson and E. Swyngedouw (eds) *The Post-Political and its Discontents. Spaces of Depoliticisation, Spectres of Radical Politics*. Edinburgh: Edinburgh University Press, pp. 1–22.

Wærness, K. (2010) 'Da husmoren forsvant', *Tidskrift for Kjønnsforskning* 34 (4): 394–404.

12

'The Handbook of Masturbation and Defloration': tracing sources of recent neo-conservatism in Poland

Agnieszka Kościańska

Since the summer of 2013, gender has become one of the most discussed terms in Poland. In spite of its scholarly roots, discussions on the concept have for the most part taken place outside the academic setting. Gender is often discussed in churches, examined in everyday conversations, and analysed as a part of public debate. On 29 December 2013, Catholics all over Poland heard about 'gender ideology'. Polish bishops explained in their letters to the faithful that 'gender ideology' is:

> the product of many decades of ideological and cultural changes deeply rooted in Marxism and neo-Marxism endorsed by several feminist movements and the sexual revolution ... According to this ideology, humans can freely determine whether they want to be men or women and freely choose their sexual orientation. This voluntary self-determination, not necessarily life-long, is to make the society accept the right to set up new types of families – for instance, families built on homosexual relations. (Shepherds of the Catholic church in Poland 2013)

The bishops stressed that 'gender ideology' was dangerous to the family and the nation: 'Humans unsure of their sexual identity are not capable of discovering and fulfilling tasks that they face in their marital, family, social and professional lives' (Shepherds 2013). They pointed to the fact that 'gender ideology has been slowly introduced into different structures of social life: education, health service, cultural and education centres and non-governmental organisations. Some media portray this ideology in a positive way: as a means to counteract violence and to aim for equality' (Shepherds 2013). They appeal 'to institutions responsible for Polish education not to yield under pressure from the few but very loud groups with not inconsiderable financial resources, which in the name of modern education carry out experiments on children and young people' (Shepherds 2013). By 'experiments', they meant sex education based on WHO standards, as well as a sex and equality education curriculum for pre-school prepared by feminists.

On another occasion, during one of their official meetings, Polish bishops discussed whether Judith Butler posed a threat to the Polish nation. In parishes all over Poland, meetings and conferences deliberating on the dangers of 'gender ideology' as well as rallies against sex and equality education in schools were organised. In 2014 in Warsaw, in one of the main city squares, a group of elderly women stood with banners that read 'Stop Gender', 'Gender Means Death'. The event was repeated almost every afternoon and called 'a prayer rally'. In the Catholic media, Priest Darius Oko explained to the faithful that gender was like Stalinism and Nazism, or even worse. He portrayed 'gender ideology' and 'homosexual propaganda' as the creations of Satan (see, for instance, Cichobłazińska 2013). Others took it more personally. During my fieldwork among Polish sex experts, a therapist told me about his patient, a Catholic priest, who came to see him because he was in love with another priest, but suffered from erectile dysfunction. The priest did not have a problem with breaking the rule of celibacy and with engaging in homosexual acts, condemned by the Catholic church. But when on the therapist's shelf he saw a two-volume-collection, which I co-edited, entitled, *Gender: An Anthropological Perspective*, he thundered with outrage: 'Why are you promoting gender ideology here!'

Not only is the church against 'gender ideology', some secular experts have likewise argued against the concept. For instance, Zbigniew Lew-Starowicz, a major Polish sexologist, who in the 1970s and 1980s was already sceptical about gender equality in relationships and in social life (for more, see Kościańska 2016), stressed on many recent occasions that although he thought gender studies were interesting as such, too much gender equality might lead to sexual problems.[1]

Among these critics, gender appears as a broad and vague concept encompassing women's rights, reproductive and sexual rights, sex education, homosexuality, transgenderism, LGBTQI rights, social construction theory, and gender performativity; all presented as threats to the family and the nation. Within this narrative, sex education is seen to pose the greatest danger as it is directed at young people, i.e. the future of the nation and the family. Political analysts have argued that the attack on 'gender ideology' significantly contributed to the electoral victory of the radical right in Poland in 2015 (Kucharczyk 2016, Graff and Korolczuk 2017: 175–176), which since then has been limiting gender, sexual, and reproductive rights. In this chapter, I try to make sense of this seemingly sudden move of a complicated academic term to the heart of public debate. I argue that the current war on gender is deeply rooted in earlier debates about gender and sexuality that can be traced back to the mid-1980s, when conservative milieux organised around sexuality and gender. This chapter is based on my ethnographic and archival research on sex education in Poland. I conducted interviews with major Polish sex educators and participated in workshops and training for sex educators. My inquiries also covered sex education handbooks and pamphlets as well as popular press debates around sexuality (the 1960s to present).

A red herring or the heart of the nation?

Scholars, activists, and journalists have offered various interpretations of the development of the attack on gender. Some argue that the church initiated the debate on gender in order to shift public scrutiny away from Catholic paedophilia and financial scandals (Sierakowski 2014). Others suggest that debates over gender and sexuality serve as 'red herrings' (for instance, Sroczyński 2014) to shift the public's attention away from real (meaning economic and social) problems. Finally, many left-oriented commentators claim that the attack on gender stems from Polish backwardness (for more on various interpretations, see Kościańska 2014a, Graff and Koroluczuk 2017).

These interpretations do not take into consideration the very fact that both modern power (Foucault 1978) and the modern nation (Yuval-Davis 1997) are highly gendered and sexualised phenomena. As I have argued elsewhere (Kościańska 2014a), the struggle over gender should be seen as a struggle over the nation: what makes a true Pole? Are feminists and homosexuals allowed to belong to the national community? Do we want a state based on equality, or one based on patriarchal religion? In his study of homophobia in Hungary, Hadley Renkin argues: 'LGBT activists propose their own competing vision for postsocialist Hungarian identity. This vision fundamentally challenges right-wing notions of identity and community and has contributed to the dramatic growth in public homophobia over the last several years, culminating in the attacks on the last two Pride Marches' (2009: 27). As such, Renkin suggests that homophobia should be understood as a struggle over national identity and cultural citizenship. Similar processes can be observed in Poland: for the last decade, feminist and LGBTQI activists have been involved in building a new version of patriotism and national history. They have done so by, for instance, rewriting Polish history to show that queers have been among the major figures of Polish literature (Tomasik 2009), or by using national symbols during feminist marches or gay pride parades (for more, Kościańska 2014a; on Hungary, Renkin 2007).

Agnieszka Graff and Elżbieta Korolczuk link 'the war on gender' to anti-colonial rhetoric.[2] They argue that although many elements of the attack on gender are global it is definitely characterised by local specificities. They point to the 'effective appropriation of the anti-colonial narrative, where "genderists" feature in the role of colonizers, while the conservative right plays the role of defender of authentic local culture' (Graff and Korolczuk 2017: 189, see also Korolczuk 2014). Because of that, Graff and Korolczuk stress that anti-gender mobilisation is not 'another wave of backlash, but a new ideological and political configuration' (Graff and Korolczuk 2017: 176), although this colonial narrative was made possible by the fact that since the mid-1990s 'gender conservatism' has been perceived 'as key to Poland's uniqueness in Europe' (2017: 184).[3]

While the war on gender is a new phenomenon, it would not be possible without earlier social mobilisation around gender and sexuality. I would argue that the war on gender is informed by earlier debates on these topics. In what follows, I will show that some arguments, including the colonisation narrative, were already formulated in the 1980s. As such, in order to fully understand the current attack on gender in the Polish context, we should start by looking for its historical sources.

My analysis is informed by feminist scholars who have pointed to a backlash in women's rights that appeared after socialism (see, for instance, Grabowska 2014, Mishtal 2015). The almost total ban on abortion in 1993 in Poland, which under socialism had offered (since 1956) its female citizens abortion on demand, represents the most visible sign of a new politics (Zielińska 2000). Scholars like Magdalena Grabowska and Joanna Mishtal have shown that due to the involvement of the Catholic church in anti-communist opposition, the church gained an incredibly strong position in the 1990s, since it 'was helping us to win freedom' (Mishtal 2015: 18). Therefore, it could pressure the state to introduce legal changes in accordance with Catholic teachings. Grabowska goes further and, drawing on historical research by Malgorzata Fidelis (2010), argues that in reference to gender and sexuality, there has been an alliance between church and state since the mid-1950s:

> The reforms introduced after 1953 aimed to reconstitute the pre-war gender contract, and in particular the gender division of labour, that is, unpaid domestic work done by women. The idea of the 'Polish road to socialism', conceived by First Secretary Władysław Gomułka, was based on the reconciliation of several seemingly contradictory legacies – those of Catholicism, nationalism, and socialism ... The socialist state was seen as based on a traditional family, to which the idea of 'Polish motherhood' remained crucial. (Grabowska 2014: 62)

The current war on gender is indeed rooted in the church/state alliance under socialism. But while we should look for historical roots in this period, we should do so not only on the state level, as Grabowska suggested. I would argue that discourses as well as social mobilisations during late state socialism are critical to understanding the foundations of the current war on gender. In what follows, I look for sources of the current attack on gender and social divisions around sexuality and gender in the heated debate over a sex education handbook in 1987. I show this to be the moment when both conservative and progressive milieux radicalised around sexuality and gender. While the handbook allowed for the unbridled expression of progressive thinking about sexuality for the first time, its publication served as the impetus for the conservative social mobilisation and the formation of ideological boundaries (Fassin 2011) around issues of sexuality, gender, and the nation (see also Pine and Haukanes, Chapter 1, this volume).

The handbook

Although under socialism sex education had been offered in Polish schools[4] since the 1960s (Lišková, Jarska and Szegedi 2019), there was no official handbook. Despite the existence of an official curriculum, each school had its own ideas of how to teach sex education. School headmasters either assigned various teachers (for instance biology teachers) to the task, or invited specialists: sexologists or other experts from the Planned Parenthood Association, a Polish branch of the International Planned Parenthood Federation that in state socialist Poland was state dependent and responsible for family planning, reproductive health, and sex education in the country.[5] As a result, sex education varied from school to school. It was only in September 1987 that a handbook (Sokoluk, Andziak and Trawińska 1987) finally appeared.

The handbook was written by three authors associated with the Planned Parenthood Association: Wiesław Sokoluk, Maria Trawińska, and Dagmar Andziak. A few years earlier, Sokoluk had worked on updating the sex education curriculum for the Ministry of Education and Upbringing by making it more focused on issues of human sexuality.[6] Next, he was asked to write the handbook. He wrote its main part (on sexuality) and invited Trawińska and Andziak to write the chapters about family and development.

Sokoluk was one of the experts from the Planned Parenthood Association who taught classes in schools. From the late 1970s, he travelled from school to school throughout Poland and answered students' questions. He also operated the youth telephone hotline and collaborated with youth magazines; in both cases he answered sexuality related questions. Moreover, he ran the youth advisory centre at the Planned Parenthood Association in Warsaw, which consisted of a walk-in clinic and a mail counselling service. While working as a teacher and at the advisory centre, he gathered a huge collection of the questions he had been asked in school, and of the letters he had received by mail. The questions he was asked covered standard issues such as anatomy, masturbation, sexual initiation, contraception, homosexuality, transsexuality, and STDs (Sokoluk 2003: 19).

When writing the handbook, Sokoluk already had a vast collection of questions and letters. He based the handbook on his experience in youth counselling. As he told me, while preparing curricula and writing the handbook he had all those students', clients', and correspondents' questions in mind.

The handbook turned out to be remarkably progressive. It went further than any available sex and marriage manual for adults or sex columns in the Polish press of late state socialism. Previous texts addressed to adults on the one hand affirmed sexuality, but on the other were rather conservative in their description of gender roles. They were also highly heteronormative, and not very sensitive when it came to issues such as sexual violence (Kościańska 2016). Sexologists who wrote those manuals usually situated sexuality within marriage. They also implicitly contributed to pronatalist state politics by encouraging married couples to have children, often by discouraging contraception and abortion (Ignaciuk 2016). Earlier sex education books addressed to young people, also authored by experts from the Planned Parenthood Association, explained in detail issues such as biological development of the body, the physiological and psychological problems of adolescence, or the physiology of reproduction, but were vague about sexuality. Similarly to the manuals for adults, they were based on a traditional understanding of gender roles. Sokoluk's 1987 handbook took a completely different approach. It was explicit about teen sexuality and affirmed it. It did not pathologise masturbation or homosexuality (calling homosexual relationships 'analogues' to heterosexual ones). It included drawings of sex positions as well as of the erogenous zones on the male and female bodies. It discussed in detail issues of sexual initiation, for instance explaining what the hymen is and how it stretches. The handbook presented birth control as a precondition to successful and pleasurable sex. It described all of the contraception methods available at the time, discussing their efficiency and providing details on how to use them. The handbook just answered the questions, without moralising about sexuality.

Against demoralisation: the reception of the handbook

The handbook had a print run of 500,000 copies and was introduced in all Polish high schools in September 1987. By November 1987, it was banned from schools. The copies that were not sold were shredded. It all started in *Słowo Powszechne*, a Catholic daily. Bogusław Jeznach, a Catholic journalist and a supporter of the National Democracy, authored a review entitled 'The Handbook of Masturbation and Defloration'.[7] He accused Sokoluk of destroying the family by encouraging children to have sex (Jeznach 1987: 7). Another critic, Maria Braun-Gałkowska, a Catholic psychologist from the Catholic University of Lublin, read the handbook as anti-family and unpatriotic.

> If their [parents'] argumentation [against sex before marriage] results only from their own emotional difficulties, related to, for example, aging, there is no reason to take into account their perspective on other issues, such as patriotism, honesty, solid work, sobriety and other values, which the older generation should try to convey to the younger ...It is clear that there is nothing joyful or encouraging about the family (as opposed to premarital sexual activity). (Braun-Gałkowska 1987: 13)

Braun-Gałkowska also suggested that in fact the handbook 'broke the law' because it was against the family and encouraged 'young people to start their sexual lives, while undermining the parents' authority' (1987: 16). She accused the handbook of promoting 'conduct contrary to what is prescribed in the Constitution, article 79 of which says that, "Marriage, motherhood and family are cared for and protected by the Polish People's Republic"' (1987: 16).

Other critics also centred their disapproval of the handbook on issues related to the nation, much the same as today. They presented the handbook as an attempt to demoralise Polish youth, and therefore to destroy the Polish Catholic nation. Bolesław Suszka, a dendrologist, professor of natural sciences, and a Catholic activist, explained: 'At present, a particularly disgusting form of atheisation has gained in significance: demoralisation. The handbook attacks the conscience of the Nation's greatest treasure – the youth' (Suszka 1987: 11).

Bishop Kazimierz Majdański, a shepherd of the church in Western Pomerania, wrote a pastoral letter to warn the faithful about the book. He called attention to the fact that at the time when the Holy Father was visiting the homeland and speaking about 'the basic concern of his pontificate: for marriage and family ... a book came out with a huge, half-million print run, which among others, contains content that negates the teachings of the Holy Father' (Majdański 1987). The bishop wondered: 'How could it happen that a "textbook" ... does not educate, but demoralize?' (Majdański 1987).

Furthermore, Suszka accused Sokoluk, and other 'anti-Christian activists', of seeking 'sexual pseudo-freedom'. He argued that Sokoluk was 'a slave to the contraceptive mentality'. This 'contraceptive mentality', Suszka claimed, 'presupposes the essential right to slay a child for the sake of the "comfort of the adult" human being' (Suszka 1987: 6).[8] Bishop Majdański argued in a similar fashion: 'The textbook is incentive for erotic experiments devoid of true selfless love, which is endowed with the power to transmit life; faithful and honest love' (Majdański 1987).

Suszka also traced the ideological and institutional roots of the handbook. The first root was what we could call the Polish progressive tradition in sex education. Suszka wrote: 'Tadeusz Boy-Żeleński[9] sends his greetings from beyond the grave'[10] (1987: 2). At the second root, as Suszka presented it, lay an anti-Christian international conspiracy, namely the International Planned Parenthood Federation. He stressed that the authors were associated with the Polish 'Planned Parenthood Association, which has acquired a monopoly on presenting sexological issues in the vast majority of state mass media in Poland' (1987: 2). The International Federation, he warned, 'promotes contraception, sterilization and the termination of pregnancy throughout the world, calling it all family planning ... It dedicates particular attention to ... developing countries and countries with a Catholic tradition' (1987: 2). This line of argument set the stage for further conceptualisation of 'genderists' as colonisers, to which Graff and Korolczuk point in their article from 2017. In the 1930s, Boy-Żeleński was also accused of being part of an international Jewish conspiracy against the Polish nation (Lechnicki 1933). As such, the idea that sexual, reproductive, and gender rights are something imposed on the Polish nation by an external power is nothing new. It had already been forged by the 1930s.

In the late 1980s, the Catholic church in Poland was particularly strong, with more than 90% of Poles considering themselves Catholic (Grabowska 2008, Mishtal 2015). The bishops were aware of their power and tried to wield influence over the situation in the country, pushing for instance for the penalisation of abortion (they finally succeeded in 1993, after the fall of communism). Reviews of the handbook by Jeznach, Braun-Gałkowska, Suszka, and others[11] published in the Catholic press and the pastoral letter by Bishop Majdański brought about mobilisation among the faithful. People returned the handbook to the publisher and meetings were organised in parishes all over Poland to discuss the sort of harm that the handbook would bring.

The official media published either positive or neutral reviews (for instance, Moszczeńska 1987). But apart from that, hardly anyone defended the handbook. Even the Planned Parenthood Association did not stand up for its members under attack. On the contrary, the president of the Polish Planned Parenthood Association tried to block its publication. He argued that the book was too explicit about sexuality and that it would cause disapproval on the part of the Catholic church. During a meeting of the Associations' members, Sokoluk was told that the book was too progressive and that it did not fit into the Polish school system. In a conversation with me, Sokoluk recalled that during the meeting there was only one colleague, a sexologist from Poznań, who took his side.

There was also a second person in the Association who defended the handbook: Anna Dodziuk, a psychologist and an editor of *Tygodnik Mazowsze*, the leading illegal (*samisdat*) magazine published by the (then banned) Solidarity trade union. Dodziuk evaluated the handbook positively in the magazine. She stressed that the handbook treated young people seriously, encouraged them to think critically on their own, and took into consideration 'the obvious fact that teenage girls and boys have feelings and needs, including sexual ones'[12] (Dodziuk 1987: 4). In Dodziuk's opinion, Polish schools did not treat youths as equals and completely ignored the existence of adolescent sexuality. She argued that moral panic around the handbook was caused not only by the drawings and the affirmative approach toward sex, but also by the fact that hardly anyone read the handbook. Outraged parents based their disapproval on drawings and critical reviews. She finished her text with a reference to Catholic doctor and author Włodzimierz Fijałkowski, showing that Catholics also affirmed sexuality. Fijałkowski had written: 'The mood around sexuality is tense, full of distrust, fear, guilt and suspicion while we tend to forget that sexuality is God's gift; an evangelical skill that should be expanded'[13] (Dodziuk 1987: 4).

In response to her review, the magazine's editors received many letters of disapproval. These criticised them in the first place for taking up the matter of sexuality, since *Tygodnik Mazowsze* was a political magazine and sex was perceived to be an inappropriate topic. Secondly, the editors were condemned for destroying the alliance between the church and the anti-communist opposition. In reading *Tygodnik Mazowsze* it was easy to see that a major value the Solidarity movement advocated at the time was plurality: public space, in which various opinions and worldviews could be expressed and deliberated. As reactions to Dodziuk's review showed, this plurality did not cover sexuality. In the field of sexuality, conservative milieux fought for monopoly.

Breaking the unholy alliance?

The Planned Parenthood Association, which, in fact, was an official state agenda responsible for sex education during state socialism, had a long tradition of dialogue with Catholic milieux. Planned Parenthood activists and Catholics (at least those more liberally inclined) agreed in many ways:

both groups believed that sex was an important social issue and that society should be educated about the need to treat it responsibly. The leading figures of the Planned Parenthood Association were in constant contact with Catholics interested in discussing sexuality. For instance, Zbigniew Lew-Starowicz, a well-known sexologist and sex columnist, was a pious Catholic in the 1970s and discussed sexuality with Karol Wojtyła (see Kościańska 2018).

Furthermore, although sexologists and sex educators from the Planned Parenthood Association generally affirmed sexuality and stressed that sexual pleasure was key to self-realisation, they placed it within marriage. They argued that traditional gender roles were good for a pleasurable sex life and frequently presented non-reproductive extramarital sexual activity as rather questionable: a bit unhealthy or leading to dysfunctions (Kościańska 2016). Furthermore, sexologists often emphasised how harmful and ineffective methods of contraception were that were not approved by the church (Kościańska 2018). The analysis of sexological/sex education literature from the 1970s and 1980s shows very clearly that sex education authors (and hence the state, as the Planned Parenthood Association represented an official state agenda, and all texts were approved by the censors) were committed to maintaining good relationships with the church. The church and the state had an agreement on various sexuality related issues. Both were concerned about population decrease (Ignaciuk 2016), and both saw a solution in limiting access to birth control and in pushing women out of the labour market. The Communist Party did not change any progressive sex related laws, but on many occasions showed its good will towards the church in other ways, including through Planned Parenthood publications (for more generally on the church/state alliance, see Grabowska 2014).

Sokoluk's 1987 sex education handbook did not fit into this climate of collaboration between the church and state. Although Sokoluk was a member of the Planned Parenthood Association, he was not very committed to its political agenda. He remained an outsider. In an interview I conducted with him, he told me about being a hippy and a hitchhiker with an anarchist worldview. He started his career in the early 1970s at an experimental psychiatry unit where humanist psychiatry was practised. Before getting a full-time job at the Association, he worked at a research institution at the Ministry of Education and Upbringing, where he had a hard time after pushing for sex education at the pre-school level. The questions Sokoluk was asked by young people in letters and at school were the same ones posed to other sex educators. The difference was that Sokoluk replied to these questions in a straightforward manner, without taking into consideration the political stance of the Association. But Sokoluk's individual agency was not enough: the publication of the handbook was not possible without approval from the Communist Party.

The question is then: why did the Communist Party suddenly, in 1987, decide to ask Sokoluk to write the handbook, publish it, and therefore break its alliance with the church? As the historian Natalia Jarska (2019) recently showed, under socialism the Communist Party sometimes tried to use sex as a leverage in its relations with the church. Therefore, it could be argued that the party published the handbook to reduce the influence of the church, which was growing in the 1980s (Grabowska 2008, Kościańska 2018), partly because of the Pope's visit to Poland in June 1987. The Communist Party decided to check if sex might pave the way to young people's hearts. Therefore, the Party allowed not only the publication of the 1987 sex education handbook but also relaxed sex related censorship in youth and student magazines. Youth magazines, some of which were written not only by professional journalists but also by young people from all over the country, provided room for discussions about issues such as homosexuality, transsexuality, sex work, and birth control. As a result, the mid-1980s was a time of vivid youth interest in sexual emancipation and the moment when activism around gender and sexuality started: the first gay and lesbian underground magazines were published (see Szulz 2017) and the first feminist informal groups began discussing issues such as female orgasm and sexual violence (on the formation of feminism in the 1980s, see Grabowska 2012).

A public opinion survey, inquiries on the part of journalists (Moszczeńska 1987), high school student protests,[14] and hundreds of letters addressed to Sokoluk indicate that young people indeed appreciated the handbook. But the Communist Party underestimated the church's power. The Catholic press published multiple disapproving reviews as discussed above. The church also criticised the handbook during secret meetings with party officials (Tajne Dokumenty… 1993: 527). The party was forced to ban the handbook from school. The unholy alliance, broken for a short while, has continued and in fact grown in strength since the fall of communism, when the church gained real political power (Mishtal 2015). While under communism Catholics could encourage Planned Parenthood people to discourage abortion, in democratic Poland under the influence of the church, abortion was banned.

From the 1987 handbook to the current moral panic over sexuality

After communism, sex education at school was designed by Sokoluk's critics. Other conservative policies were also introduced. Under socialism, gender reassignment surgery and the psychological therapy that goes with it were fully sponsored by the state. In the 1980s, a sexology unit in Warsaw hired a priest to help its transsexual patients to transition spiritually (Kościańska 2014b). Since the early 1990s, however, patients have had to pay for their own surgery and therapy. Since 1989, the legal procedure has become significantly more complicated and requires a lawsuit against one's parents (Debińska 2013). Contraception and in vitro fertilisation were subsidised by the socialist state. This was also changed in the 1990s (Radkowska-Walkowicz 2013, Mishtal 2015).

But, as I argued above, this backlash had already started in 1987. This was when conservative milieux organised themselves around issues of sexuality and gender and won their first battle. But at the same time, in 1987, a completely new, liberal approach towards sex education materialised in the form of a handbook. Official sex education in Poland has never again had such a progressive handbook.[15] Currently, the only approved handbook represents a highly conservative approach towards sexuality, placing it exclusively in the context of marriage, traditional gender roles, and procreation. Proponents of progressive sex education lost the battle over schools.

However, since the early 1900s, progressive sex education has been organised by feminist and LGBTQI NGOs in various spaces such as schools, the internet, or in public areas. For instance, the peer sex education group Ponton, which is affiliated with the Federation for Women and Family Planning (a major Polish feminist organisation of which the Planned Parenthood Associations is a member), has been running sex education workshops in schools all over Poland and a phone hotline since its foundation in 2002. The Foundation for Modern Education Spunk has pushed for sex education based on WHO standards at the local level in Łódź (central Poland) and has also organised workshops for young people. Furthermore, since the early 1990s, many teachers have taken part in the progressive postgraduate sex education programme at the University of Warsaw. Alumni of the programme often teach sex education without any reference to the approved conservative programme. Some of them even use the forbidden 1987 handbook. Informal means of sex education have been successful in many ways. Municipal governments have gradually started to hire organisations such as Spunk and Ponton to run sex education in schools.

At the same time, the conservative camp that mobilised itself so well in 1987 has become increasingly more interested in sexuality and gender. Conservatives have made use of church networks (premarital courses, religion classes in schools, youth associations) and Catholic media to disseminate their views about sexuality. These groups criticise progressive milieux employing well-worn arguments about demoralisation and the foreign attack on the Polish nation and the Polish family. In fact, the same authors who condemned the handbook now write about the dangers of 'gender ideology' (see, for example, Jeznach 2017). In the last decade, conservative educational initiatives started to compete with progressive NGOs for municipal funding. At first, they were not successful, but once moral panic over gender and sexuality started targeting progressive sex education and equality education in 2013, conservative initiatives managed to get municipal funding. After church hierarchs called on school authorities 'not to yield under pressure from the few but very loud groups ... which in the name of modern education carry out experiments on children and young people' (Shepherd 2013), the Foundation for Modern Education Spunk ceased to run sex education in Łódź. In its place, sex education is now organised by the highly conservative Archipelag Skarbów (The Archipelago of Treasures, see also Zimniak-Hałajko 2017), which presents abstinence as the best means of birth control and HIV prevention.[16]

Conclusion

The fight over sex education in Poland, which started in 1987, has continued. Arguments against progressive sex education and gender and sexual equality have been recycled over and over again. The recent war against gender did not start in 2013, and the colonisation discourse is not new, despite the claim of Graff and Koroloczuk (2017) to the contrary. It was designed and developed over a period of more than 30 years: not after the fall of socialism, as most people tend to think, but from the mid-1980s, when the socialist state was unable to break the alliance with the Catholic church it had formed in the 1950s (Grabowska 2014) and implement secular progressive ideas about sexuality and gender against the Catholic church. The current war on gender is possible because of an explicit framing of sexuality vis-à-vis the nation, its youth, and the foreign powers that want to destroy and colonise both the nation and its young people. Within this narrative, sex education is not about sex, but rather about Polishness. This conceptualisation, combined with progressive informal sex education and the success of the progressive reframing of the nation, discussed at the beginning of this chapter, brought about the construction of ideological boundaries and the social mobilisation around sexuality and led to the current attack on 'gender ideology'.

Acknowledgements

An earlier version of this chapter was presented at the Rights, Reproduction and Care Workshop held at the University of Bergen in December 2017. Many thanks to Frances Pine and Haldis Haukanes for organising it, inviting me, and commenting on my first draft as well as to all participants for their insightful comments. Writing this chapter was possible thanks to an Imre

Kertész Kolleg Jena fellowship. I would like to thank Marta Rozmysłowicz for polishing my English writing and translating the most difficult quotations.

Notes

1 'Expert Approaches toward Gender', a conference organised by the Catholic News Agency, 24 January 2014.
2 Because of the lack of national independence in the nineteenth century, Poland has a long tradition of thinking through an anti-colonial lens (Janion 2006).
3 In her other writings, Graff has pointed to governmental (no matter if a government was on the political right or left) reluctance to introduce any gender equality laws (Graff 2001).
4 The first sex education class was held in Warsaw in 1904 by Wacław Jezierski. Although he took great pains to make sex education widely accessible, his activity was ultimately rather local. Sex education was introduced in Polish schools by the newly established Polish state right after the First World War (Kościańska 2017).
5 In existence in Poland since the mid-1950s (for more information, see Kuźma-Markowska 2013).
6 He was experienced in constructing sex education curricula. In the 1970s, he worked at a research institute at the Ministry of Education and Upbringing and was responsible for developing pre-school education. In this period, he wrote, for instance, a progressive sex education curriculum for kindergartens. The programme was never implemented.
7 Unless noted otherwise, quotes cited in this section have been translated by Marta Rozmysłowicz.
8 It is worth noting that in the handbook Sokoluk explained that it was better to prevent pregnancy than to terminate it.
9 Tadeusz Boy-Żeleński was the major figure of Polish sexual reform and of the pro-choice movement in the interwar period (see Gawin 2009, Kościańska 2017).
10 My translation.
11 See for example Luft 1987.
12 My translation.
13 My translation.
14 For instance, at a Warsaw high school, students wore protest badges: 'Give us back the handbook' (Jaczewski 2014: 180).
15 Progressive sex educators in Poland have of course authored and published handbooks after 1987. But their books never really made it in to schools. Some of them were not accepted by the Ministry of Education, while others were approved as one of two or three alternatives, with the ministry ultimately withdrawing the approval after a short period.
16 This is not (only) about state funding, but also about changes in feminist and LGBTQI thinking, their often successful claiming of cultural citizenship and their attempts to reframe thinking about the nation – a sort of 'progressive'

nationalism. Gradually, sexuality has become an important element of how people think about the nation (Kościańska 2014a).

References

Braun-Gałkowska, M. (1987) *Omówienie Podręcznika Szkolnego pt. Przysposobienie do Życia w Rodzinie*. Warszawa: KMW WNK.

Cichobłazińska, A. (2013) 'Gender – Ideologia Totalitarna, an Interview with Father Dariusz Oko', *Niedziela* 24: 40–43, www.niedziela.pl/artykul/106423/nd/ (accessed 1 October 2018).

Dębińska, M. (2013) 'Natura, Kultura i Hybrydy. Prawne Konstrukcje Transseksualizmu i Sprawy o Ustalenie Płci', *Lud* 97: 221–244.

Dodziuk, A. (1987) 'W Obronie zdrowego rozsądku', *Tygodnik Mazowsze* 227: 4.

Fassin, D. (2011) 'Policing Borders, Producing Boundaries. The Governmentality of Immigration in Dark Times', *Annual Review of Anthropology* 40: 213–226.

Fidelis, M. (2010) *Women, Communism, and Industrialization in Postwar Poland*. Cambridge: Cambridge University Press.

Foucault, M. (1978) *The History of Sexuality*, Vol. 1: *The Will to Knowledge*. New York: Pantheon Books.

Gawin, M. (2009) 'The Social Politics and Experience of Sex Education in Early Twentieth-Century Poland (1905–39)'. In: Lutz Sauerteig and R. Davidson (eds) *Shaping Sexual Knowledge: A Cultural History of Sex Education in Twentieth Century Europe*. London: Routledge, pp. 219–235.

Grabowska, M. (2008) 'Ruchy Odnowy Religijnej Przełomu Lat Siedemdziesiątych i Osiemdziesiątych: Społeczne Przyczyny i Konsekwencje'. In: T. Szawiel (ed.) *Pokolenie JP2. Przeszłość i Przyszłość Zjawiska Religijnego*. Warszawa: Wydawnictwo Naukowe SCHOLAR, pp. 22–49.

Grabowska, M. (2012) 'Bringing the Second World In: Conservative Revolution(s), Socialist Legacies, and Transnational Silences in the Trajectories of Polish Feminism', *Signs* 37 (2): 385–411.

Grabowska, M. (2014) 'Cultural War or Business as Usual? Recent Instances and the Historical Origins of the Backlash Against Women's Rights and Sexual Rights in Poland'. In: Heinrich Böll Foundation (ed.) *Anti-Gender Movements on the Rise? Strategizing for Gender Equality in Central and Eastern Europe*. Berlin: Heinrich Böll Foundation, pp. 54–64.

Graff, A. (2001) *Świat bez Kobiet. Płeć w Polskim Życiu Publicznym*. Warszawa: W.A.B.

Graff, A. and E. Korolczuk (2017) '"Worse than Communism and Nazism Put Together": War on Gender in Poland'. In: R. Kuhar and D. Patenotte (eds) *Anti-Gender Campaigns in Europe: Mobilizing against Equality*. London: Rowman & Littlefield, pp. 175–194.

Ignaciuk, A. (2016) 'Reproductive Policies and Women's Birth Control Practices in State-socialist Poland (1960s–1980s)'. In: L. Niethammer and S. Satjuko (eds) *'Wenn die Chemie stimmt': Gender Relations and Birth Control in the Age of the 'Pill'*. Göttingen: Wallstein, pp. 271–294.

Jaczewski, A. (2014) *Seksualność Dzieci i Młodzieży. Pół Wieku Badań i Refleksji*. Warszawa: Difin.

Janion, M. (2006). *Niesamowita Słowiańszczyzna*. Kraków: Wydawnictwo Literackie.
Jarska, N. (2019) 'Modern Marriage and the Culture of Sexuality: Experts between the State and the Church in Poland, 1956–1970', *European History Quarterly* 49 (3): 467–490.
Jeznach, B. (1987) 'Podręcznik Masturbacji i Defloracji', *Słowo Powszechne*, 26–28 September.
Jeznach, B. (2017) 'Cywilizacja dewiacji'. http://jeznach.neon24.pl/post/140885, cywilizacja-dewiacji (accessed 16 February 2018).
Korolczuk, E. (2014). 'The War on Gender from a Transnational Perspective – Lessons for Feminist Strategising'. In: Heinrich Böll Foundation (ed.) *Anti-Gender Movements on the Rise? Strategising for Gender Equality in Central and Eastern Europe*. Berlin: Heinrich Böll Foundation, pp. 43–53.
Kościańska, A. (2014a) 'Panika wokół Gender – Temat Zastępczy czy Spór o Obywatelstwo Kulturowe', *Ars Educandi* 11: 259–268. https://doi.org/10.26881/ae.2014.11.20.
Kościańska, A. (2014b) 'Beyond Viagra: Sex Therapy in Poland', *Sociologický Časopis/ Czech Sociological Review* 50 (6): 919–938.
Kościańska, A. (2016) 'Sex on Equal Terms? Polish Sexology on Women's Emancipation and "Good Sex" from the 1970s to Present', *Sexualities* 19 (1–2): 236–256.
Kościańska, A. (2017) *Zobaczyć łosia. Historia Polskiej Edukacji Eeksualnej od Pierwszej Lekcji do Internetu*. Wołowiec: Czarne.
Kościańska, A. (2018) 'Humanae Vitae, Birth Control and the Forgotten History of the Catholic Church in Poland'. In: A. Harris (ed.) *The Schism of '68. Genders and Sexualities in History*. Cham: Palgrave Macmillan, pp. 187–208.
Kucharczyk, J. (2016) 'Resisting Backlash Against Democracy', paper presented at 'An un-Conference at the 25th Anniversary Democracy & Diversity Institute in Wroclaw', Poland, Transregional Center for Democratic Studies, The New School for Social Research, July 16–17.
Kuźma-Markowska, S. (2013) 'Międzynarodowe Aspekty Działalności Towarzystwa Świadomego Macierzyństwa w lLtach 50. i 60. XX w'. In: B. Płonka-Syroka and A. Szlagowska (eds) *Problem Kontroli Urodzeń i Antykoncepcji. Krytyczno-porównawcza Analiza Dyskursów*. Wrocław: Uniwersytet Medyczny im. Piastów Śląskich we Wrocławiu, pp. 263–282.
Lechnicki, C. (1933, ed.) *Prawda o Boyu-Żeleńskim. Głosy Krytyczne*. Warszawa: Skład Główny, Dom Książki Polskiej.
Lišková K., N. Jarska, and G. Szegedi (2019) 'Sexuality and Gender in School-based Sex Education in Czechoslovakia, Hungary and Poland in the 1970s and 1980s', *The History of the Family* DOI: 10.1080/1081602X.2019.1679219.
Luft, B. (1987) 'Znaleźć Odpowiedź', *Gość Niedzielny*, 25 October.
Majdański, K. (1987) 'Przeciw Demoralizacji. List Pasterski Biskupa Szczecińsko-Kmieńskiego Kazimierza Majdańskiego', *Gość Niedzielny*, 8 November.
Mishtal, J. (2015) *The Politics of Morality: The Church, the State, and Reproductive Rights in Postsocialist Poland*. Athens, GA: Ohio University Press.
Moszczeńska, R. (1987). '"Straszna" Książka. O Prawidłowościach Życia Człowieka', *Życie Warszawy*, 10 November.
Radkowska-Walkowicz, M. (2013) *Doświadczenie in Vitro. Niepłodność i Nowe Technologie Reprodukcyjne w Perspektywie Antropologicznej*. Warszawa: Wydawnictwa Uniwersytetu Warszawskiego.
Renkin, H.Z. (2007) 'Predecessors and Pilgrims: Lesbian History-making and Belonging in Postsocialist Hungary'. In: J. Takács and R. Kuhar (eds) *Beyond*

the Pink Curtain: The Everyday Life of LGBTs in Eastern and Central Europe. Ljubljana: Peace Institute, pp. 269–286.

Renkin, H.Z. (2009) 'Homophobia and Queer Belonging in Hungary', *Focaal – European Journal of Anthropology* 53: 20–37.

Shepherds of the Catholic Church in Poland (2013) Pastoral letter of the Bishops' Conference of Poland to be used on the Sunday of the Holy Family 2013. https://episkopat.pl/pastoral-letter-of-the-bishops-conference-of-poland-to-be-used-on-the-sunday-of-the-holy-family-2013/ (accessed 1 October 2018).

Sierakowski, S. (2014) 'The Polish Church's Gender Problem', *The International New York Times*, 27 January. www.nytimes.com/2014/01/27/opinion/sierakowski-the-polish-churchs-gender-problem.html (accessed 1 October 2018).

Sokoluk, W. (2003) *Wychowanie do Życia w Rodzinie. Poradnik Metodyczny dla Nauczycieli*. Warszawa: Wydawnictwa Szkolne i Pedagogiczne.

Sokoluk W., D. Andziak, and M. Trawińska (1987) *Przysposobienie do Życia w Rodzinie*. Warszawa: Wydawnictwa Szkolne i Pedagogiczne.

Sroczyński, G. (2014) 'Byliśmy Głupi, an Interview with Marcin Król', *Gazeta Wyborcza*, 7 February, http://wyborcza.pl/magazyn/1,124059,15414610,Bylismy_glupi.html. (accessed 1 October 2018).

Suszka, B. (1987) *Podręcznik Szkolny „Przysposobienie do Życia w Rodzinie" – Zagrożenie czy Wyzwanie?*. Poznań: Duszpasterstwo Rodzin Archidiecezji Poznańskiej.

Szulc, L. (2017) *Transnational Homosexuals in Communist Poland: Cross-Border Flows in Gay and Lesbian Magazines*. New York: Palgrave Macmillan.

Tajne Dokumenty…. (1993) *Tajne Dokumenty. Państwo – Kościół 1980–1989*. London, Warszawa: Wydawnictwo Aneks, Polityka.

Tomasik, K. (2009) *Homobiografie. Pisarki i Pisarze Polscy XIX i XX wieku*. Warszawa: Wydawnictwo Krytyki Politycznej.

Yuval-Davis, N. (1997) *Gender and Nation*. London: Sage Publications.

Zielińska, E. (2000) 'Between Ideology, Politics, and Common Sense: The Discourse of Reproductive Rights in Poland'. In: S. Gal and G. Kligman (eds) *Reproducing Gender. Politics, Publics, and Everyday Life after Socialism*. Princeton: Princeton University Press, pp. 23–57.

Zimniak-Hałajko, M. (2017) *Ciało i Wspólnota*. Warszawa: Wydział Polonistyki UW.

Index

Note: 'n.' after a page reference indicates the number of a note on that page

EU authorised representative for GPSR:
Easy Access System Europe, Mustamäe tee 50,
10621 Tallinn, Estonia
gpsr.requests@easproject.com

www.ingramcontent.com/pod-product-compliance
Lightning Source LLC
Chambersburg PA
CBHW052000270326
41929CB00015B/2726
* 9 7 8 1 5 2 6 1 7 4 6 2 8 *